The Eastern Christian Churches

THE EASTERN CHRISTIAN CHURCHES

A Brief Survey
(6th edition)

Ronald Roberson

Edizioni «Orientalia Christiana»
1999

1st edition   - 1986
2nd edition - 1988
3rd edition - 1990
4th edition - 1993
5th edition - 1995

cover: Pentecost, miniature from a Syriac Evangeliary
(1227) kept at Mor Gabriel, near Midyat, Turkey.

ISBN 88-7210-321-5

Edizioni Orientalia Christiana
Pontificio Istituto Orientale
Piazza S. Maria Maggiore, 7
00185 Roma, Italy

Finito di stampare nel mese di gennaio 1999 presso la
Tipolitografia 200 sas di De Magistris R. & C.
Via Trento, 46 – 00046 Grottaferrata (Rm)
tel. fax 06-941 04 73 – E mail: rdemagistris@pelagus.it

TABLE OF CONTENTS

Introduction   9

I. The Assyrian Church of the East   15

II. THE ORIENTAL ORTHODOX CHURCHES   23
    A. The Armenian Apostolic Church   24
    B. The Coptic Orthodox Church   27
    C. The Ethiopian Orthodox Church   30
    D. The Syrian Orthodox Church   34
    E. The Malankara Orthodox Syrian Church   37
    F. The Eritrean Orthodox Church   40

III. THE ORTHODOX CHURCH   43

    A. The Autocephalous Churches   44
        1. The Patriarchate of Constantinople
                  (The Ecumenical Patriarchate)   45
        2. The Patriarchate of Alexandria   51
        3. The Patriarchate of Antioch   54
        4. The Patriarchate of Jerusalem   57
        5. The Orthodox Church of Russia   60
        6. The Orthodox Church of Serbia   68
        7. The Orthodox Church of Romania   72
        8. The Orthodox Church of Bulgaria   76
        9. The Orthodox Church of Georgia   80
      10. The Orthodox Church of Cyprus   83
      11. The Orthodox Church of Greece   86
      12. The Orthodox Church of Poland   89
      13. The Orthodox Church of Albania   92
      14. The Orthodox Church in the Czech and
                    Slovak Republics   96
      15. The Orthodox Church in America   98

    B. The Autonomous Churches   102
        1. The Orthodox Church of Mount Sinai   103
        2. The Orthodox Church of Finland   105
        3. The Orthodox Church of Japan   107

4. The Orthodox Church of China   108
5. The Estonian Apostolic Orthodox Church   109

C. Canonical Churches Under Constantinople   112
1. The American Carpatho-Russian Orthodox Greek
                              Catholic Church   112
2. The Ukrainian Orthodox Church of the USA and Diaspora   113
3. The Russian Orthodox Archdiocese in Western Europe . . .   116
4. The Albanian Orthodox Diocese of America   118
5. The Belarusan Council of Orthodox Churches
                              in North America   118
6. The Ukrainian Orthodox Church of Canada   119

D. Churches of Irregular Status   120
1. The Old Believers   121
2. The Russian Orthodox Church Outside Russia   123
3. The Ukrainian Orthodox Church-Kiev Patriarchate
        and Ukrainian Autocephalous Orthodox Church   . . .   126
4. The Belarusan Autocephalous Orthodox Church   129
5. The Macedonian Orthodox Church   130
6. The Old Calendar Orthodox Churches   133

IV. THE CATHOLIC EASTERN CHURCHES   139

A. Churches with No Counterpart   142
1. The Maronite Catholic Church   142
2. The Italo-Albanian Catholic Church   145

B. From the Assyrian Church of the East   146
1. The Chaldean Catholic Church   146
2. The Syro-Malabar Catholic Church   149

C. From the Oriental Orthodox Churches   151
1. The Armenian Catholic Church   151
2. The Coptic Catholic Church   154
3. The Ethiopian Catholic Church   156
4. The Syrian Catholic Church   157
5. The Syro-Malankara Catholic Church   159

D. From the Orthodox Church   161
1. The Melkite Catholic Church   161
2. The Ukrainian Catholic Church   165
3. The Ruthenian Catholic Church   169
4. The Romanian Catholic Church   173

5. The Greek Catholic Church 177
6. Byzantine Catholics in former Yugoslavia 178
7. The Bulgarian Catholic Church 179
8. The Slovak Catholic Church 182
9. The Hungarian Catholic Church 184
10. Eastern Catholic Communities Without Hierarchies 185

Appendix I
  Catholic-Orthodox Relations in Post-Communist Europe:
  Ghosts from the Past and Challenges for the Future 189

Appendix II
  The Contemporary Relationship between the Catholic
  and Oriental Orthodox Churches 237

Bibliography 267

Index of Churches and Their Heads 273

Introduction

Many western Christians are baffled by the complexity of the Christian East, which can appear to be a bewildering array of national churches and ethnic jurisdictions. The purpose of this survey is to provide a clear overview of the eastern churches for the nonspecialist by furnishing basic information about each of them and indicating the relationships among them. Each church is placed in its historical, geographical, doctrinal, and liturgical context. Because this book is primarily intended for an English-speaking audience, details are also provided regarding the presence of each of these churches in North America, Britain, and Australia.

The principle used in this book for the classification of churches is communion. That is, it describes groups of churches that are in full communion with one another, rather than categorizing them according to other criteria such as liturgical tradition.

This approach yields four distinct and separate eastern Christian communions: (1) the Assyrian Church of the East, which is not in communion with any other church; (2) the six Oriental Orthodox churches, which, even though each is independent, are in full communion with one another; (3) the Orthodox Church, which is a communion of national or regional churches, all of which recognize the Patriarch of Constantinople as a point of unity enjoying certain rights and privileges; and (4) the Eastern Catholic churches, all of which are in communion with the Church of Rome and its bishop. The order in which these four communions are listed is of no particular significance; it reflects only the chronological sequence in which they emerged as distinct entities.

The only exception here to the principle of communion for the classification of churches is the Orthodox Churches of Irregular Status [see III.D]. They have been included as a subcategory of the

Orthodox Church, but they are not in full communion with it. All of them are of Orthodox origin, but today the Orthodox view them as at least uncanonical if not fully schismatic.

I have endeavored in this book to present these churches as they are, and to describe disputed matters without making judgments as to the rightness or wrongness of the various points of view. For instance, the order in which the autocephalous Orthodox churches should be listed presents a problem because the Orthodox are not in unanimous agreement among themselves as to the precedence of their churches after the four ancient patriarchates. I have listed them in the order recognized by the Patriarchate of Constantinople and most other Orthodox churches, and have added the Orthodox Church in America, which has been granted autocephalous status by the Moscow Patriarchate but is not recognized as such by Constantinople. The four ancient patriarchates are followed by the five patriarchates of more recent origin, and then by the other autocephalous churches that do not have the rank of patriarchate.

A word needs to be said about the status of the Orthodox Church in America (the OCA), which I have included among the autocephalous Orthodox churches. In doing this I am aware that Constantinople and most other Orthodox churches do not recognize the OCA as autocephalous. This is why it is not allowed to take part in such pan-Orthodox activities as international dialogues with other Christian churches. Nevertheless, it functions as an autocephalous church, and its inclusion in the American Standing Conference of Canonical Orthodox Bishops indicates that it has achieved a certain level of legitimacy among other Orthodox churches in the United States. It seemed appropriate to include this church among the autocephalous Orthodox churches, along with a description of the controversy about its status. It is not my intention to take a position on the problem, but only to describe it.

The membership statistics provided for these churches must be treated with great caution. Many eastern churches exist in areas where no census has been taken or where the true size of church membership could have explosive political implications. Thus one is forced to rely on estimates which at times are of limited value. In the case of churches that are members of the World Council of Churches, I usually report the figures that were provided by them to the WCC and published in its 1985 revised *Handbook of Member Churches*, edited by Ans J. van der Bent. For other churches and jurisdictions I have most often relied on the data provided in *The World Christian Encyclopedia*, edited by D. Barrett and published in 1982. This work claims to present the most accurate statistics on church membership available. Both these sources have now become dated, and in some cases I have either modified the membership statistics on the basis of compelling new data or acknowledged other estimates in the text. For the Eastern Catholic churches, I have taken figures exclusively from the 1998 *Annuario Pontificio*, the annual yearbook of the Vatican. It provides official membership statistics for every Catholic diocese. I have added up the membership figures of all the dioceses of each Eastern Catholic Church and rounded off the sum to the next highest thousand. It should be kept in mind that these figures will be lower than the real membership of churches that have a significant presence in the diaspora. This is because the statistics do not include faithful of those churches who, lacking sufficient numbers to form their own dioceses, come under the jurisdiction of the local Latin bishops.

It may be noticed that the entries for some smaller churches are more extensive than those of other larger or more prestigious ones. This is because I have endeavored to supply more information regarding some churches whose histories are less known and less readily accessible. A number of the most important works in English that treat the larger churches are indicated in the bibliography. Given the large amount of information that is now available on the internet, this edition also includes a number of web site addresses maintained by the various churches. I have not included web sites of local jurisdictions such as the Greek Orthodox Archdiocese of America, but these can often be found as links on the pages of the mother churches. A useful list of official Orthodox web site and e-mail addresses can be found on the site of the Orthodox Church of America at http://www.oca.org/Orthodox-Churches/#autocephalous.

I have treated the ecumenical relationships between these four communions at various points in the main text. The Catholic and Orthodox churches have been engaged in an international theological dialogue since 1980. A series of unofficial consultations between the Catholic Church and Oriental Orthodox churches has been underway since the 1970s, and significant common statements have been issued by Popes and Oriental Orthodox hierarchs concerning christological doctrine and other issues dividing their churches. A commission for dialogue between the Catholic Church and the Coptic Orthodox Church was set up in 1973, and a dialogue with the Malankara Orthodox Syrian Church in India has been in progress since October 1989. Moreover, the Orthodox Church has been engaged in dialogue with the Anglican Communion since 1976, and an official dialogue began between the Orthodox Church and the Oriental Orthodox churches in December 1985. Sources on these dialogues can be found in the bibliography, along with books on other aspects of the eastern churches.

This sixth edition includes as appendices two articles on ecumenical themes that I have published elsewhere. The first, entitled "Catholic-Orthodox Relations in Post-Communist Europe: Ghosts from the Past and Challenges for the Future," is from a conference given at Rome's Centro Pro Unione on March 18, 1993. It was published in the *Centro Pro Unione Semi-Annual Bulletin* 43 (Spring 1993) 17-31. The original text has been very slightly revised for this edition, and it appears with a postscript describing developments up to mid-1998. The second article, "The Contemporary Relationship between the Roman Catholic and Oriental Orthodox Churches," first appeared as "The Modern Roman Catholic-Oriental Orthodox Dialogue" in *One in Christ* 21 (1985) 238-254. In an updated form and with the present title it appeared in *The Vienna Dialogue: Five Pro Oriente Consultations with Oriental Orthodoxy*, Booklet Nr. 1 (Vienna: Pro Oriente, 1991) 23-38. The version found here first appeared in *Oriental Orthodox-Roman Catholic Interchurch Marriages and Other Pastoral Relationships* (Washington, DC: United States Catholic Conference, 1995) 81-103. New information was added to take into account the visit of Armenian Catholicos Karekin I to Rome in December 1996. Some of the material presented in this edition on the Eastern Catholic churches also appears in *Encyclopedia of Catholicism*, published by HarperCollins in 1995 under the general editorship of Richard P. McBrien.

Any constructive comments that readers may wish to make on this text are welcomed, as well as updated information that could be considered for inclusion in subsequent editions of this book. Letters can be addressed to the author at St. Paul's College, 3015 Fourth Street NE, Washington, DC 20017 USA.

I would like to extend my sincere thanks to the many people I consulted while preparing this survey and its five previous editions. In particular I would like to acknowledge the assistance of Protodeacon Lawrence Cross of the Australian Catholic University who supplied much useful information about Eastern Christians in Australia.

An extremely varied and complex history is covered in this work, and I have striven to present it as clearly as possible. I have done my best to remain objective and fair in treating what at times are tragic and painful situations in the history of these churches and the relationships between them. I hope that this survey will in some small way help western Christians to understand more about our sisters and brothers in the East, so that one day the Church might learn — using the image often evoked by Pope John Paul II — to again breathe fully with two lungs, one eastern and one western.

October 1998

I. The Assyrian Church of the East

It is not known exactly when Christianity first took root in upper Mesopotamia, but a Christian presence had certainly been established there by the mid-2nd century. In the 3rd century, the area was conquered by the Persians. Although this was to be a multi-ethnic church, the Assyrian people traditionally played a central role in its ecclesial life. Its geographical location caused it to become known simply as "the Church of the East."

Around the year 300, the bishops were first organized into an ecclesiastical structure under the leadership of a Catholicos, the bishop of the Persian royal capital at Seleucia-Ctesiphon. He later received the additional title of Patriarch.

In the 5th century, the Church of the East gravitated towards the radical Antiochene form of christology that had been articulated by Theodore of Mopsuestia and Nestorius, and fell out of communion with the church in the Roman Empire. This was due in part to the significant influx of Nestorian Christians into Persia that took place following the condemnation of Nestorian christology by the Council of Ephesus in 431, and the expulsion of Nestorians from the Roman Empire by Emperor Zeno (474-491). In addition, the Persian Christians needed to distance themselves from the official church of the Roman Empire, with which Persia was frequently at war. In this way they were able to maintain their Christian faith while avoiding suspicions that they were collaborating with the Roman enemy.

Synods in the 5th century also decreed that celibacy should be obligatory for no one in this church, including bishops. A number of bishops and even patriarchs were married until the early 6th century, when the decision was taken to ordain only celibate monks to the episcopate. Priests, however, have always been allowed to marry, even after ordination.

The Church of the East was always a minority in largely Zoroastrian Persia, but nevertheless it flourished for many centuries, with its rich scholarly activity centered on the famous school of Nisibis. The church expanded through missionary activity into areas as far away as India, Tibet, China, and Mongolia. This continued even after the Mesopotamian homeland was conquered by the Muslim Arabs in the 7th century. The Patriarchate was moved to the new city of Baghdad after it became the capital in 766. By 1318 there were some 30 metropolitan sees and 200 suffragan dioceses. But during the invasions of Tamerlane in the late 14th century, these Christians were almost annihilated. By the 16th century, they had been reduced to a small community of Assyrians in what is now eastern Turkey. The church was then further weakened by the formation of a Catholic counterpart known as the Chaldean Catholic Church [see IV.B.1].

During World War I, the Assyrians suffered massive deportations and massacres at the hands of the Turks who suspected them of supporting the British enemy. About one third of the Assyrian population perished. Most of the survivors fled south into Iraq, hoping to be protected by the British. But in 1933, after the end of the British mandate in Iraq, a clash between Assyrians and Iraqi troops ended in another massacre and a further scattering of the community. The Iraqi authorities then stripped Assyrian Patriarch Mar Simon XXIII of his citizenship and expelled him. He went into exile in San Francisco, California, USA.

In 1964 a dispute arose within the church, triggered by Mar Simon's decision to adopt the Gregorian calendar. But the real issue was the person of Mar Simon and the centuries-old practice by which he was elected. By 1450, the office of Patriarch and some other episcopal sees had become hereditary within one family, usually being passed down from uncle to nephew. This often produced unqualified leaders of the church who at times were elected at a very young age: Mar Simon himself had been elected at age 12. The dissidents also held that a Patriarch was needed who could live with his community in Iraq.

Those opposed to Mar Simon were supported by Mar Thomas Darmo, the Assyrian Metropolitan of India. In 1968 he traveled from India to Baghdad and ordained three new bishops. They then met in synod and elected him Patriarch over against Mar Simon. Mar Thomas Darmo died in the following year, and was succeeded in 1970 by Mar Addai of Baghdad.

But in 1973 Mar Simon resigned as Patriarch and married. As no successor could be agreed upon, the Assyrian bishops in communion with him attempted to persuade him to resume his office despite his marriage. But in the midst of these negotiations, on November 6, 1975, Mar Simon was assassinated in San Jose, California. The bishop of Tehran, Iran, was elected Patriarch in 1976 and adopted the name Mar Dinkha IV. He took up residence in the United States.

Mar Dinkha made it clear that with his election, the patriarchal dynasty had ended. This removed the major reason for the schism between the two groups. Although the rift has not yet been healed, recent meetings between bishops of the two sides appear to have made substantial progress towards resolving the dispute. Currently Mar Dinkha's side has eleven bishops and Mar Addai's side has five bishops.

Meeting in Australia in July 1994, the Assyrian Holy Synod reached a number of important decisions concerning the life of this church. The bishops established a Commission on Interchurch Relations and Education Development under the guidance of Bishop Bawai Soro to prepare for theological dialogues with other churches and develop programming in religious education. The Synod also officially sanctioned the residence of the Patriarch in Morton Grove, Illinois, USA.

A milestone in relations with the Roman Catholic Church was reached on November 11, 1994, when Mar Dinkha IV and Pope John Paul II signed a Common Christological Declaration in the Vatican.

The statement affirms that Catholics and Assyrians are "united today in the confession of the same faith in the Son of God..." and envisages broad pastoral cooperation between the two churches, especially in the areas of catechesis and the formation of future priests. The Pope and Patriarch also established a mixed committee for theological dialogue and charged it with overcoming the obstacles that still prevent full communion. It began meeting annually in 1995.

This international theological dialogue between the Assyrians and the Catholic Church as a whole has been accompanied by an improvement in relations between the Assyrian Church of the East and its Catholic counterpart, the Chaldean Catholic Church. In November 1996 Mar Dinkha IV and Chaldean Patriarch Raphael I Bidawid met in Southfield, Michigan, and signed a Joint Patriarchal Statement that committed their two churches to working towards reintegration and pledged cooperation on pastoral questions such as the drafting of a common catechism, the setting up of a common seminary in the Chicago-Detroit area, the preservation of the Aramaic language, and other common pastoral programs between parishes and dioceses around the world.

On August 15, 1997, the two Patriarchs met again, in Roselle, Illinois, and ratified a "Joint Synodal Decree for Promoting Unity," that had been signed by the members of both Holy Synods. It restated the areas of pastoral cooperation envisaged in the Joint Patriarchal Statement, recognized that Assyrians and Chaldeans should come to accept each other's diverse practices as legitimate, formally implemented the establishment of an Assyrian-Chaldean "Joint Commission for Unity," and declared that each side recognized the apostolic succession, sacraments and Christian witness of the other. The text also spelled out the central concerns of both sides in the dialogue. While both churches wanted to preserve the Aramaic language and culture, the Assyrians were intent on retaining their freedom and self-governance, and the Chaldeans affirmed the necessity of maintaining full communion with Rome.

In mid-1997 it was announced that the Assyrian Church of the East and the Syrian Orthodox Church [see II.D] had agreed to establish a bilateral theological dialogue. As a gesture to foster better relations with the Oriental Orthodox churches, the Assyrian Holy Synod decided in 1997 to remove from the liturgy all anathemata directed against others.

Although the Assyrians accept only the first two ecumenical councils, recent ecumenical discussions held under the auspices of the *Pro Oriente* foundation have concluded that in substance the faith of the Assyrian Church is consistent with the christological teaching of the Council of Chalcedon (451). Officially the church adheres to extreme Antiochian christological terminology, according to which in Christ there are two natures and two *qnoma* (a Syriac term with no Greek equivalent that refers to an individual but never personalized concrete nature) in one person. The synod of bishops has requested that their church not be called nestorian, since this term has been used in the past to insult them. The Assyrians are not in communion with any other church.

The East Syrian rite of the Assyrian Church appears to have been an independent development from the ancient Syriac liturgy of Edessa. It may also preserve elements of an ancient Persian rite that has been lost. Services are still held predominantly in Syriac.

In North America, the Patriarch resides in the Chicago area (8908 Birch Avenue, Morton Grove, Illinois 60053). Mar Aprim Khamis is Bishop of the Eastern United States and also administers the parishes of the Western United States (680 Minnesota Avenue, San Jose, California 95125). Mar Bawai Soro (at the same San Jose address) retains episcopal oversight of two English-speaking parishes located in Seattle, Washington, and Sacramento, California. Altogether there are 16 parishes in the country. Mar Emmanuel Joseph is Bishop of Canada, where there are four parishes and two missions (165 Thistle Down Boulevard, Etobicoke, Ontario M9V 1J7). Assyrians in Australia and New Zealand, who have three parishes and two missions, are headed by Mar Meelis Zaia (PO Box 621, Fairfield NSW 2165). There is also one Assyrian parish in London under the jurisdiction of Mar Odisho Oraha, who resides in Sweden.

> LOCATION: Iraq, Iran, Syria, Lebanon, North America, Australia, India
> HEAD: Mar Dinkha IV (born 1935, elected 1976)
> Title: Catholicos-Patriarch of the Church of the East
> Residence: Morton Grove, Illinois, USA
> MEMBERSHIP: 400,000
> WEB SITE: http://www.cired.org

The Thomas Christians

When the Portuguese arrived in India at the end of the 15th century, they encountered a Christian community claiming to have been founded by the Apostle Thomas when he evangelized India following the death and resurrection of Christ. Located on the southwest coast, in what is now Kerala State, they were fully integrated into Indian society as a separate caste. They were in full communion with the Assyrian Church of the East, which in early centuries had regularly sent bishops to India to ordain deacons and priests. In the 8th century India received its own Metropolitan who was assigned the tenth place in the Assyrian hierarchy. But because the Metropolitans generally did not speak the local language, real jurisdiction was placed in the hands of an Indian priest with the title "Archdeacon of All India." He was effectively the civil and religious superior of the entire community until the arrival of the Portuguese.

Portuguese colonization was the beginning of a sad history of forced latinization that caused unrest and schisms among the Thomas Christians. Today their descendants, who number about 5,000,000, are divided into five oriental churches, including about 15,000 who still belong to the Assyrian Church of the East. For the

others see the Syrian Orthodox Church [II.D], the Malankara Orthodox Syrian Church [II.E], the Syro-Malabar Catholic Church [IV.B.2],
and the Syro-Malankara Catholic Church [IV.C.5].

Another interesting feature of the Thomas Christians is the existence of a distinct ethnic community known as the "Southists," or
"Knanaya." According to tradition, their origins can be traced to a
group of 72 Jewish Christian families who immigrated to India from
Mesopotamia in the year 345 AD. There is historical evidence to support this claim. The descendants of these ancient immigrants, who do
not intermarry with those outside the community and now number
about 200,000, are divided into two ethnic dioceses in Kerala, one
belonging to the Syro-Malabar Catholic Church and the other to the
Syrian Orthodox Patriarchate. A Syrian Orthodox Knanaya Diocese
was established for North America in 1982. Rev. Abraham Thomas
Vazhayil Cor-Episcopa is currently the Administrator of the diocese,
which has nine parishes in the USA and Canada. In addition, there
are three Catholic Knanaya communities in the United States.

II. THE ORIENTAL ORTHODOX CHURCHES

The term "Oriental Orthodox churches" is now generally used to describe a group of six ancient eastern churches. Although they are in communion with one another, each is fully independent and possesses many distinctive traditions.

The common element among these churches is their rejection of the christological definition of the Council of Chalcedon (451), which asserted that Christ is one person in two natures, undivided and unconfused. For them, to say that Christ has two natures was to overemphasize the duality in Christ and to compromise the unity of his person. Yet they reject the classical monophysite position of Eutyches, who held that Christ's humanity was absorbed into his single divine nature. They prefer the formula of St. Cyril of Alexandria, who spoke of "the one incarnate nature of the Word of God" (μία φύσις τοῦ Θεοῦ Λόγου σεσαρκωμένη).

During the period following Chalcedon, those who rejected the council's teaching made up a significant portion of the Christians in the Byzantine Empire. Today, however, they are greatly reduced in number. Some of these churches have existed for centuries in areas where there is a non-Christian majority, and more recently others have suffered from many decades of persecution by communist governments.

Because they denied Chalcedon's definition of two natures in Christ, these Christians have often erroneously been called "monophysites," from the Greek word meaning "one nature." The group has also been referred to as "the Lesser Eastern churches," "the Ancient Oriental churches," "the Non-Chalcedonian churches," or "the Pre-Chalcedonian churches." Today it is widely recognized by theologians and church leaders on both sides that the christological differences between the Oriental Orthodox and those who accepted Chalcedon were only verbal, and that in fact both parties profess the same faith in Christ using different formulas.

II. A. The Armenian Apostolic Church

Ancient Armenia was located in present-day eastern Turkey and in bordering areas of the former Soviet Union and Iran. This country became the first nation to adopt Christianity as its state religion when King Tiridates III was converted to the Christian faith by St. Gregory the Illuminator at the beginning of the 4th century. A cathedral was soon built at Etchmiadzin which to this day remains the center of the Armenian Church. It is widely believed that the monk St. Mesrob invented the Armenian alphabet around the year 404, making it possible for the Bible to be translated into that language.

In 506 an Armenian synod rejected the christological teachings of the Council of Chalcedon (451), which no Armenian bishop had attended. At that time the Armenian Church was more concerned with countering the nestorianizing tendencies of the neighboring church in the Persian Empire.

Long a vulnerable buffer state between the hostile Roman and Persian empires, the ancient Armenian kingdom was destroyed in the 11th century. Many Armenians then fled to Cilicia (in south central Asia Minor), where a new Armenian kingdom was established. Here the Armenians had extensive contacts with the Latin Crusaders. Although this new kingdom also ceased to exist by the 14th century and the Armenian people were dispersed, they survived in spite of foreign domination. Their identity as a people centered on their language and their church.

In the late 19th and early 20th centuries, the Armenians in Turkey suffered a series of massacres and expulsions that led to the death of large numbers of them. It is widely believed that altogether between

1.5 and 2 million Armenians died in the genocide. The survivors fled to neighboring countries and to Istanbul.

Today the Armenian Apostolic Church is centered in the Republic of Armenia which declared its independence on September 23, 1991. The holy see of Etchmiadzin, the ancient residence of the Armenian Catholicos, is near Yerevan, the capital. The collapse of Soviet communism has provided conditions for a renaissance of this ancient church in its homeland. New dioceses and parishes are being opened, new organizations founded, religious periodicals published, and religious instruction introduced in the schools. Preparations are underway to celebrate in 2001 the 1700th anniversary of the acceptance of Christianity as Armenia's state religion, which is to include the consecration of a large new cathedral in Yerevan. But the church is experiencing a lack of sufficient clergy, and feels threatened by the new activity of other religious groups that are now free to function in the country. By 1997, it was estimated that as much as 10% of the population belonged to fast-growing sects, and the government was taking action to restrict the activity of religious groups other than the Armenian Apostolic Church.

The Armenian liturgy includes elements of the Syriac, Jerusalem, and Byzantine traditions. While a distinctive Armenian liturgical tradition was being formed in the 5th to the 7th centuries, there was strong liturgical influence from Syria and Jerusalem. Later there was a period of byzantinization, and finally, during the Middle Ages, many Latin usages were adopted.

Although the Armenian Catholicos in Etchmiadzin is recognized by all Armenian Orthodox as the spiritual head of their church, three other Armenian jurisdictions have survived the centuries. Two Catholicosates are in full communion but administratively independent, while two Patriarchates are dependent in spiritual matters on Etchmiadzin. *The Catholicosate of Etchmiadzin* has jurisdiction over Armenians throughout the former USSR and much of the diaspora, including Iraq, India, Egypt, Syria, Sudan, Ethiopia, Europe, Australia, and the Americas. It includes about 5,000,000 faithful. *The Patri-archate of Jerusalem* has its headquarters at St. James monastery in that city and is responsible for the holy places that belong to the Armenian Church. It includes the perhaps 10,000 Armenian faithful in Israel, Jordan, and the Palestinian Autonomous Region and is under the pastoral guidance of Patriarch Torkom II Manoogian (born 1919, elected 1990). *The Patriarchate of Constantinople* has jurisdiction over Turkey and the Greek island of Crete. In 1914 this patriarchate included 12 archdioceses, 27 dioceses, and six monasteries with approximately 1,350,000 faithful. Today only the Patriarchate itself remains, with a flock of about 82,000. Patriarch Mesrob II Mutafyan was born in 1956 and elected in 1998.

The Catholicosate of Cilicia, now based in Antelias, Lebanon, has jurisdiction in Lebanon, Syria, Cyprus, Iran, Syria and Greece, and has about 800,000 members. Cilicia has had a history of tension with Etchmiadzin, and both maintain separate jurisdictions in North America, Greece and Syria. In 1997 delegations from the two Catholicosates met in Etchmiadzin to try to overcome those differences and strengthen the unity of the Armenian Church. Efforts to draft a common constitution for the Armenian Church that would normalize relations between Etchmiadzin and Cilicia are also underway. Catholicos Aram I Keshishian (born 1947) was elected in 1995.

The Armenian Apostolic Church currently maintains four seminaries: Kevorkian Seminary in Etchmiadzin, a seminary of the Catholicosate of Cilicia in Bikfaya, Lebanon, St. James Seminary in Jerusalem, and St. Nersess Seminary in New Rochelle, New York, which is associated with St. Vladimir's Orthodox Seminary in nearby Crestwood, New York.

The Catholicosate of Etchmiadzin has bishops throughout the diaspora. The Armenians in the United Kingdom, who have three parishes, are under the pastoral supervision of Archbishop Yeghishe Gizirian (St. Sarkis Church, Iverna Gardens, London W8 6TP). Archbishop Aghan Baliozian is Primate of Australia and New Zealand

(Holy Resurrection Armenian Church, 10 Marquarie Street, PO Box 694, Chatswood NSW 2067). There are parishes in Sydney and Melbourne. In North America, the Eastern USA Diocese (St. Vartan's Cathedral, 630 Second Avenue, New York, New York 10016) is headed by Archbishop Khajag Barsamian, while Archbishop Vatche Hovsepian of Los Angeles is Primate of the Western USA Diocese (1201 North Vine Street, Hollywood, California 90038). Altogether there are 65 parishes in the USA. The Diocese of Canada (615 Stuart Avenue, Montréal, Québec H2V 3H2), which has five parishes, is under the pastoral care of Archbishop Hovnan Derderian.

The Catholicosate of Cilicia also has two dioceses in the United States: the Prelacy of the Eastern United States and Canada is headed by Bishop Oshagan Choloyan (138 East 39th Street, New York, New York 10016), and the Western Prelacy is administered by Bishop Moushegh Martirossian (4401 Russell Avenue, Los Angeles, California 90027). Altogether there are 33 parishes in the USA, and four in Canada.

LOCATION: Armenia, large diaspora
HEAD: Catholicos Karekin I (born 1932, elected 1995)
Title: Supreme Patriarch and Catholicos of All Armenians
Residence: Etchmiadzin, Armenia
MEMBERSHIP: 6,000,000

II. B. The Coptic Orthodox Church

The foundation of the church in Egypt is closely associated with St. Mark the Evangelist who, according to tradition, was martyred in Alexandria in 63 AD. Eventually Egypt became a Christian nation and Alexandria an extremely important center of theological reflection. Moreover, monks in the Egyptian desert provided the first models for the Christian monastic tradition, having been nourished by the spiritual insights of the early "desert fathers."

But the christological teachings of the Council of Chalcedon in 451, partially because of opposition to Byzantine domination, were rejected by much of the Egyptian hierarchy and faithful. Persecutions intended to force acceptance only reinforced the resistance. Eventually a separate "Coptic" (from the Arabic and Greek word for "Egyptian") Church emerged with a distinct theological and liturgical tradition. From the 5th to the 9th centuries the Greek Patriarchs lived in the city of Alexandria, while the Coptic Patriarchs resided in the desert monastery of St. Macarius.

After the Arab invasion in 641, the Copts slowly diminished in numbers, becoming a minority in Egypt around the year 850. Arabic replaced Coptic as the official language of the country in the 8th century. Islamic rule was marked by long periods of persecution, but also by periods of relative freedom, during which the church flourished again and produced outstanding theological and spiritual works in Arabic.

The Copts are the largest Christian community in the Middle East and are still a significant minority in Egypt. There is strong evidence that the official membership figure reported below is underestimated: Pope Shenouda III reported in February 1995 that his church had eight million members.

There are many separate Coptic schools in Egypt, and a Sunday School movement flourishes. Presently an encouraging revival of monasticism is taking place, and many young monks, involved in agriculture and publishing, inhabit the ancient desert monasteries. There are currently twelve monasteries with close to 600 monks, and six convents with about 300 nuns. The largest concentration of monasteries is at Wadi Natrun, about 60 miles northwest of Cairo.

The Coptic Church's main seminary is in Cairo next to St. Mark's Cathedral. About half of the church's priests were educated there, and many laypeople participate in evening courses in scripture and theology. A Coptic Institute of Higher Studies, founded in 1954 and situated at the patriarchal compound, is an important ecumenical center for the study of the Coptic Christian tradition.

The recent rise of Islamic fundamentalism in Egypt has created new problems for the Coptic Church. Following anti-Coptic outbursts by fundamentalists in the late 1970s, President Sadat in 1981 placed Pope Shenouda III under house arrest in one of the desert monasteries. He was not released until 1985. It was generally surmised that this action resulted from the government's need to appear even-handed in dealing with conflicting groups. Nevertheless, this interference in the affairs of the Coptic Church disturbed many Egyptian Christians. There were increasing attacks against Copts by Islamic militants in Egypt in 1997.

The Coptic liturgy grew from the original Greek rite of Alexandria, developing by the 4th century its own native characteristics. This process took place mainly in the monasteries, and to this day the Coptic liturgy has many monastic characteristics. It is celebrated in both Coptic and Arabic.

In 1995 the Coptic Holy Synod divided the single Archdiocese of the United States into six dioceses. Bishops were named for Los Angeles (Amba Serapion) and Dallas (Amba Youssef). The other dioceses awaiting bishops were named Western United States, East Coast, Mid-Continent and New York-New Jersey. Altogether there are more than 70 parishes and 100 priests in the USA and 15 parishes in Canada. Further information can be obtained from Rev. Jacob Ghaly, Virgin Mary Coptic Orthodox Church, 41 Main Street South, Spring Valley, New York 10977. In Australia there are 14 Coptic parishes, also under the direct supervision of Pope Shenouda. The Secretary of the Coptic Board of Deacons can be reached at 70 Wollongong Road, Arncliffe, NSW 2205.

In the British Isles, Bishop Misael leads the Diocese of Birmingham (Hill Park House, Lapworth Street, Solihull, Warwickshire B94 5QS), and Bishop Antony (40 Kingston Drive, Whitley Bay NE26 1JJ) heads the Diocese of Scotland, Ireland and Northeast England that was established in 1995. Copts in other areas of England fall under the direct jurisdiction of Pope Shenouda III. Altogether there are 12 parishes and 16 priests in the United Kingdom, and one parish with a priest in Ireland. The Secretary of the Coptic Church Council is Dr. Fuad Megally, 509 Duncan House, Dolphin Square, London SW1. On June 19, 1994, the Coptic Orthodox Patriarchate formally received the small Orthodox Church of the British Isles into its jurisdiction as a distinct diocese covering the United Kingdom and Ireland. It was renamed The British Orthodox Church, and its head, Metropolitan Seraphim of Glastonbury, was given the new name of Abba Seraphim El Souriani (10 Heathwood Gardens, Charlton, London SE7 8EP). It currently has seven parishes served by nine priests.

> LOCATION: Egypt and diaspora in Europe, Africa, Australia, the Americas
> HEAD: Pope Shenouda III (born 1923, elected 1971)
> Title: Pope of Alexandria, Patriarch of the See of St. Mark
> Residence: Cairo, Egypt
> MEMBERSHIP: 3,900,000

II. C. The Ethiopian Orthodox Church

According to an ancient tradition, the first great evangelizer of the Ethiopians was St. Frumentius, a Roman citizen from Tyre who had been shipwrecked along the African coast of the Red Sea. He gained the confidence of the emperor at Aksum and eventually brought about the conversion of his son, who later became Emperor Ezana. Ezana later introduced Christianity as the state religion around the year 330. Frumentius was ordained a bishop by St. Athanasius of Alexandria and returned to Ethiopia to help with the continued evangelization of the country.

Around the year 480 the "Nine Saints" arrived in Ethiopia and began missionary activities. According to tradition they were from

Rome, Constantinople and Syria. They had left their countries because of their opposition to Chalcedonian christology and had probably resided for a time at St. Pachomius monastery in Egypt. Their influence, along with its traditional links with the Copts in Egypt, probably explains the origin of the Ethiopian Church's rejection of Chalcedon. The Nine Saints are credited with largely wiping out the remaining paganism in Ethiopia, with introducing the monastic tradition, and with making a substantial contribution to the development of Ge'ez religious literature by translating the Bible and religious works into that classical Ethiopian language. Monasteries quickly sprang up throughout the country and became important intellectual centers.

The Ethiopian Church reached its zenith in the 15th century when much creative theological and spiritual literature was produced and the church was engaged in extensive missionary activity.

The very negative experience of contact with Portuguese Roman Catholic missionaries in the 16th century [see IV.C.3] was followed by centuries of isolation from which the Ethiopian Church has only recently emerged.

This church is unique in retaining several Jewish practices such as circumcision and the observance of dietary laws and Saturday as well as Sunday sabbath. This is probably due to the fact that the earliest presence of Christianity in Ethiopia had come directly from Palestine through southern Arabia. But there is a tradition that Judaism was practiced by some Ethiopians even before the arrival of Christianity. There have also been some unusual christological developments, including a school of thought that holds that the union of Christ's divine and human natures took place only upon his anointing at Baptism. These teachings were never officially adopted and have mostly died out.

The Ethiopian liturgy is of Alexandrian (Coptic) origin and influenced by the Syriac tradition. The liturgy was always celebrated in the ancient Ge'ez language until very recent times. Today a translation of the liturgy into modern Amharic is being used increasingly in the parishes. A strong monastic tradition continues.

From ancient times, all bishops in Ethiopia were Egyptian Copts appointed by the Coptic Patriarchate. Indeed, for many centuries the only bishop in Ethiopia was the Coptic Metropolitan. In the early 20th century the Ethiopian Church began to press for greater autonomy and the election of native Ethiopian bishops. In 1929 four native Ethiopian bishops were ordained to assist the Coptic Metropolitan. With the support of Emperor Haile Selassie (reigned 1930-1974), an agreement was reached with the Copts in 1948 which provided for the election of an ethnic Ethiopian Metropolitan upon the death of Metropolitan Qerillos. Thus when he died in 1951, an assembly of clergy and laity elected an Ethiopian, Basilios, as Metropolitan, and the autonomy of the Ethiopian Church was established. In 1959 the Coptic Patriarchate confirmed Metropolitan Basilios as the first Patriarch of the Ethiopian Orthodox Church.

An Ethiopian Orthodox faculty of theology, Trinity College, functioned as part of the University of Addis Ababa until it was closed by the government in 1974. In the same year, the church established St. Paul Theological College in Addis Ababa to provide a theological education for candidates for the priesthood. It has long been common for many Ethiopian Orthodox men to seek ordination; it was estimated in 1988 that there were 250,000 clergymen in the country. In order to provide them with an adequate level of education, six Clergy Training Centers have recently been established in various parts of Ethiopia. Every parish is now expected to have a Sunday School program.

Especially in recent years, the Ethiopian Church has assumed an active role in serving those in need. It has sponsored relief efforts on behalf of refugees and victims of drought, and a number of church-sponsored orphanages have been set up.

The Ethiopian Orthodox Church was the state religion of the country until the 1974 Marxist revolution, which overthrew the Em-

peror and placed Colonel Mengistu Haile Mariam at the head of government. Soon after the revolution, church and state were officially
separated and most church land was nationalized. This signaled the
beginning of a campaign against all the religious groups in the country.

Following the collapse of the communist government in May
1991, Patriarch Merkorios (elected in 1988) was accused of collaboration with the Mengistu regime. In September, under pressure, he
resigned his duties as Patriarch. On July 5, 1992, the Holy Synod
elected Abune Paulos as fifth Patriarch of the Ethiopian Orthodox
Church. He had been imprisoned for seven years by the Marxist
authorities after Patriarch Theophilos (deposed in 1976 and murdered in prison in 1979) ordained him a bishop without government
approval in 1975. Paulos was released in 1983 and had spent the intervening years in the United States. Meanwhile, Patriarch Merkorios, who took refuge in Kenya, has refused to recognize the election
of Paulos.

In October 1994 Patriarch Paulos presided over the reopening of
Trinity Theological College in the Ethiopian capital. The college began functioning again with 50 students in its degree program and 100
studying for diplomas in theology.

The total membership figure reported below was provided by the
World Council of Churches. But some credible sources in Ethiopia
believe that the true figure may be as high as 30 million, based on estimates that the Ethiopian Orthodox make up about 60% of the total
population of 55 million.

In Australia there are Ethiopian Orthodox communities in each of
the state capitals. Contact Fr. Mangsha Dessie at PO Box 176, Ascot
Vale, Victoria 3032. Three parishes in Great Britain were supervised
by Bishop Yohannes until his death in December 1997. Rev. Berhanu
Beserat (33 Juniper Crescent, London, NW1 8HA) was then named
acting head of the Ethiopian Orthodox Church in Europe.

In the United States, Ethiopian Archbishop Yesehaq did not recognize the election of Patriarch Paulos and broke communion with the Patriarchate in 1992. In response, the Ethiopian Holy Synod suspended him, and also decided to divide the existing Archdiocese of the Western Hemisphere into three jurisdictions (USA and Canada, Latin America and the Caribbean, and Western Europe). It appointed Abuna Matthias as new Archbishop of the United States and Canada (PO Box 77262, Washington, DC 20013). Canada was later established as a separate diocese under the supervision of Bishop Matthias who resides in London, Ontario. However, Archbishop Yesehaq continues to hold the allegiance of many Ethiopian Orthodox in the Americas and still maintains his office at 140-142 West 176th, Bronx, New York 10451. Altogether there are about 90,000 Ethiopian Orthodox in the western hemisphere, including a significant number of converts in the West Indies.

LOCATION: Ethiopia, small diaspora
HEAD: Patriarch Paulos (born 1935, elected 1992)
Title: Patriarch of the Ethiopian Orthodox Church
Residence: Addis Ababa, Ethiopia
MEMBERSHIP: 16,000,000

II. D. The Syrian Orthodox Church

The Syrian Church traces its origins back to the early Christian community at Antioch, which is mentioned in the Acts of the Apostles. The Antiochene Church became one of the great centers of Christianity in the early centuries. But the Council of Chalcedon in 451 provoked a split in the community. The council's teachings were enforced by the Byzantine imperial authorities in the cities, but they were largely rejected in the countryside.

In the 6th century, the Bishop of Edessa, Jacob Baradai, ordained many bishops and priests to carry on the faith of those who rejected

Chalcedon in the face of imperial opposition. Consequently, this church became known as "Jacobite," with its own liturgy (called "West Syrian" or "Antiochene") and other traditions using the Syriac language spoken by the common people. Some communities were also established outside the Byzantine Empire in Persia.

The conquest of the area by the Persians and later the Arabs ended Byzantine persecution and created conditions favoring further development of the Syrian Church. There was a great revival of Syrian Orthodox scholarship in the Middle Ages, when the community possessed flourishing schools of theology, philosophy, history, and science. At its height, the church included twenty metropolitan sees and 103 dioceses extending as far to the east as Afghanistan. There is also evidence of communities of Syrian Orthodox faithful without bishops as distant as Turkestan and Sinkiang during this period.

But the Mongol invasions under Tamerlane in the late 14th century, during which most Syrian churches and monasteries were destroyed, marked the beginning of a long decline. Terrible losses were suffered again during and after World War I because of persecutions and massacres in eastern Turkey. This led to a widespread dispersion of the community.

Even now the Syrian Orthodox population is shifting. In the 1950s and 1960s many emigrated from Iraq and Syria to Lebanon. Within Iraq, they have been moving from the northern city of Mosul to Baghdad. The most serious erosion of the community has taken place in southeast Turkey, where only a few Syrian Orthodox remain. Earlier in this century many Syrian Orthodox also immigrated to Western Europe and the Americas for economic and political reasons.

The Syrians have a strong monastic tradition, and a few monasteries remain in the Mardin province of Turkey and other parts of the Middle East. There are now three monasteries in the diaspora, located in the Netherlands, Germany, and Switzerland.

The Syrian Patriarchs resided in Antioch until 1034. Since that time they have resided in Mar Barsauma monastery (1034-1293), Der ez-Za'faran monastery (1293-1924), Homs, Syria (1924-1959), and finally Damascus (since 1959).

Some theological education is still provided by the monasteries. But St. Ephrem Syrian Orthodox Seminary is the major theological institute of the Patriarchate. It was founded in Zahle, Lebanon, but moved to Mosul, Iraq, in 1939. It moved back to Zahle in the 1960s, and relocated to Atchaneh, near Beirut, in 1968. The outbreak of civil war in Lebanon forced the removal of the students to Damascus, Syria. New facilities for the seminary at Sayedniya, near Damascus, were consecrated by the Syrian Patriarch on September 14, 1996.

Since the mid-17th century, the Syrian Patriarchate has included an autonomous church in India, a part of which is now called the "Malankara Syrian Orthodox Church." The head of that church, Catholicos Mar Baselios Paulos II, died in September 1996. No successor had been elected by the beginning of 1998. See also the Malankara Orthodox Syrian Church: II.E.

A Syrian Orthodox Archdiocese of the United States and Canada was founded by Archbishop Mar Athanasius Yeshue Samuel in 1957. After his death in April 1995, the Syrian Holy Synod divided the Archdiocese into three jurisdictions. The Patriarchal Vicariate for the Eastern United States (49 Kipp Avenue, Lodi, New Jersey 07644), is headed by Mor Kyrilos Ephrem Karim (born 1965, elected 1995). It has 13 parishes. The Patriarchal Vicariate for the Western United States (417 East Fairmount Road, Burbank, California 91502), which has five parishes, is under the pastoral care of Mor Climis Eugene Kaplan (born 1955, elected 1995). The Patriarchal Vicar for Canada (999 Montpellier #102, St. Laurent, Quebec H4L 5E5), where there are five parishes, is Mor Timotheos Ephrem Aboodi (born 1930, elected 1995). In 1993 the Syrian Holy Synod separated the parishes of Indian faithful from the Syrian Archdiocese and established the Malankara Archdiocese of the Syrian Orthodox Church in North America under the pastoral guidance of Metropolitan Mar Nicolovos Zachariah (175 Ninth Avenue, New York, New York 10011). It includes 23 parishes, served by 25 priests. The Patriarchal Vicariate of Australia and New Zealand (PO Box 257, Lidcombe 2141) did not have a bishop in late 1997. There are eight parishes in Australia and one in New Zealand. The Syrian Orthodox Church in Britain is represented by Fr. Thomas H. Dawood (5 Canning Road, Croydon, CR0 6QB), and the Malankara Church by Fr. Eldhose Koungampillil (1 Roslyn Court, Roslyn Avenue, East Barnet, Hertsfordshire, EN4 8DJ).

> LOCATION: Syria, Lebanon, Turkey, Israel, India, diaspora
> HEAD: Patriarch Ignatius Zakka I Iwas (born 1933, elected 1980)
> Title: Syrian Orthodox Patriarch of Antioch and All the East
> Residence: Damascus, Syria
> MEMBERSHIP: 250,000, plus 1,000,000 in India

II. E. The Malankara Orthodox Syrian Church

In the mid-17th century, most of the Thomas Christians in India (see Assyrian Church of the East, I) had become increasingly upset with the latinization of their church by the Portuguese. This led thousands of faithful to gather at the Coonan Cross in Mattancherry on January 16, 1653, and take an oath to submit no longer to the authority of Rome. The leader of the dissidents may have attempted to reestablish communion with the Assyrian Church of the East, but in any case this was not achieved. Then in 1665, the Syrian Patriarch agreed to send a bishop to head the community on the condition that its leader and his followers agree to accept Syrian christology and follow the West Syrian rite. This group was eventually administered as an autonomous church within the Syrian Patriarchate.

However, in 1912 there was a split in the community when a significant section declared itself an autocephalous church and announced the re-establishment of the ancient Catholicosate of the East in India. This was not accepted by those who remained loyal to the Syrian Patriarch. The two sides were reconciled in 1958 when the

Indian Supreme Court declared that only the autocephalous Catholicos and bishops in communion with him had legal standing. But in 1975 the Syrian Patriarch excommunicated and deposed the Catholicos and appointed a rival, an action that resulted in the community splitting yet again. In June 1996 the Supreme Court of India rendered a decision that (a) upheld the Constitution of the church that had been adopted in 1934 and made it binding on both factions, (b) stated that there is only one Orthodox church in India, currently divided into two factions, and (c) recognized the Syrian Orthodox Patriarch of Antioch as the spiritual head of the universal Syrian Church, while affirming that the autocephalous Catholicos has legal standing as the head of the entire church, and that he is custodian of its parishes and properties.

The precise size of these two communities is extremely difficult to determine and is hotly disputed by the two sides. Many outside observers believe that roughly half of the Oriental Orthodox in India, who altogether number about 2,000,000, are part of this autocephalous church, while the other half makes up an autonomous church under the supervision of the Syrian Orthodox Patriarchate [see above, II.D].

There are two other churches in Kerala that originated in the Malankara Orthodox community. Due in part to the activity of Anglican missionaries, a reform movement grew up within this church in the 19th century. Those who adhered to the movement eventually formed *The Mar Thoma Syrian Church of Malabar*, which to a great extent conserves oriental liturgical practice and ethos. This church, whose episcopal succession derives from the Syrian Orthodox Church, tends to accept reformed theology and has been in communion with the Anglican Provinces since 1974. It now has about 700,000 members.

In the late 18th century, a Syrian prelate from Jerusalem ordained a local monk as bishop, but he was not accepted by the Malankara Metropolitan. This bishop then fled to the north and established his own group of followers at the village of Thozhiyoor. Less than 10,000 faithful make up this church today, which is called *The Malabar Independent Syrian Church of Thozhiyoor*. While preserving its oriental heritage, this group has links with the Mar Thoma Church and increasingly with the Anglican Communion.

The Malankara Orthodox Syrian Church administers the Orthodox Theological Seminary at Kottayam, which was founded in the early 19th century and now has about 140 students. New facilities have recently been built, including the "Sophia Centre" for the theological training of lay men and women, and a School for Liturgical Music affiliated with Kottayam's Mahatma Gandhi University. The church also operates a number of colleges, schools, hospitals and orphanages.

This church also has a modest monastic tradition. There are four communities of men that follow a monastic rule and eleven for celibate priests and laity without a definite monastic order. There are also ten convents where nuns live a dedicated life of service and worship.

Metropolitan Thomas Mar Makarios is the Senior Metropolitan of the Malankara Orthodox Church in America (1114 Delaware Avenue, Buffalo, New York 14209). There are 56 priests and 56 parishes within that jurisdiction. Mar Makarios also serves as Metropolitan of Canada and Europe. The Malankara Orthodox Church has a parish in Great Britain (Fr. M. S. Skariah, 44 Newbury Road, Newbury Park, Ilford, Essex 1G2 7HD). There is also a parish in Australia that can be reached through Fr. Skariah at 73 Little George Street, Fitzroy, Victoria 3065.

LOCATION: India, small diaspora
HEAD: Baselius Mar Thoma Matthews II (born 1915, elected 1991)
Title: Catholicos of the East; Catholicos of the Apostolic Throne of
    St. Thomas
and Malankara Metropolitan
Residence: Kottayam, Kerala State, India
MEMBERSHIP: 1,000,000

II. F. The Eritrean Orthodox Church

Eritrea, located along the southwest coast of the Red Sea, was the site of the ancient Christian kingdom of Aksum. It began to decline in the 7th century in the wake of Muslim invasions, and a new Ethiopian kingdom was subsequently established in the interior. The region retained a certain independence until it fell under Ottoman rule in the 16th century. Eritrea was an Italian colony from 1890 to 1941, when it was captured by the British. It entered a federation with Ethiopia in 1952, and was annexed as an Ethiopian province in 1962. A lengthy struggle for self-rule culminated with the country's declaration of independence on May 24, 1993.

In July 1993, the bishops of the country (with the support of the government) appealed to Pope Shenouda III of the Coptic Orthodox Church to obtain separation from the Ethiopian Orthodox Church and autocephalous status. On September 28, 1993, the Coptic Holy Synod responded favorably to this request and authorized the training of as many as ten future bishops for the Eritrean Church in Coptic monasteries. On June 19, 1994, Pope Shenouda ordained five of these new bishops in Cairo.

The process of the establishment of an independent Eritrean Orthodox Church took place in accord with the Ethiopian Orthodox Church. In early September 1993 Patriarch Paulos and Archbishop Philipos (the ranking bishop in Eritrea) sanctioned the separation of their churches, while stating their desire to work closely together. In February 1994 an agreement was signed in Addis Ababa that reaffirmed the autocephalous status of both the Ethiopian and Eritrean churches, and recognized a primacy of honor of the Coptic Church among the Oriental Orthodox churches in Africa.

After intensive discussions among government and church leaders in April 1998, Abba Philipos, the bishop of Asmara, was chosen as the first Patriarch of the Eritrean Orthodox Church. He was ordained Patriarch by Coptic Pope Shenouda III in Cairo on May 8, 1998. A protocol between the Holy Synods of the Eritrean and Coptic churches was also signed. It provided for close cooperation between the two churches, including the holding of a common general synod at least every three years, the commemoration of the heads of both churches in all liturgies, the formation of a common delegation in theological dialogues with other churches, and the establishment of a standing committee of the two synods to promote cooperation in such areas as theological education, social services, and development projects.

The Eritrean Orthodox Church has approximately 1,500 churches, 22 monasteries, and 15,000 priests. The Eritrean Orthodox Church in Great Britain is represented by Bishop Markos, Secretary to the Holy Synod, 11 Anfield Close, Weir Road, London SW12 0NT. Bishop Makarios (5 Woodstone Drive, Cedar Grove, New Jersey 07009-0373), an ethnic Eritrean and a member of the Coptic Holy Synod, is responsible for Eritrean Orthodox faithful in the United States.

LOCATION: Eritrea
HEAD: Patriarch Philipos I (born 1905, elected 1998)
Title: Patriarch of Eritrea
Residence: Asmara, Eritrea
MEMBERSHIP: 1,700,000

III. THE ORTHODOX CHURCH

Orthodox Christians consider themselves to be part of one church in the sense that they share the same faith and sacraments, as well as the Byzantine liturgical, canonical, and spiritual tradition. All Orthodox recognize the first seven ecumenical councils as normative for doctrine and church life. A number of later councils are also considered to express the same original faith. Although referred to most commonly as the Orthodox Church, this communion is also frequently called the Eastern Orthodox Church to distinguish it from the Oriental Orthodox churches described in the previous section.

At the level of church government, Orthodoxy is a communion of churches, all of which recognize the Patriarch of Constantinople as *primus inter pares,* or "first among equals." Although he does not have authority to intervene in the affairs of local churches outside his own Patriarchate, he is considered first in honor and the symbolic center of all the Orthodox churches. Thus the Patriarchate of Constantinople (also known as the Ecumenical Patriarchate) enjoys a certain priority among the various Orthodox churches. It sees this status as a service that provides a mechanism for promoting conciliarity and mutual responsibility. This role includes convoking the churches and coordinating their activity, and at times intervening in situations in an effort to find solutions to specific problems.

The schism between what are now known as the Orthodox and Catholic churches was the result of a centuries-long process of estrangement. Such events as the excommunications in 1054 between the Patriarch of Constantinople and the papal legate were only high points in this process. Moreover, each Orthodox church has its own history concerning the rift with Rome. There was never, for example, a formal separation between Rome and the Patriarchate of Antioch, although Antioch came to share the common Byzantine perception of the schism. Today it is widely agreed that there were significant non-theological factors at play in this gradual alienation between East and West. These included the interruption of regular communication that resulted from political developments and the loss of the ability to understand the Greek or Latin of the other church. But doctrinal issues were also involved, especially regarding the nature of the Church. The most important of these concerned the eternal procession of the Holy Spirit (related to the addition of the *filioque* to the Creed by the western church), and the meaning of the role of the bishop of Rome as first bishop in the Church.

Two major attempts to reestablish communion between Catholics and Orthodox took place at the Second Council of Lyons in 1274 and the Council of Florence-Ferrara in 1438-1439. Although formal reunions were proclaimed in both cases, they were ultimately rejected by the general Orthodox population. Many centuries of mutual isolation have been ended only in the contemporary period. An official international dialogue between the two churches has been in progress since 1980.

III. A. THE AUTOCEPHALOUS ORTHODOX CHURCHES

There are thirteen Orthodox churches that are generally accepted as "autocephalous," which in Greek means "self-headed." An autocephalous church possesses the right to resolve all internal problems on its own authority and the ability to choose its own bishops, including the Patriarch, Archbishop or Metropolitan who heads the church. While each autocephalous church acts independently, they all remain in full sacramental and canonical communion with one another.

Today these autocephalous Orthodox churches include the four ancient Eastern Patriarchates (Constantinople, Alexandria, Antioch, and Jerusalem), and ten other Orthodox churches that have emerged over the centuries in Russia, Serbia, Romania, Bulgaria, Georgia, Cyprus, Greece, Poland, Albania, and the Czech and Slovak Republics. On its own initiative, the Patriarchate of Moscow has granted autocephalous status to most of its parishes in North America under the name of the Orthodox Church in America. But since the Patriarchate of Constantinople claims the exclusive right to grant autocephalous status, it and most other Orthodox churches do not recognize the autocephaly of the American church.

Nine of these autocephalous churches are Patriarchates: Constantinople, Alexandria, Antioch, Jerusalem, Russia, Serbia, Romania, Bulgaria and Georgia. The others are headed by an Archbishop or Metropolitan.

III. A. 1. The Patriarchate of Constantinople (The Ecumenical Patriarchate)

In New Testament times, Greek culture was predominant in the eastern regions of the Roman Empire. The early growth of the Church, beginning with the missionary activity of St. Paul, eventually led to the Christianization of this Greek civilization.

The Emperor Constantine began a process that led to the adoption of Christianity as the imperial state religion by Emperor Theodosius in the late 4th century. Constantine also moved the empire's capital from Rome to the small Greek city of Byzantium in 330 and renamed it Constantinople, or New Rome.

Because of Constantinople's new status as capital of the empire, its church grew in importance. Canon 3 of the First Council of Constantinople (381) stated that the bishop of that city "shall have primacy of honor after the Bishop of Rome because Constantinople is the New Rome." Thus it assumed a position higher than the more ancient Patriarchates of Alexandria and Antioch. In its disputed 28th Canon, the Council of Chalcedon in 451 recognized an expansion of the boundaries of the Patriarchate of Constantinople and of its authority over bishops of dioceses "among the barbarians," which has been variously interpreted as referring either to areas outside the Byzantine Empire or to non-Greeks. In any case, for almost a thousand years the Patriarch of Constantinople presided over the church in the eastern Roman (Byzantine) Empire and its missionary activity that brought the Christian faith in its Byzantine form to many peoples north of the imperial borders. The cathedral church of Constantinople, Hagia Sophia (Holy Wisdom), was the center of religious life in the eastern Christian world.

The schism between Rome and Constantinople developed slowly over a long period, and is often described in older books as culminating in 1054 with the mutual excommunications between Patriarch Michael Cerularius and Cardinal Humbert, the papal legate. But for the common people in the Empire, the rift took on real meaning only after the 1204 sacking of Constantinople by the Latins during the Fourth Crusade. As communion with Rome was breaking down, Constantinople began to assume the first position among the churches of the Byzantine tradition.

Constantinople fell to the Ottoman Turks in 1453. While they placed many restrictions on Christians, in some ways the Turks enhanced the Patriarch's authority by making him the civil leader of the multi-ethnic Orthodox community within the Empire, and he retained his position as the first of the Orthodox Patriarchs. This gave him a certain authority over the Greek Patriarchates of Alexandria, Antioch, and Jerusalem, which were also within Ottoman territory. But the assumption of civil authority carried a heavy price: when the Greeks rebelled against Turkish rule in 1821, the Ottoman sultan held Patriarch Gregory V responsible and had him hanged at the gates of the patriarchal compound. Two metropolitans and 12 bishops followed him to the gallows.

In 1832 an independent Greek state was established, and a separate autocephalous Church of Greece was set up in 1833. After World War I, there was a major exchange of populations between Greece and Turkey. Anti-Greek riots in Istanbul (the new Turkish name for Constantinople) in the 1950s precipitated another exodus of Greeks from Turkey. Now very few remain.

Today the Patriarchate of Constantinople includes the 4,000 to 5,000 Greeks who remain in Turkey, as well as some sections of Greece (Mount Athos, the semi-autonomous Church of Crete, and the Dodecanese Islands). There was an important theological school on the island of Halki, near Istanbul, until it was closed by the government in 1971. Securing the re-opening of the school is a major priority of the current Patriarch. The Patriarchate administers certain theological academic institutions in Greece, including a school at the monastery of John the Theologian on the island of Patmos, the Patriarchal Institute for Patristic Studies in Thessalonika, and the Orthodox Academy of Crete. In addition, in 1993 the Holy Synod of the Ecumenical Patriarchate designated the Patriarch Athenagoras Orthodox Institute at the Graduate Theological Union in Berkeley, California, as an official patriarchal institute. The Patriarchate also maintains an Orthodox Center at Chambésy, Switzerland, near Geneva. A new Institute of Orthodox Theology opened its doors at Chambésy in late 1997.

The monastic republic of Mount Athos, although located in Greece, is under the jurisdiction of the Ecumenical Patriarchate. The Greek constitution recognizes the administrative autonomy of the monasteries, and the civil governor of the peninsula, appointed by the Greek government, is not to interfere in their internal life. The fortunes of Mount Athos have varied in recent years. While there were 6,345 monks on the peninsula in 1913, the number had fallen to 1,191 in 1980. But a recent influx of young monks to the Holy Mountain raised the total number to about 1,300 in 1995. In the mid-1960s a decisive movement away from the idiorhythmic and towards the

cenobitic style of life began in the monasteries. At that time there
were 11 cenobitic and nine idiorhythmic communities. But as of
1992, when Pantocrator monastery officially adopted the cenobitic
style, no idiorhythmic communities remained. Mount Athos has long
had a multi-ethnic character, with many monks coming from the
Slavic, Romanian and Georgian churches as well as the Greek. The
fall of the communist regimes in Eastern Europe has made it possible
for monks to come to Athos from those countries once again. But
there is some evidence that the Greek government has been trying to
limit the number of new non-Greek monks in the monasteries.

In December 1989 the Patriarchate inaugurated a new administrative headquarters at the Phanar (a section of Istanbul), replacing the
original 17th-century building that had been destroyed in a fire in
1941. It was only in 1987 that the Turkish government had granted
permission to rebuild the edifice. Making use of this facility and the
otherwise unused complex of the Halki theological school, the Patriarchate has recently resumed sponsoring important church events.

Patriarch Bartholomew has brought new vigor to his church's role
within Orthodoxy and beyond. He has been calling all the bishops of
the Patriarchate together for meetings at the Phanar on a regular basis. In March 1992 he convoked the heads of all the autocephalous
churches in Istanbul, and again on the island of Patmos in September
1995. The Ecumenical Patriarch addressed the European Parliament
in Strasbourg in April 1994, has visited most of the autocephalous
Orthodox churches, and visited Pope John Paul II in the Vatican in
June 1995. In December 1995 he visited the Archbishop of Canter-
bury in England and the World Council of Churches in Geneva. In
January 1994 the Patriarch was able, in conjunction with the Patriarchal Institute in Thessalonika, to revive the patriarchal review
Ὀρθοδοξία, which had appeared regularly from 1926 to 1963. At the
Patriarch's initiative, an Orthodox office was opened at the headquar-
ters of the European Community in Brussels on January 10, 1995.

The Patriarch has also become a strong advocate of measures to protect the environment.

However, the situation of the Greek community in Turkey remains precarious. This was made evident by such recent events as the profanation of a Greek cemetery in Istanbul and the setting ablaze of a Greek school. Konrad Raiser, the General Secretary of the World Council of Churches, wrote to Turkish Prime Minister Tansu Ciller on November 4, 1993, to express his concern about the restriction of certain fundamental rights of the Greek minority in the country. He pointed out growing public animosity towards Greeks in Turkey and the lack of education in minority schools. He called upon the Turkish government to protect the Greek minority against religious intolerance, to guarantee its right to its own language and culture, to avoid using the community as a pawn in international disputes, and to show good will by allowing the reopening of the Halki theological school. But problems have continued: three bombs were defused at the patriarchal compound just before they were set to detonate in May 1994, a hand grenade was thrown into the patriarchal complex and exploded without causing injury in September 1996, and a bomb exploded within the grounds of the Patriarchate on the night of December 2-3, 1997, causing extensive damage and injuring a deacon. In January 1998 a church in downtown Istanbul was looted and set afire, and the caretaker was killed.

Even in these circumstances, Patriarch Bartholomew has rejected proposals that the Patriarchate move to another city such as Thessalonika in Greece. He recalls that aside from a brief interruption in the 13th century, the Patriarchate has always been located in ancient Constantinople. Moreover, while transferring to Thessalonika would be to identify with Greece, remaining in Istanbul, at the crossroads of many civilizations and languages, allows the Patriarchate to stand above nationalistic rivalries. Indeed, the Patriarch has vigorously condemned excessive nationalism as detrimental to Orthodoxy and peace in the world. For these reasons the Patriarch believes that the

Patriarchate's location in a secular state with a Muslim majority is advantageous for the Orthodox Church.

The Patriarchate is governed by the Permanent Holy Synod, over which the Patriarch presides. It is made up of twelve active metropolitan bishops whose dioceses are within Turkey. There has been no direct lay participation in the administration of the Patriarchate since a mixed council was abolished in 1923.

The Greek Orthodox in the diaspora are part of the Ecumenical Patriarchate, as well as a number of other jurisdictions of various ethnic backgrounds [see section III.C below]. Archbishop Gregorios of Thyateira and Great Britain has offices at Thyateira House, 5 Craven Hill, W2 3EN London. There are four monasteries and 100 parishes and chapels in Britain, and one parish in Dublin, Ireland.

Archbishop Stylianos presides over Greek Orthodox faithful in Australia (242 Cleveland Street, Redfern, Sydney, NSW 2016). The Australian Archdiocese, which includes 120 parishes and two monastic communities, opened St. Andrew's Greek Orthodox Theological School in Sydney in 1986. The Archdiocese is divided into five districts, three of which are headed by an assistant bishop who is responsible to the Archbishop in Sydney. Greek Orthodox in New Zealand (7 parishes) as well as Korea and Japan, are under the pastoral care of Metropolitan Dionysios (365 Broadway, Miramar, Wellington, N.Z.). A Metropolis of Hong Kong was established in 1996. It is headed by Metropolitan Nikitas (2205 Queens Place, 74 Queens Road Central, Hong Kong), whose jurisdiction includes Greek Orthodox communities in the rest of China, Singapore, India, Indonesia, and the Philippines.

In 1996 the Holy Synod of the Ecumenical Patriarchate divided the former Archdiocese of North and South America into four separate metropolitanates: (1) America (United States), (2) Toronto and All Canada (3) Buenos Aires and South America, and (4) Panama and Central America. The Greek Orthodox Archdiocese of America is led by Archbishop Spyridon (10 East 79th Street, New York, New York

10021). In the USA there are eight dioceses, 570 parishes and eight monastic communities. The Greek Orthodox Metropolis of Canada has 76 parishes and two monasteries under the guidance of Metropolitan Sotirios (86 Overlea Boulevard, East York, Ontario M4H 1C6). The Archdiocese of America administers Hellenic College/Holy Cross Greek Orthodox School of Theology in Brookline, Massachusetts, and the Canadian Metropolis opened a Greek Orthodox Theological Academy in Toronto in September 1998.

LOCATION: Turkey, Greece, the Americas, Western Europe, Australia
HEAD: Patriarch Bartholomew I (born 1940, elected 1991)
Title: Archbishop of Constantinople/New Rome, Ecumenical Patriarch
Residence: Istanbul (Constantinople), Turkey
MEMBERSHIP: 3,500,000
WEB SITE: http://www.patriarchate.org

III. A. 2. The Patriarchate of Alexandria

Until the period following the Council of Chalcedon (451 AD), the Christians in Egypt were united in a single Patriarchate. The controversy surrounding Chalcedon's christological teaching, however, led to a split between the majority that rejected the Council [the Coptic Orthodox Church, see II.B], and the largely Greek minority that accepted it. The Greek Orthodox Patriarchate of Alexandria is descended from the latter group. By the 7th century, it has been estimated that there were 17 or 18 million Copts in Egypt, and approximately 200,000 (mostly imperial officials, soldiers, merchants and other Greeks) who accepted Chalcedon. At this time both groups used the ancient Alexandrian liturgy, but in the Greek Patriarchate it was gradually replaced by the Byzantine liturgy, and the Alexandrian rite died out by the 12th century.

With the Arab conquest and the withdrawal of the Byzantine armies in 642, the Greeks in Egypt suffered persecution because of their links with the Byzantine Empire. This difficult situation became even worse with the Turkish conquest of Egypt in 1517. The Greek Patriarchs of Alexandria began to live off and on in Constantinople, and the Ecumenical Patriarchate often appointed them to office. Only in 1846, with the election of Patriarch Hierotheos I, did the Patriarchs reside consistently in Alexandria again. The involvement of the Ecumenical Patriarchate in the administration of the Church of Alexandria ended with the death of Hierotheos I in 1858.

Patriarch Melitios II (1926-1935) compiled the bylaws of the Patriarchate and submitted them to the Egyptian government. Under these bylaws the Patriarchate remained independent and enjoyed government protection. Melitios was the first Patriarch to be recognized by royal decree, as Egypt was by then no longer part of the Ottoman Empire. Melitios also founded St. Athanasios seminary, systematized the ecclesiastical courts, and established the jurisdiction of the Patriarchate throughout Africa, introducing "All Africa" in place of "All Egypt" in his title.

In the early years of the 20th century, a significant immigration of Greeks and Orthodox Arabs into Egypt and other parts of Africa increased the membership of the Patriarchate. In 1907 the number of Greeks in Egypt was estimated to be 192,000, but by 1997 the number had dropped to some 1,650. Today the Patriarchate has jurisdiction over all the Orthodox faithful in Africa.

In the 1930s a spontaneous movement of indigenous Africans towards the Orthodox Church began in Uganda under the leadership of a former Anglican, Reuben Spartas. He was received into full communion with the Greek Orthodox Patriarchate of Alexandria in 1946, and the Orthodox communities in East Africa that had been founded under his leadership were organized into the Archdiocese of Irinoupolis with headquarters in Nairobi in 1958. This group is now served by a growing native African clergy, including three bishops. In 1998 there were 80 priests in Kenya, 22 in Uganda and 11 in Tanzania. In November 1994 the Patriarchate's Holy Synod created a separate diocese for Uganda and elected the auxiliary bishop of Irinoupolis for Uganda, Theodore Nagiama, as its first Metropolitan. He was the first black bishop to be elected head of a diocese anywhere in the Orthodox Church.

Pope Parthenios III, who was in office from 1987 until his death in 1996, was a strong exponent of the ecumenical movement and was one of the Presidents of the World Council of Churches at the time of his death. Pope Petros VII, his 47-year-old successor, reaffirmed his church's participation in the WCC and the African Council of Churches at his enthronement. Petros also pledged to reorganize the administrative structure of the Patriarchate, to pay special attention to the mission in black Africa, to reopen the Patriarchal Institute of Eastern Studies in Alexandria, and to revive the patriarchal review, *Analecta*.

The Patriarchate is governed on the basis of a series of regulations that were originally adopted at the end of the 19th century. It established a synodal system of administration in contrast to the previous governance by the Patriarch alone, and provided that the Patriarch should be elected by both clergy and laity. The Holy Synod, which is made up of at least seven metropolitans, must meet at least once a year, but ordinarily gathers every six months.

Through the efforts of Archbishop Makarios III of Cyprus, a seminary was opened in Nairobi in 1981. Originally named after Makarios, it was renamed the Orthodox Patriarchal School in 1998. In that year it had 42 students from various parts of Africa. There are two Greek religious communities and two composed of ethnic Arabs. The total membership of the Patriarchate is composed of approximately 100,000 black Africans and 150,000 others, mostly ethnic Greeks.

LOCATION: Egypt, the rest of Africa
HEAD: Pope Petros VII (born 1949, elected 1997)

Title: Pope and Patriarch of Alexandria and All Africa
Residence: Alexandria, Egypt
MEMBERSHIP: 250,000
WEB SITE: http://www.greece.org/gopatalex

III. A. 3. The Patriarchate of Antioch

Antioch was a very important urban center in the ancient world, and it was there, according to the Book of Acts, that the followers of Jesus were first called Christians. Antioch eventually became the seat of a Patriarchate that included all the Christians in the vast Eastern Province of the Roman Empire and beyond.

Reactions to the Council of Chalcedon triggered a schism in the Patriarchate. The larger group, which repudiated the council, eventually formed the Syrian Orthodox Church [see II.D]. This church is descended from those who accepted Chalcedon, mostly Greeks and hellenized sections of the indigenous population.

Such was the situation when Antioch fell to the Arab invaders in August 638. Perceived as allies of the Byzantine enemy, the local Greeks now underwent a long period of persecution, and the patriarchal throne was often vacant or occupied by a non-resident during the 7th and first half of the 8th centuries.

The Byzantines regained possession of the city in 969, and until 1085, when Antioch fell to the Seljuk Turks, the Greek Patriarchate prospered under Byzantine rule. During this period, the West Syrian liturgy was gradually replaced by the Byzantine liturgy, a process that would be complete by the 12th century.

In 1098, the Crusaders took Antioch and set up a Latin kingdom in Syria that would last nearly two centuries. A Latin Patriarchate of Antioch was established, while a line of Greek Patriarchs continued in exile.

After Antioch was taken by the Egyptian Mamelukes in 1268, the Greek Patriarch was able to return to the area. Because Antioch itself had long ago been reduced to a small town, the Patriarchate was permanently transferred to Damascus in the 14th century. The area was taken from the Mamelukes by the Ottoman Turks in 1517 and remained under Turkish control until the end of World War I. The church was greatly weakened by a schism in 1724, when many of its faithful became Catholic and formed what would become the Melkite Greek Catholic Church [see IV.D.1].

By this time the great majority of the faithful of this Patriarchate were Arabs. In 1898 the last Greek Patriarch was deposed, and an Arab successor was elected in 1899. Thus the Patriarchate became fully Arab in character. A strong renewal movement, involving Orthodox youth in particular, has been under way since the 1940s.

The St. John of Damascus Academy of Theology, located near Tripoli, Lebanon, was established by the Patriarchate in 1970. In 1988 it was officially incorporated into Balamand University.

The Holy Synod of the Antioch Patriarchate is composed of the Patriarch and all the active Metropolitans. It meets at least yearly, and has the function of electing the Patriarch and other bishops, preserving the faith and taking measures against certain violations of ecclesiastical order. In addition, a general community council is made up of the Holy Synod and lay representatives. Meeting twice a year, this body is responsible for financial, educational, judicial and administrative matters. When a new Patriarch needs to be chosen, it selects three candidates, one of which is then elected by the Holy Synod.

The present Patriarch has been active in the ecumenical movement and has been involved in efforts to reestablish the unity of all those whose roots can be traced back to the ancient undivided Antioch Patriarchate. With this in mind he met on July 22, 1991, with the Syrian Orthodox Patriarch, Ignatius Zakka I Iwas [see II.D]. They signed a document that called for "complete and mutual respect between the two churches." It also forbade the passing of faithful from one church to the other, envisaged joint meetings of the two Holy Synods when appropriate, and provided guidelines for intercommunion of the faithful and even Eucharistic concelebration by the clergy of the two churches.

The Patriarchate has been participating in a special bilateral theological commission for dialogue with the Melkite Greek Catholic Church to explore ways of healing the schism of 1724. In an unprecedented act, the Melkite Greek Catholic Patriarch, Maximos V, addressed a meeting of the Antiochene Holy Synod in October 1996. The Antiochene Patriarch has vigorously supported the continuation of the international dialogue with the Catholic Church.

There has been extensive immigration to the new world in recent years, and dioceses have been established in North America, Argentina, Brazil, and Australia. In North America the Antiochian Orthodox Christian Archdiocese is under the supervision of Metropolitan Philip Saliba (358 Mountain Road, Englewood, New Jersey 07631). The Archdiocese has 204 parishes in the USA and 16 in Canada. This jurisdiction includes a Western Rite Vicariate composed mostly of former Episcopalians (Anglicans) with a total of about 10,000 members, as well as a distinct Antiochian Evangelical Orthodox Mission, which originated in the Campus Crusade for Christ and uses the Byzantine rite.

The Australian Antiochian Orthodox Diocese is headed by Bishop Gibran of Larissa (PO Box 241, Punchbowl, NSW 2196). It has nine parishes in addition to three communities in New Zealand. An English-speaking Russian parish in Melbourne (Moscow Patriarchate) is also under Bishop Gibran and is served by clergy of the Antiochian Diocese.

There is one Antiochian Orthodox worshiping community in London, England. In addition, a group of former Anglicans in Great Britain with about 700 members grouped in nine communities, called "Pilgrimage to Orthodoxy," has been received into the Orthodox

Church under the jurisdiction of the Antiochian bishop in Paris. In April 1995 he ordained two ex-Anglican priests from this group as Orthodox priests, and several more ordinations were later held. Some of these communities use the Byzantine rite, the others a modified form of the Western liturgy.

> LOCATION: Syria, Lebanon, Iraq, Kuwait, Iran, the Americas, Australia
> HEAD: Patriarch Ignatius IV (born 1920, elected 1979)
> Title: Patriarch of Antioch and All the East
> Residence: Damascus, Syria
> MEMBERSHIP: 750,000

III. A. 4. The Patriarchate of Jerusalem

Given its association with the life of Jesus and his first community of disciples, Jerusalem has always been of great importance to Christians. As the Christian faith gained wider acceptance in the Roman Empire, the prestige of Jerusalem grew as well. Emperor Constantine, who was very favorable to Christianity, caused magnificent basilicas to be built over some of the holy places in the 4th century. Monasticism had come to Palestine very soon after the first Christian communities were founded in Egypt, and monasteries continued to flourish in the area, especially in the desert between Jerusalem and the Dead Sea.

In 451 the Council of Chalcedon decided to raise the Church of Jerusalem to the rank of Patriarchate. In doing so, three ecclesiastical provinces with about sixty dioceses were detached from the Patriarchate of Antioch, to which the area had previously belonged. Under Greek Byzantine rule, Jerusalem continued to thrive as the destination of countless Christian pilgrims as "the Mother church." The invasions of the Persians in 614 and the Arabs in 637 brought this prosperity to an end. Many Christian churches and monasteries were destroyed, and much of the population gradually converted to Islam.

In 1099 the Crusaders took over Jerusalem and established a Latin kingdom that would endure for almost a century. During this period Rome created a Latin Patriarchate of Jerusalem. A line of Greek Patriarchs continued in exile, usually residing in Constantinople. The Greek Patriarchs began living at or near Jerusalem again following the collapse of the Crusader kingdom.

Jerusalem fell to the Seljuk Turks in 1187, but was soon taken by the Egyptian Mamelukes. The Ottoman Turks gained control of the city in 1516. During the 400 years of Ottoman rule there were many struggles between Christian groups over possession of the holy places. In the mid-19th century, the Turks confirmed Greek control over most of them. This arrangement has remained unchanged during the British mandate, which began in 1917, and under subsequent Jordanian and Israeli administrations.

The Patriarchate is governed by a Holy Synod presided over by the Patriarch. Its members, which cannot exceed 18, are all clerics and appointed by the Patriarch. In addition, there is a mixed council that allows for lay input in the decision-making process of the Patriarchate.

The fact that the hierarchy of the Patriarchate is Greek while the faithful are Arab has been a source of contention in recent times. Since 1534 all the Patriarchs of Jerusalem have been ethnic Greeks. At present the Patriarch and bishops are drawn from the Brotherhood of the Holy Sepulcher, a Jerusalem monastic community founded in the 16th century that has 90 Greek and four Arab members. The married clergy are entirely drawn from the local Arab population. This explains why the Byzantine liturgy is celebrated in Greek in the monasteries but in Arabic in the parishes.

The long-standing tensions resulting from this situation came into the open once again in May 1992 when the Arab Orthodox Initiative Committee was founded to press for the arabization of the Patriarchate as the only way to preserve an authentic Orthodox witness in the region. Since that time it has also called into question the alienation of church property and other financial dealings of the Patriarchate and demanded that church accounts be made public. It also claimed that the Greek hierarchy showed little concern for the welfare of the Arab Orthodox community, symbolized by the fact that the number of schools had dropped from six in 1967 to three. In September 1994 the group warned that the situation was moving towards confrontation. The activities of the committee, however, were being vigorously resisted by Patriarch Diodoros and the Holy Synod, who asserted the hierarchy's freedom of action and the historically Greek character of the Patriarchate.

The Jerusalem Patriarchate has also taken a rather negative stance towards the ecumenical movement: in 1989 it withdrew its delegates from all the bilateral theological dialogues in which the Orthodox Church is engaged. The Patriarch stated that other Christians were using the dialogues as a means of proselytism, and that, since the Orthodox Church already possesses the fullness of Christian truth, it had no need to participate in such discussions.

However, the Jerusalem Patriarchate continues to take part in the activities of the World Council of Churches and the Middle East Council of Churches, and Patriarch Diodoros has willingly signed joint statements with other local church leaders, especially in regard to the situation of Christians in the Holy Land. These local ecumenical initiatives prepared the way for the drafting of a common memorandum entitled "The Significance of Jerusalem for Christians" that was signed by the Patriarchs and heads of all the traditional churches present in Jerusalem, including the Franciscan Custos of the Holy Land, on November 23, 1994. Since then, the same church leaders meet about every two months in the Greek Orthodox Patriarchate, under the presidency of Patriarch Diodoros. They have also created an ecumenical committee for the preparation of the celebrations of the year 2000.

LOCATION: Israel, Jordan and areas under the control of the Palestinian Authority
HEAD: Patriarch Diodoros I (born 1923, elected 1981)
Title: The Greek Orthodox Patriarch of Jerusalem
Residence: Jerusalem
MEMBERSHIP: 130,000

III. A. 5. The Orthodox Church of Russia

In the late 10th century, according to the legend, the pagan Grand Prince Vladimir of Kiev sent envoys to different parts of the world to examine the local religions and to advise him which would be best for his kingdom. When the envoys returned, they recommended the faith of the Greeks, for they reported that when they attended the divine liturgy in the cathedral of Hagia Sophia in Constantinople, "we did not know if we were in heaven or on earth." After the baptism of Prince Vladimir, many of his followers were baptized in the waters of the Dnieper river in 988. Thus Byzantine Christianity became the faith of the three peoples who trace their origins to Rus' of Kiev: the Ukrainians, Belarusans, and Russians.

Christian Kiev flourished for a time, but then entered a period of decline that culminated in 1240 when the city was destroyed during the Mongol invasions. As a result of the Mongol destruction, large numbers of people moved northward. By the 14th century a new center grew up around the principality of Moscow, and the Metropolitans of Kiev took up residence there. Later, Moscow was declared the metropolitan see in its own right.

When Constantinople fell to the Turks in 1453, Russia was throwing off Mongol rule and becoming an independent state. Because the first Rome was said to have fallen into heresy and the New Rome had fallen under the Turks, some Russians began to speak of Moscow as the "Third Rome" which would carry on the traditions of Orthodoxy and Roman civilization. The tsar (caesar) was now the champion and protector of Orthodoxy just as the Byzantine Emperor once had been. The Russian church had already begun to develop its own style of iconography and church architecture and its own theological and spiritual traditions.

In the mid-17th century a schism took place in this church when Patriarch Nikon reformed a number of Russian liturgical usages to make them conform with those of the Greek church. Those who refused to submit to the reform and insisted on continuing these uniquely Russian traditions came to be known as "Old Believers" [see III.D.1].

A Russian Orthodox Patriarchate was officially established by Constantinople in 1589, but it was abolished by Peter the Great in 1721. The church was then administered by a Holy Synod under regulations that brought the church under close state supervision. During this period, especially in the 19th century, a great revival of Russian Orthodox theology, spirituality, and monasticism took place.

In August 1917, after the abdication of the tsar but before the Bolshevik Revolution, a synod of the Russian Orthodox Church began in Moscow. It reestablished the Russian Patriarchate and elected Metropolitan Tikhon of Moscow to that office. But before the synod ended, it was learned that the Metropolitan of Kiev had been murdered and that persecutions had begun. Patriarch Tikhon was outspoken in his criticism of the communists in his early years as Patriarch, but moderated his public position after a year in prison. Patriarch Tikhon and his successor Patriarch Sergius worked out a *modus vivendi* with the government that set the tone of church-state relations under communism: the Russian Orthodox Church publicly supported the government on all issues, and the state agreed to allow the church a very restricted sphere of activity, limited in practice to liturgical worship.

The persecution took different forms in different periods: virtually all the theologans and leaders of the church were either exiled in the 1920s or executed in the 1930s. In 1937 alone some 136,000 clerics

were arrested and 85,000 killed. In the period from 1917 to 1939, between 80% and 85% of the pre-revolutionary Russian Orthodox
clergy disappeared. Conditions improved somewhat during World
War II and in Stalin's later years, until Khrushchev began to intensify
the persecutions in 1959.

Many churches were closed after the revolution, and another massive wave of church closings took place under Khrushchev in 1959-
1962. While in 1917, the Russian Orthodox Church had 77,767
churches (parishes and monasteries), in the late 1970s there were
only about 6,800. The number of functioning monasteries (1,498 in
1914) was down to 12, and the 57 theological seminaries operating in
1914 had been reduced to three in Moscow, Leningrad (St. Petersburg), and Odessa, with theological academies of higher studies in
the first two cities.

After 1990, however, thanks to the reforms set in motion by President Mikhail Gorbachev, the situation of the Russian Orthodox
Church began to improve dramatically. In late 1997 Patriarch Aleksy
II stated that the church numbered 124 dioceses with 148 bishops,
18,000 priests and 1,737 deacons. There were over 430 monasteries,
in addition to over 60 monastery annexes in cities. Five theological
academies, 23 seminaries, 21 ecclesiastical schools, one theological
institute, two Orthodox universities, five courses for preparing pastors, and two diocesan women's ecclesiastical schools were also serving the church. In addition, there were choral and icon-painting departments and a multitude of church parish schools. In October 1992
the St. Tikhon of Moscow Theological Institute opened in Moscow
for training Orthodox laity. The students, more or less evenly divided
between women and men, numbered some 650 in the first year. On
February 24, 1993, the Russian Orthodox Church established St. John
the Theologian University in Moscow to continue the Russian hu-
manist educational tradition and to offer an in-depth study of the
theological disciplines as well.

In December 1993 the University of Chicago's National Opinion Research Center released the results of a poll that documented an extraordinary growth of religious faith in Russia. It showed that between one half and three quarters of the Russian people believed in God, depending on how the question was worded. Although 11% said they were Orthodox when growing up, 28% reported themselves as Orthodox now, indicating that the Russian Orthodox Church had more than doubled its membership. The trend towards theism was strongest in the 17-24 age group, where 30% had converted from atheism to belief in God. An astonishing 75% of those surveyed reported having "a great deal of confidence in the church." But a survey conducted by the Russian Center of Public Opinion Studies in August 1994 revealed that while 52% of those surveyed considered themselves believers, only 2% attended church services at least once a week. In another poll by the same organization in late 1997, 46% of respondents described themselves as nonbelievers, and 45% considered themselves Orthodox Christians. Explaining their religious convictions, about 31% said they have always believed in God, 13% said they began to believe in God after professing atheism, 26% said they have never believed in God and 2% said they once believed in God but lost their faith. Ninety-six percent of respondents said they had been baptized, 83% as small children and 13% by choice when they were older. The poll of 2,400 people had a margin of error of 2 percentage points.

Assuming the accuracy of the 1997 poll's finding that 45% of the Russian population considers itself Orthodox, there would now be a total of about 66 million Orthodox in Russia alone. In view of the lack of reliable information about Orthodox membership in the other newly independent former Soviet states with large Russian minorities, the total membership of the Moscow Patriarchate reported below is only an approximation.

At present the Russian church is struggling to adapt to the rapid changes taking place in Russian society. It has strictly enforced a ban on the participation of clergy in politics, but has been developing a closer relationship with the Russian military. In the fall of 1994 the Russian government agreed to help finance the reconstruction of the Cathedral of Christ the Savior, a massive 19th-century structure leveled by Stalin in 1931 that once dominated the Moscow skyline. Patriarch Aleksy laid the new cornerstone on January 7, 1995, and Easter services were held in the structure in 1996.

At the late 1994 meeting of the Russian Orthodox Council of Bishops, Patriarch Aleksy commented that the church had gone through a very difficult period since the previous meeting in 1992. It had had to deal with problems relating to liturgical practice, proper theological and pastoral formation, and ecclesial service to society. The assembly turned down a call from conservative elements for the Moscow Patriarchate to withdraw from all ecumenical organizations, but it condemned the missionary activity being carried out in Russia by American Methodist, Evangelical and Presbyterian groups, and by certain South Korean Protestants. The bishops sanctioned the beginning of a vast effort to catechize and evangelize the Russian population and set up a special commission to review liturgical practice and texts to make the liturgy more easily understood by the faithful.

The Council met again in February 1997 and decided against recommending the proposed canonization of Tsar Nicholas II and his family. The bishops again turned down efforts to bring about the withdrawal of the Russian church from the World Council of Churches, and called for pan-Orthodox discussions on the advisability of WCC membership. The bishops also took account of the bilateral dialogue with the Catholic Church, assailed what they perceived as continued Catholic proselytism among the Orthodox, and asked the Synodical Theological Commission to study the Balamand Document produced by the international Catholic-Orthodox dialogue. High-level delegations from the Vatican and the Moscow Patriarchate have been meeting regularly twice each year. The bishops also warmly acknowledged progress in relations with the Oriental

Orthodox churches and called for greater clarity in the christological formulations produced by the dialogue.

The perceived threat from foreign religious groups was one of the factors that led the Russian Orthodox Church to lend its strong support to a new Law on Religion that President Yeltsin signed on September 26, 1997. The law identifies Orthodoxy, Islam, Buddhism, Judaism and Christianity as traditional religions, and places restrictions on the activities of some groups, including a 15-year waiting period for registration; the limitation of unregistered groups to informal, private practice; and the placing of severe constraints on the activity of foreign missionaries. The law's restriction of religious freedom raised major concerns in the West but appeared to reflect a consensus on the question within Russian society.

The highest authority in the Russian Orthodox Church is the Local Council. It is convened periodically and made up of bishops, other clergy and the laity. Ordinary administration of the church is carried out by the Holy Synod. It is composed of the Patriarch and six diocesan bishops, three of them permanent and three temporary members. The Council of Bishops, which gathers together the entire episcopate as well as the heads of Holy Synod departments and rectors of the theological academies and seminaries, convenes approximately every two years.

The disintegration of the communist system and the Soviet Union created centrifugal forces that threatened the unity of the Moscow Patriarchate. In January 1990, when conditions were already changing, the Bishops' Council of the Russian Orthodox Church met in Moscow and decided to grant a certain measure of autonomy to the Orthodox churches in Ukraine and Byelorussia (now Belarus). Each of these was made an exarchate of the Moscow Patriarchate, with the optional names "the Ukrainian Orthodox Church" and "the Byelorussian (now Belarusan) Orthodox Church." Following the dissolution of the Soviet Union on December 25, 1991, and the independence of the various successor states, the Patriarchate granted similar autonomous status to the Orthodox churches in Estonia, Latvia and Moldova.

Responding to demands in Ukraine for greater autonomy, on October 27, 1990, the Bishops' Council abolished the exarchate and granted "independence and self-government" to the Ukrainian Orthodox Church. But the church remained linked to Moscow, and the Metropolitan of Kiev still served as a member of the Holy Synod of the Moscow Patriarchate. After Ukraine declared its independence on August 24, 1991, Metropolitan Filaret of Kiev began to seek complete separation of his church from the Moscow Patriarchate. The Russian Orthodox Bishop's Council turned down this request in April 1992. But Filaret continued to seek autocephaly for his church, and matters came to a head in May 1992 when the Moscow Patriarchate deposed Filaret and appointed Metropolitan Volodymyr (Sabodan) of Rostov as new Metropolitan of Kiev. In June the Patriarchate defrocked Filaret and reduced him to the lay state. Subsequently Filaret joined the non-canonical Ukrainian Autocephalous Church and was elected its Patriarch [see III.D.3].

There was another problem in the newly independent republic of Moldova which (then known as Bessarabia) had been a part of Romania before 1812 and again from 1918 to 1944. In spite of the fact that the Moscow Patriarchate had granted autonomous status to its Moldovan diocese, the Holy Synod of the Romanian Orthodox Church decided in December 1992 to reconstitute its own Metropolitanate of Bessarabia in the same territory. Thus the Orthodox in Moldova were split between the two rival jurisdictions. The Romanian and Russian Patriarchates have held discussions in an effort to resolve the dispute, but these had been unsuccessful by mid-1998. The Moldovan government has refused to allow the registration of the Bessarabian Metropolitanate linked to Bucharest.

In Estonia, an autonomous Orthodox church under the Patriarchate of Constantinople existed from 1923 until it was absorbed into the Moscow Patriarchate in 1945 after the country was annexed by the Soviet Union. In the wake of Estonian independence in 1991, there were calls for the re-establishment of this church, which had maintained its headquarters in Stockholm in exile. The newly independent Estonian government officially recognized it as the legal continuation of the Estonian Orthodox Church that existed in the interwar period. On February 20, 1996, the Ecumenical Patriarchate formally re-established the autonomous Estonian Orthodox Church under its jurisdiction, and thus provoked a major crisis in relations with the Moscow Patriarchate, which then refused to commemorate the Ecumenical Patriarch in the diptychs. The crisis was resolved on May 16, 1996, when the two Holy Synods announced an agreement sanctioning the existence of two separate jurisdictions in Estonia. The majority of Orthodox parishes joined the newly restored autonomous church under Constantinople, but the majority of the faithful opted for the diocese dependent on Moscow [See the Estonian Apostolic Orthodox Church, III.B.5].

The 31 parishes in North America under the Moscow Patriarchate are administered by Bishop Paul of Zaraisk (15 East 97th Street, New York, New York 10029). The 25 Patriarchal Canadian parishes (all in Alberta and Saskatchewan) fall under the pastoral care of Bishop Mark of Kashira (St. Barbara Church, 10105 96th Street, Edmonton, Alberta T5H 2G3). The Patriarchate's 20 places of worship in Britain are presided over by Metropolitan Anthony Bloom of Sourozh (67 Ennismore Gardens, London SW7 1NH). Moscow has also recently established two parishes in Australia. Contact Fr. Peter Hill, Glen Iris Road, Glen Iris VIC 3146.

See also the Orthodox Church in America [III.A.15], the Russian Orthodox Archdiocese in Western Europe [III.C.3], and the Russian Orthodox Church Outside Russia [III.D.2].

LOCATION: Russia and the other countries of the Commonwealth of
    Independent States, diaspora
HEAD: Patriarch Aleksy II (born 1929, elected 1990)
Title: Patriarch of Moscow and All Russia

Residence: Moscow, Russia
MEMBERSHIP: 80,000,000
WEB SITE: http://www.russian-orthodox-church.org.ru

III. A. 6. The Orthodox Church of Serbia

The origins of Christianity in Serbia are obscure. It is known that
Latin missionaries were active along the Dalmatian coast in the 7th
century, and that by the 9th century Byzantine missionaries were at
work in Serbia, having been sent by Emperor Basil I the Macedonian.
Eventually the Serbian people became entirely Christian.

Due in part to its geographical location, the Serbian church vacil-
lated between Rome and Constantinople for a time, but finally gravitated towards the Byzantines. In 1219, St. Sava was consecrated the
first Archbishop of a self-governing Serbian Orthodox Church by the
Patriarch of Constantinople, then residing at Nicaea during the Latin
occupation of his city.

The Serbian kingdom reached its apogee during the reign of
Stevan Dushan, who extended Serbian rule to Albania, Thessaly,
Epirus, and Macedonia. Dushan was crowned Emperor of the Serbians and established a Serbian Patriarchate at Peč in 1346. This state
of affairs was recognized by Constantinople in 1375.

The Serbians were defeated by the Turks in 1389, and subse-
quently they were gradually integrated into the Ottoman Empire. The
Turks suppressed the Serbian Patriarchate in 1459, only to restore it
in 1557. But it was suppressed again in 1766, when all the bishops in
Serbia proper were replaced by Greeks subject to the Patriarchate in
Constantinople.

The emergence of an autonomous Serbian state in 1830 was coupled with the establishment of an autonomous Orthodox metropolia
based at Belgrade and the replacement of Greek bishops by Serbs. In
1878 Serbia gained international recognition as an independent na-

tion, and in 1879 the Patriarchate of Constantinople recognized the Serbian church as autocephalous. In 1918 the multinational state of Yugoslavia was formed, making possible the amalgamation of various Orthodox jurisdictions now within Yugoslavia (the formerly autonomous Serbian metropolias of Belgrade, Karlovci, Bosnia, Montenegro, and the diocese of Dalmatia) into a single Serbian Orthodox Church. In 1920 Constantinople recognized this union and raised the Serbian Church to the rank of Patriarchate.

The Serbian church suffered heavily during World War II, especially in regions under the control of the fascist Croatian state. Altogether it lost some 25% of its churches and monasteries and about one-fifth of its clergy. Following the establishment of a communist Yugoslav government in 1945, the Serbian church had to work out a new relationship with the officially atheist state. Much church property was confiscated, religious education was banned in the schools, and there was disagreement about the role of Serbia in multi-ethnic Yugoslavia. Tito's break with the Soviet Union in 1948 and the development of better relations with the West led to greater tolerance of religion and an improved situation for the church. Nevertheless, subtle forms of persecution continued, with the government supporting a schism within the Serbian Orthodox Church [see the Macedonian Orthodox Church, III.D.5].

Following the breakup of Yugoslavia, the Serbian Orthodox Church has become more involved in political matters. It has strenuously denounced the anti-religious practices of past communist regimes and, in May 1992, began to distance itself from the Milosevic government. But, while it frequently called for peace during the war in Bosnia-Herzegovina, the church hierarchy also vigorously supported the efforts of Serbian minorities in that country and in Croatia to achieve political union with Serbia itself. In 1994 the Serbian Orthodox bishops met in Banja Luka, in the Serb-held section of Bosnia. At the meeting they asserted that, since many Serbs found themselves in new republics outside Serbia as a result of borders that had been artificially imposed by totalitarian regimes for administrative purposes, those borders could not be accepted as final. They rejected both the international sanctions placed on Yugoslavia and the sanctions that had been placed by the Yugoslav government on the Serbs in Bosnia. They pledged to remain with the Serbian people "on the cross upon which they are being crucified."

In 1996 the Serbian bishops called for the moral renewal of the Serbian people, but said that this process was hindered by the educational system which was still Marxist in spirit. They also denounced "the reappearance of old totalitarian methods" in society and continued to claim that the actions of the international community in Bosnia and the Hague Tribunal are biased against Serbia. In early January 1997 the Serbian Holy Synod condemned in the strongest terms the efforts of the Milosevic government to suppress the results of the November 1996 local elections and called upon the authorities to respect democratic principles. Later in January Patriarch Pavle led more than 300,000 demonstrators in the streets of Belgrade in support of the pro-democracy movement.

In mid-1997 an assembly of all the Serbian bishops encouraged Serbian exiles from Croatia and Bosnia to return to their homes and demanded that the governments of those countries guarantee their safety. The bishops also called for a dialogue with the Yugoslav government on the restitution of church property seized after 1945, and for the teaching of catechism in public schools. On the question of ecumenism, the bishops stated that their church is always open to dialogue and does everything possible to promote reconciliation and unity among Christians. They also called for a pan-Orthodox consultation on the ecumenical movement and Orthodox participation in the World Council of Churches. The assembly met again in November 1997 to consider the reorganization of the church's educational system. The bishops also reiterated their call for the introduction of religious education in the public schools and the promotion of Christian ethical values among the people.

The highest authority in the Serbian church is the Holy Assembly of Bishops, composed of all the diocesan bishops. It meets once a year in May. The standing Holy Synod of Bishops, made up of the Patriarch and four bishops, governs the church on a day-to-day basis. There is a theological institute in Belgrade (founded 1921), four seminaries, and a school for the training of monks. Fifteen religious publications are sponsored by the Patriarchate and other dioceses.

Dioceses for Serbian Orthodox abroad have been established in North America, Western Europe, and Australia. The community in the diaspora experienced a split in 1963 over the relationship between the Serbian Patriarchate and the communist Yugoslav government. Those in whose judgment the relationship included unacceptable government interference in church affairs formed the Free Serbian Orthodox Church, later known as the New Gracanica Metropolitan-ate, and broke all canonical links with Belgrade. It was only in 1991 that there was a reconciliation between the two groups under Patri-arch Pavle, although for a time both ecclesiastical structures contin-ued to exist. The two groups adopted a common constitution in 1998, paving the way for future administrative unity.

The New Gracanica jurisdiction was headed by Metropolitan Ireney (PO Box 371, Grayslake, Illinois 60030) until the Serbian Holy Synod appointed Bishop Longin of Dalmatia as administrator in May 1998 due to Ireney's ill health. The ranking hierarch of the three dio-ceses in the United States that remained linked to the Serbian Patri-archate is Metropolitan Christopher (Midwestern American Metro-politanate, St. Sava Monastery, Box 519, Libertyville, Illinois 60048). The diocese of Canada is under the pastoral care of Bishop Georgije (2520 Dixie Road, Mississauga, Ontario L4Y 2A5). Altogether there are 73 parishes or missions in the United States and 20 in Canada. In addition, Bishop Luka (PO Box 172, Brunswick East, Victoria 3057) presides over 17 parishes in Australia and New Zealand. In the United Kingdom there are 22 Serbian Orthodox worshiping communities under the jurisdiction of Bishop Dositej of Britain and Scandinavia, who resides in Sweden.

LOCATION: Yugoslavia and former republics, Western Europe, North America, Australia
HEAD: Patriarch Pavle I (born 1914, elected 1990)
Title: Archbishop of Peč, Metropolitan of Belgrade and Karlovči, Patriarch of the Serbs
Residence: Belgrade, Yugoslavia
MEMBERSHIP: 8,000,000
WEB SITE: http://www.spc.org.yu

III. A. 7. The Orthodox Church of Romania

The Romanian Orthodox Church is unique among the Orthodox churches because it alone exists within a Latin culture. Romanian is a romance tongue, directly descended from the language of the Roman soldiers and settlers who occupied Dacia and intermarried with its inhabitants following its conquest by Emperor Trajan in 106 AD.

Christianity in the area has been traced back to apostolic times, but the history of its development during the millennium following the withdrawal of Roman administration in 271 is obscure. Certainly both Latin and Byzantine missionaries had been active in the area. In any case, by the time the Romanian principalities of Moldavia and Wallachia emerged as political entities in the 14th century, Romanian ethnic identity was already closely identified with the Orthodox Christian faith. Approval was given for the liturgy to be celebrated in Romanian at a local synod in 1568.

The following centuries witnessed the development of a distinct Romanian theological tradition in spite of the fact that Wallachia and Moldavia were vassals of the Ottoman Empire from the 16th to the 19th centuries. The two principalities were united under a single prince in 1859, and Romania gained full independence in 1878. Consequently, the Patriarchate of Constantinople, which had exercised jurisdiction over the Romanians while they were within the Ottoman Empire, recognized the autocephalous status of the Romanian Church in 1885. Transylvania, which included large numbers of Orthodox Romanians, was integrated into the Romanian kingdom after World War I, and the Romanian Church was raised to the rank of Patriarchate in 1925.

The establishment of a communist government in Romania after World War II required a new *modus vivendi* between church and state. In general, the Romanian Orthodox Church adopted a policy of close cooperation with the government. Whatever the merits of that decision may have been, the church was able to maintain an active and meaningful existence in the country. A strong spiritual renewal movement took place in the late 1950s. A large number of churches were left open, and there were many functioning monasteries, although all church activity was kept under strict government supervision. There were six seminaries and two theological institutes (in Sibiu and Bucharest). High-quality theological journals were published--including three by the Patriarchate itself and one by each of the five metropolitanates--and important theological works as well.

Following the overthrow of the government of Nicolae Ceauşescu in December 1989, the Romanian Orthodox hierarchy was severely criticized from many quarters for having cooperated with the communist regime. Patriarch Teoctist resigned his office in January 1990, but was reinstated by the Holy Synod the following April. Since that time the Romanian Orthodox Church seems to have stabilized its position and is experiencing a sustained growth in its activity. Relations with the Romanian government became much more constructive after the election of Emil Constantinescu as President in 1996, and plans were being laid for the contruction for an enormous Cathedral of the Nation's Salvation in Bucharest. But the church has been locked in a continuing struggle with the Romanian Greek Catholic Church over the return of former Greek Catholic churches that had been confiscated by the communist government in 1948 and turned over to the Orthodox [see IV.D.4].

In February 1997 the Romanian Orthodox Church reported having 23 dioceses and 9,208 parishes. By that time 72 Orthodox chapels had been opened in hospitals, 29 in prisons, 18 in military installations and 13 in homes for the elderly and children. There were 296 monasteries (173 male and 123 female) and 97 sketes (81 male and 16 female) with 2,414 monks and 4,090 nuns. The church was being served by 9,174 priests and eight deacons. One hundred and one priests were serving as hospital chaplains, 33 in prisons and 23 in the armed forces. In 1995 there were 28 seminaries with a total of 5,524 students, including nuns and laypeople. Higher studies in theology had been integrated into the state university system, with 14 faculties of Orthodox theology around the country. Altogether there were 3,206 male and 2,419 female students. In addition, there were 12 schools for church cantors with 451 students. Thirty-three church periodicals were being published in the dioceses.

According to the Romanian census taken in 1992, 87% of the population identified itself as Orthodox. Opinion polls since 1989 have shown consistently that the Romanian population held the church in high regard, with 86% describing its activity as "good or very good" in a late 1997 survey.

In 1993 the Romanian Patriarchate reestablished jurisdictions in areas that were part of Romanian territory in the interwar period: in northern Bukovina (now in Ukraine) and Bessarabia, most of which is now the independent republic of Moldova. The Orthodox Church in Moldova had been part of the Russian Orthodox Church since World War II, and had just been granted autonomous status by Moscow. Thus Moldovan Orthodox faithful were now divided between the two competing jurisdictions. The Moldovan government supported the jurisdiction linked to Moscow and did not allow the new Romanian jurisdiction to register officially. Romanian Metropolitan Petru of Bessarabia complained of discrimination and persecution, but in December 1997 Moldova's Supreme Court ruled in favor of the government. Metropolitan Petru claimed the allegiance of 110 parishes around the country.

The highest authority in the Romanian Orthodox Church in canonical and spiritual matters is the Holy Synod, composed of all the bishops in the country. Meetings take place at least once a year. At other times the normal administration of the church falls to the Permanent Holy Synod, made up of the Patriarch and the active Metropolitans. On financial and administrative matters, the highest authority is the National Ecclesiastical Assembly, made up of one cleric and two lay persons from each diocese as well as the members of the Holy Synod.

Altogether the Romanian Patriarchate has four dioceses and two vicariates with a total of 167 parishes served by three bishops and 170 priests outside Romania. An autonomous diocese in North America is headed by Archbishop Victorin Ursache (Romanian Orthodox Archdiocese in America and Canada, 19959 Riopelle Avenue, Detroit, Michigan 48203). It has 13 parishes in the USA and 21 in Canada. Romanian Orthodox in Britain are cared for by Fr. P. Pufulete who resides at 8 Elsynge Road, Battersea London SW 18. The community in Australia, which has five parishes, can be contacted through Fr. Gabriel Popescu, PO Box 558, Campsie NSW 2194. Metropolitan Nicolae Corneanu of Banat has been named by the Holy Synod as Exarch for all Orthodox Romanians in the diaspora.

Another Romanian Orthodox jurisdiction is part of the Orthodox Church in America [see III.A.15]. It is presided over by Bishop Nathaniel Popp (Romanian Orthodox Episcopate of America, Vatra Româneasca, 2522 Grey Tower Road, Jackson, Michigan 49201). There are 41 parishes in the USA and 16 in Canada. In 1993 the two Romanian Orthodox jurisdictions in North America agreed to establish full normal ecclesial relations, ending decades of hostility.

LOCATION: Romania, Western Europe and North America
HEAD: Patriarch Teoctist I (born 1915, elected 1986)

Title: Archbishop of Bucharest, Metropolitan of Ungro-Wallachia,
Patriarch of the Romanian Orthodox Church
Residence: Bucharest, Romania
Membership: 19,800,000

III. A. 8. The Orthodox Church of Bulgaria

A Christian presence in the territory of modern Bulgaria can be
traced back to early centuries, as a council of bishops met in Sardica
(now Sofia) in 343. The region was subsequently occupied by Bulgar
tribes who, although pagan, had already had some contacts with
Christian missionaries. The decisive moment in the development of
Christianity among the Bulgarians was the baptism of King Boris I by
a Byzantine bishop in 865, which was followed by the gradual Christianization of the Bulgarian people. Bulgaria wavered between Rome
and Constantinople for a time and became the subject of a major dispute between the two churches. But in the end Bulgaria opted for
Constantinople and Byzantine civilization.

The Bulgarian state became very powerful in the 10th century. In
927 Constantinople recognized the king as Emperor of the Bulgarians
and the Archbishop of Preslav as Patriarch of the Bulgarian Church.
But the Byzantines gained strength and invaded the Bulgarian Empire in 971, at which time the Patriarch left Preslav and took up residence at Ohrid, Macedonia. The Byzantines conquered Macedonia in
1018 and reduced the patriarchate to the rank of autocephalous
archbishopric.

Bulgaria regained its independence in 1186 with the establishment
of the second empire based at Turnovo. After lengthy negotiations the
Bulgarian church recognized the supremacy of the Pope in 1204. But
this agreement ended in 1235 when the Bulgarian Emperor made an
alliance with the Greeks against the Latin Empire in Constantinople,

and the Byzantine patriarch recognized a second Bulgarian Orthodox patriarchate in return.

With the beginning of Turkish domination in 1393, the Bulgarian church lost its autocephalous character and was integrated into the Patriarchate of Constantinople. In 1870 the Ottoman government allowed the reestablishment of a national Bulgarian church as an autonomous exarchate. Constantinople reacted strongly and declared the Bulgarian church schismatic in 1872. This rift continued long after Bulgaria became a principality in 1878 and an independent kingdom in 1908. It was only in 1945 that the Ecumenical Patriarchate recognized the Bulgarian church as autocephalous and ended the schism. The Metropolitan of Sofia assumed the title of Patriarch in 1953 and he was recognized as such by Constantinople in 1961. During the period of communist rule, which began in 1944, the government followed a religious policy similar to that of the Soviet Union, and the church was compelled to play a largely passive role in society.

The Bulgarian Orthodox Church has not escaped the turmoil that followed the collapse of the communist system. In 1991 the new government created a Board of Religious Affairs that began to initiate reforms in the country's religious institutions. In March 1992 it ruled that the 1971 election of Patriarch Maxim had been illegal because he had been appointed by the communist government in an uncanonical manner. This triggered a division among the bishops, with three of them under the leadership of Metropolitan Pimen of Nekrop publicly calling for Maxim's deposition. In January 1993 a delegation from the Ecumenical Patriarchate visited Sofia to try to facilitate a solution, but without success. The dispute hardened into a schism when, on July 4, 1996, Metropolitan Pimen was installed as rival Patriarch and anathematized by Maxim's Holy Synod. When Petar Stoyanov was sworn in as Bulgarian President in January 1997, Pimen conducted a blessing ceremony, and in March 1997 the Supreme Administrative Court ruled that the registration of Maxim's Holy Synod was invalid.

In January 1998 President Stoyanov called upon both Patriarchs to resign to provide for the election of a single successor that would end the schism.

An "extraordinary and enlarged synod" of the Bulgarian Orthodox Church was held in Sofia from September 30 to October 1, 1998. It was presided over by Ecumenical Patriarch Bartholomew and attended by six other Patriarchs and 20 metropolitans, including Patriarch Aleksy II of Moscow and Patriarch Petros VII of Alexandria. The synod reaffirmed Maxim's position as Patriarch, and achieved a reconciliation between the opposing groups. Patriarch Pimen and the other dissident bishops repented for their actions and were received back into communion with the Orthodox Church as bishops along with their clergy and laity. It was not immediately clear, however, how the agreement would be received among the faithful, who had been deeply divided over the dispute.

In July 1997 the first Bulgarian Orthodox general council in 40 years was held in Sofia under the leadership of Patriarch Maxim. The council focused on new possibilities open to the church in the new conditions of a democratic society. It called upon the government to allow it to develop its ministry in various areas of public life including the media. It asked the authorities to guarantee religious instruction in schools, to establish chaplaincies in the armed forces, in prisons and hospitals, and to return property confiscated by the communists. Measures were adopted to begin a process of renewal of church life, including the development of catechetical programs and theological formation, the setting up of a large program of social action, the strengthening of the role of the laity in the church, and the renewal of monasticism. New church statutes were to be drafted to replace those instituted in 1953 under communist pressure. Religious instruction in the schools resumed in September 1997.

New theology faculties have been created since the fall of communism. At present there are Bulgarian Orthodox seminaries in Plovdiv and Sofia, and faculties of theology at the University of Sofia and at

St. Cyril and Methodius University in Veliko Tarnovo. In mid-1997 the Bulgarian Orthodox Church had 11 dioceses in the country and two abroad, with 2,600 parishes served by about 1,500 priests. In addition, there were 120 functioning monasteries with a total of 200 monks and nuns.

The Bulgarian Orthodox Holy Synod, made up of the Patriarch and all the diocesan bishops, is the supreme clerical, juridical and administrative authority in the church. It functions in two bodies. The Full Synod meets each June and November and whenever else it is judged necessary. The Lesser Synod is composed of the Patriarch and four other bishops elected by the Full Synod to four-year terms, meets almost continually and deals with current church affairs. The Patriarch presides over both bodies and handles relations with the state and other churches.

Metropolitan Joseph of America, Canada and Australia resides at 550-A West 50th Street, New York, New York 10019. Altogether there are nine parishes in the USA, two in Canada and two in Australia. The community in Australia can be reached through Fr. Todor Popov at St. Petka Church, 1 Merlin Road, Fulham, Adelaide SA 5024. Bulgarian Orthodox in Britain can be contacted through Fr. Simeon Spassov Iliev via the Bulgarian Embassy, 188 Queens Gate - The Mews, London SW 5 HL.

Another Bulgarian Orthodox diocese is part of the Orthodox Church in America [III.A.15]. It is presided over by Archbishop Kyrill, whose address is 519 Brynhaven Drive, Toledo, Ohio 43616. There are 14 parishes in the USA and two in Canada.

LOCATION: Bulgaria, small diaspora in Europe and America
HEAD: Patriarch Maxim (born 1914, elected 1971)
Title: Metropolitan of Sofia, Patriarch of All Bulgaria
Residence: Sofia, Bulgaria
MEMBERSHIP: 8,000,000
WEB SITE: http://bulgarian.orthodox-church.org

III. A. 9. The Orthodox Church of Georgia

Georgia, which is centered in the Caucasus mountains at the eastern end of the Black Sea, has a civilization that reaches back to ancient times. Due in large part to the missionary activity of St. Nino, a slave girl from Cappadocia, the kingdom of Iberia (East Georgia) adopted the Christian faith as its state religion in 337. West Georgia, then a part of the Roman Empire, became Christian through a gradual process that was virtually complete by the 5th century.

The Jerusalem liturgy of St. James was celebrated in Iberia, at first in Greek, but in Georgian by the 6th century. The Byzantine liturgy was always used in West Georgia, changing from Greek to Georgian in the 8th or 9th century. East Georgia adopted the Byzantine liturgy soon after East and West Georgia were combined into a single kingdom and Catholicosate in 1008.

The church in Iberia was at first dependent on the Patriarchate of Antioch, but it was established as an independent church by King Vakhtang Gorgaslan in 467. For a time following the Council of Chalcedon (451), the Georgians of Iberia joined the neighboring Armenians in rejecting its teachings. But in 607 they broke with the Armenians and accepted it.

Monasticism began to flourish in Georgia in the 6th century and reached its zenith in the 8th and 9th centuries. The monasteries became important centers of missionary and cultural activity. Georgians founded the Iviron monastery on Mount Athos, where many important religious works were translated from Greek into Georgian.

From the 11th to the 13th centuries, Georgia underwent a golden age during which a rich Christian literature was developed in the Georgian language. But this came to an end when the country was devastated by the invasions of Genghis Khan in the 13th century and Tamerlane in the 15th century. In the period from 1500 to 1800 Georgia underwent a cultural renaissance, largely because the rival

Ottomans and Persians kept each other from gaining full control over the country. New contacts were developed with the West and Russia.

In 1801 Georgia was annexed by Russia, and when the Patriarch died in 1811 the Russians abolished the Patriarchate. The Georgian church was then administered from St. Petersburg by the Holy Synod of the Russian Orthodox Church through a special exarch. The 30 dioceses of the church were reduced to five, and the Georgian language was suppressed in the seminaries and in the liturgy, being replaced by Russian or Slavonic.

After the abdication of Tsar Nicholas II on March 1, 1917, the authority of the Russian Orthodox Church in the non-Russian areas of the empire was seriously undermined. On March 12, 1917, a meeting of Georgian bishops, clergy and laity announced the re-establishment of autocephaly. The following September a council of the Georgian Orthodox Church elected a new Catholicos-Patriarch. These actions were not accepted by the Russian Orthodox Church. After the Bolshevik revolution in October 1917, Georgia briefly regained its independence, from May 1918 to February 1921, when it was annexed by the Soviet Union. But the Georgian church retained its independence from the Moscow Patriarchate in spite of intense persecution by the Soviets. The Moscow Patriarchate formally granted autocephaly to the Georgian church in 1943.

The situation of this church under Soviet rule was similar to that of the Russian Orthodox Church: while in 1917 there were 2,455 churches open in Georgia, only 80 were functioning by the mid-1980s, along with four or five monasteries and a seminary. The Georgian church was compelled to follow the Moscow Patriarchate in its ecumenical and international policies.

But the reform policies of Mikhail Gorbachev in the Soviet Union also affected the church of Georgia. Many churches were re-opened, and on October 1, 1988, a Georgian Orthodox Theological Academy was formally inaugurated in Tbilisi, the capital, with 150 students studying in sections dealing with theology, Christian anthropology

and Christian art. There is now a second theological academy in Ge-
lati and six seminaries around the country, as well as an institute for
the formation of laypeople. Each diocese has set up a center for the
training of catechists and missionaries to work for the re-evangeliza-
tion of the nation.

On March 4, 1990, the Ecumenical Patriarchate granted autocephalous status to the church of Georgia and confirmed its patriarchal rank. The status of the Georgian church had been in dispute between Moscow and Constantinople for some time: the Ecumenical
Patriarchate did not recognize Moscow's authority to grant autocephaly in 1943 and had continued to consider it an autonomous
church. This regularized the position of the Georgian church
throughout the Orthodox world.

The process of renewal intensified after Georgia became an independent nation in 1991. Vocations to the priesthood were ample, a
renewal of monastic life was beginning, and many new churches
were opened. The baptism of the Georgian President, Eduard
Shevardnadze, into the Georgian Orthodox Church in late 1992 symbolized the augmented role that the church may be able to play in the
newly independent republic. In 1994 the Orthodox Church and the
Georgian government reached an agreement to require the teaching
of religion in public schools using a program elaborated in conjunction with the church. A large new cathedral dedicated to the Holy
Trinity was being built in Tbilisi with government assistance. The
cornerstone was laid by Patriarch Ilia in March 1996.

A council of the Georgian Orthodox Church, which gathered together the entire hierarchy along with clerical and lay delegates, met
in September 1995. It made several decisions to foster a pastoral and
spiritual renewal of the church. It also requested a clarification of the
position of the Georgian Church in the dyptics and proceeded to the
canonization of five new saints.

By 1997 anti-ecumenical attitudes had gained much ground in
Georgia, and serious divisions began to appear over the participation

of the church in the ecumenical movement. In an open letter published on May 17, 1997, the abbots of five monasteries threatened to break communion with Patriarch Ilia, who had served as one of the presidents of the World Council of Churches from 1979 to 1983, because of his ecumenical activities. Tensions were running very high, and in order to avoid a possible schism, the Holy Synod voted on May 20, 1997, to withdraw from both the WCC and the European Council of Churches. This did not entirely resolve the situation, however, and some of the leaders of the opposition, who appeared to be in close contact with Old Calendarist groups in Greece, called upon the church to break communion with those Orthodox churches that continued to participate in ecumenical organizations. There was a significant political factor in this dispute: Patriarch Ilia has forged a close alliance with President Shevardnadze's government, while the anti-ecumenical group is linked to supporters of ousted President Zviad Gamsakhurdia.

Out of a total Georgian population of about 5,500,000, 65% identified themselves as Georgian Orthodox in 1993, 11% Muslim, 10% Russian Orthodox, and 8% Armenian Apostolic. In 1997 it was reported that there were 500 parishes within the Orthodox Church of Georgia, served by about the same number of priests. There were 27 monasteries.

LOCATION: Georgia, small diaspora
HEAD: Catholicos Ilia II (born 1932, elected 1977)
Title: Catholicos-Patriarch of All Georgia
Residence: Tbilisi, Georgia
MEMBERSHIP: 3,500,000

III. A. 10. The Orthodox Church of Cyprus

The church of Cyprus traces its origins back to apostolic times, the island having been evangelized by Sts. Paul and Barnabas according to the Book of Acts (13:4-13). Because the island was administered as part of the civil province of the East, whose capital was Antioch, the Patriarchs of Antioch for a time claimed jurisdiction over the Cypriot church and the right to appoint its Archbishop. But the Council of Ephesus in 431 recognized the church's independence and directed that the Archbishops of Cyprus should be elected by the synod of Cypriot bishops.

From the mid-7th century to the mid-10th century, there were frequent Arab attacks against Cyprus that often wrought widespread devastation. Because of this Arab threat, Byzantine Emperor Justinian II evacuated the Christian population of the island from 688 to 695 and settled many of them in a new city on the Dardanelles called Nea Justiniana. The Archbishop of Cyprus took up residence there and was given the additional title of Archbishop of Nea Justiniana, an honor that he retains to this day. The decisive victory of Byzantine Emperor Nicephorus II Phocas (963-969) over the Arabs inaugurated a period of peace during which churches and monasteries were rebuilt and the church flourished. In the 11th and 12th centuries, however, there was growing resentment against the oppressive rule of successive Byzantine governors who often used Cyprus as a basis for rebellion against the Emperors in Constantinople.

In 1191 the island was conquered by King Richard the Lionhearted of England, who had come to the area on a crusade. A few months later, Richard sold the island to the Knights Templar, who then sold it in 1192 to the Frenchman Guy de Lusignan, the exiled King of the Crusader state of Jerusalem. He established a western feudal society in Cyprus and a dynasty that would last nearly 300 years. A Latin hierarchy was soon erected, to the detriment of the Orthodox. By 1260 the Orthodox monasteries had been made subject to the Latin bishops, the number of Orthodox bishops on the island had been reduced from 15 to four, and all of them had been placed under the authority of the new Latin Archbishop of Cyprus. Several western monastic orders founded houses on the island, often benefiting from the confiscation of Orthodox ecclesiastical property. This situation changed little with the conquest of Cyprus by Venice in 1489.

In 1571 the island fell to the Ottoman Turks. The Turks ended the feudal social system, banished the Latin hierarchy, and recognized the Orthodox. Although the Orthodox were allowed to resume electing their own Archbishop, they retained only the four dioceses the Latins had allowed them. As was true elsewhere in the Ottoman Empire, the Orthodox bishops became civil as well as spiritual leaders of their own Greek people. Thus when the Greek revolution broke out in 1821, the bishops were considered sympathetic to the Greek cause. In the same year, all the bishops and many other prominent churchmen were summoned to the governor's palace and murdered by the guards. Later a new hierarchy was sent to the island by the Patriarchate of Antioch. These bishops were able to improve the situation of the Greek community somewhat, but it still suffered under very heavy taxation.

In 1878 Great Britain leased the island from Turkey and in 1914 annexed it outright. A political movement soon developed on Cyprus among the majority Greek community in favor of *enosis*, or union with Greece. Orthodox religious leaders were involved in this movement, in keeping with their now traditional role in political affairs. When Britain granted independence to the island in 1960, the Archbishop of Cyprus, Makarios III, was elected its first president. Clashes between the Greek and Turkish communities culminated in 1974 with a Turkish invasion of the island and the establishment of the "Turkish Republic of Northern Cyprus." Many churches and monasteries in the northern part of the island were destroyed or looted in the process, and the Orthodox were denied all access to churches or monasteries in the area. It was only on November 30, 1994, that two priests were allowed to cross into the north and celebrate the Eucharist at St. Andrew monastery on the Karpas peninsula, the first such event in 20 years.

In April 1973 a crisis began in the church of Cyprus when the three Metropolitans of the island declared the deposition of Archbishop Makarios because his role as President was considered incompatible with being a bishop. But in July the three Metropolitans were themselves deposed by a "major synod" made up of bishops from the Patriarchates of Alexandria, Antioch, Jerusalem, and the church of Greece. New bishops were appointed, and the number of dioceses in Cyprus was later increased from four to six.

In the church of Cyprus in late 1997 there were nine men's monasteries with a total of 84 monks, and 14 women's communities with 142 nuns. The most prominent male community is Kykkos monastery located high in the Troodos mountains. Its monks staff the church's seminary, Barnabas the Apostle Theological School in Nicosia.

LOCATION: Cyprus
HEAD: Archbishop Chrysostomos (born 1927, elected 1977)
Title: Archbishop of Nea Justiniana and All Cyprus
Residence: Nicosia, Cyprus
MEMBERSHIP: 442,000
WEB SITE: http://www.church.cy.net

III. A. 11. The Orthodox Church of Greece

The Greek revolution against Turkish rule began in 1821 and culminated, after European intervention, in the recognition of the independence of a small Greek state by Turkey in 1832. The Orthodox Church played a prominent role in the revolution and paid a heavy price for it: the Patriarch of Constantinople Gregorios V and a number of Metropolitans had been hanged by the Turks as traitors soon after the revolt broke out.

The new Greek government, in spite of traditional allegiances, was reluctant for the Orthodox Church in Greece to remain under the jurisdiction of the Patriarch of Constantinople, whose see remained in Ottoman territory. For this reason in 1833 the church of Greece was declared autocephalous and placed under the authority of a permanent five-member Synod of Bishops and the King, who was declared head of the church. The autocephalous status of the Greek church was recognized in 1850 by Constantinople in a Patriarchal *Tomos* which also specified that the Archbishop of Athens should be the permanent head of the synod of bishops.

As additional territory was incorporated into Greece at the expense of the Ottomans, new Orthodox dioceses were assimilated into the new Greek church. The Orthodox in the extensive territory in northern Greece conquered from Turkey in 1912 remained directly under the jurisdiction of the Ecumenical Patriarchate until 1928, when by agreement it was "provisionally" placed under the administration of the church of Greece.

State control over the Greek church has been gradually reduced with the implementation of subsequent ecclesiastical regulations, although the latest constitution (1975) recognizes Orthodoxy as the "predominant religion in Greece." It also recognizes the right of other religions to worship without interference, but the worship of non-Orthodox must not disturb public order, and all proselytism is forbidden. As opposed to earlier constitutions, the President of Greece no longer must be an Orthodox Christian, and he is no longer required to swear to protect the predominant religion in the country. The constitution also states that the Orthodox Church of Greece "is autocephalous and governed by the Holy Synod of all functioning bishops, and by the permanent Holy Synod which is made up of members of the first." This structure explicitly respects the provisions of the 1850 *Tomos* of autocephaly. Today the Permanent Holy Synod is made up of 13 bishops, including the Archbishop of Athens who presides over it. In view of a projected revision of the Greek constitution, in 1995 the church and state initiated a dialogue about possible further changes in their relationship. But in May 1996 the government announced that the constitutional provisions already in place would not be changed. Official statistics show that 96% of the population of Greece is Orthodox, 1% Catholic and Protestant, and 2% Muslim.

Orthodox dioceses in Greece tend to be small: there are 80 within the Church of Greece, plus eight in Crete and four in the Dodecanese Islands that are under the jurisdiction of the Ecumenical Patriarchate.

Monasticism, which had been in steady decline since the 19th century, has recently witnessed a modest revival. In 1986 it was estimated that there were about 2,000 Orthodox monks and another 2,000 nuns in the church of Greece. The monastic republic of Mount Athos, although within Greece, is under the jurisdiction of the Ecumenical Patriarchate (see III.A.1).

There was a significant renewal movement within the Greek church following World War II. This was boosted by the "new monasticism," or lay brotherhoods that started at the beginning of the century. The most prominent of these groups, *Zoi*, reached its height in the mid-1960s when it had about 130 members, virtually all theologians, some 34 of them being priests. The community worked to reform the attitudes of Greeks towards the Orthodox Church by placing strong emphasis on personal piety. *Zoi* combined monastic spirituality with an active apostolate, and in some ways resembles the apostolic religious communities that developed in the western church. In 1960 the more traditionalist members broke away from *Zoi* to form a smaller new brotherhood called *Sotir*. Although today these movements are in decline and most of the members are elderly, they provided a new model of Orthodox religious life and had a profound influence on the church of Greece.

The church has also been heavily involved in philanthropic activity, not only by issuing statements expressing the church's teaching on social justice, but also by maintaining many orphanages, homes for the aged, hospitals, etc.

Theological scholarship in Greece is centered at the two theological faculties at the universities of Athens and Thessalonika. There are also several seminaries for the training of parish priests. Many of the most distinguished theologians of the Greek church are laymen.

Archbishop Christodoulos of Athens and All Greece was elected in April 1998 to succeed Archbishop Seraphim, who had headed the church since 1974. At his enthronement on May 9, the vigorous new Archbishop, who had helped found the church's radio and television stations, pledged to increase the church's role in society, to eradicate manifestations of xenophobia or racism, to increase the church's outreach to young people, to improve relations with the Ecumenical Patriarchate, and to affirm Greece's role in Europe by advocating full accession to the European Union.

The Greek Orthodox in the diaspora are under the jurisdiction of the Patriarchate of Constantinople [see III.A.1].

LOCATION: Greece
HEAD: Archbishop Christodoulos (born 1939, elected 1998)
Title: Archbishop of Athens and All Greece
Residence: Athens, Greece
MEMBERSHIP: 9,025,000

III. A. 12. The Orthodox Church of Poland

When Poland was restored as an independent country in the wake of World War I, nearly 4,000,000 Orthodox Christians were included within its new boundaries. Most of these were ethnic Belarusans and Ukrainians in the eastern parts of the country who had been under the jurisdiction of the Moscow Patriarchate.

Soon after its independence, however, the Polish government began to promote the idea that Orthodox in Poland should constitute an autocephalous Orthodox church independent of Moscow. This position was supported by the first Orthodox Metropolitan of Warsaw, George Yoroshevsky, who had been recently appointed by Moscow and granted a certain degree of autonomy. But in 1923 he was assassinated by a Russian monk who held the opposite view.

The Polish government then appealed the question to the Patriarchate of Constantinople which, after lengthy consideration, issued a document granting autocephalous status to the Polish Orthodox Church on November 13, 1924. In 1927 Constantinople also granted the Metropolitan of Warsaw the title of "Beatitude." The Moscow Patriarchate, however, considered this action as interference in its affairs and refused to recognize the Polish church's autocephalous status.

During the interwar period there was some tension within the Polish Orthodox Church deriving from the fact that all its bishops were Russian, while 70% of the faithful were Ukrainian. The bishops rejected demands for Ukrainian bishops and the use of the Ukrainian language in the liturgy, but took measures to satisfy many of these aspirations. During this period there were five dioceses, two seminaries (at Vilnius and Krzemieniec) with 500 students, a Faculty of Orthodox Theology at Warsaw with 150 students, 1,624 parishes, and 16 monasteries.

In the 1930s there were also some unfortunate conflicts between Catholics and Orthodox in Poland. Metropolitan Dionysy of Warsaw formally protested anti-Orthodox incidents, saying that Orthodox priests were being forced to preach in Polish, Orthodox churches were being forcibly closed and many destroyed, and pressure was being placed on Orthodox faithful to become Catholic. The Ukrainian Catholic Metropolitan Andrew Sheptytsky corroborated these accusations and added his own voice to the Orthodox protests in a pastoral letter to his faithful.

When Eastern Poland was annexed by the Soviet Union in 1939, most Polish Orthodox again found themselves in the Soviet Union and reincorporated into the Moscow Patriarchate. Thus the Polish Orthodox Church was greatly reduced in size.

In 1948, following the communist takeover of Poland, the Orthodox Metropolitan of Warsaw was deposed because of his opposition to communism. In the same year, at the request of the synod of Polish Orthodox bishops, the Moscow Patriarchate simultaneously declared Constantinople's 1924 proclamation of autocephaly null and void, and issued its own declaration of autocephaly. Nevertheless, the office of Metropolitan of Warsaw remained vacant until 1951, when the Polish Orthodox bishops asked the Moscow Patriarchate to name a new Metropolitan. Moscow then appointed Archbishop Makary Oksaniuk of Lviv in Ukraine, who had presided over the dissolution of the Ukrainian Catholic Church in 1946-1947, as new Metropolitan. Since that time, the Polish Orthodox Church has continued to have a close relationship with the Moscow Patriarchate.

There are three small Polish Orthodox monasteries at Jabłeczna, Supraśl (near Białystok), and Mount Grabarka. The Supraśl monastery complex has been at the center of a dispute between the Orthodox and Catholic churches in Poland. Founded in the late 15th century, the monastery has changed hands between Roman Catholics, Orthodox and Greek Catholics several times. In 1944 part of the complex was given to the Orthodox as a monastery, and in September 1993 the Polish Council of Ministers decided to return the entire complex to the Orthodox Church. Transfer of the property was delayed because of protests from both the Roman and Greek Catholic churches. But in February 1996 the Polish government reaffirmed its decision to give the complex to the Orthodox.

In recent years, the Polish Orthodox Church has become more integrated into Polish culture, and Polish is being used in the liturgy more often. Four church periodicals are published, and the church is becoming increasingly involved in charitable works. Currently the church has six dioceses and 410 churches within 250 parishes served by 259 priests and deacons. The Orthodox Theological Seminary in

Warsaw has about 80 students, and there is an Orthodox faculty of theology at the Christian Theological Academy in the same city with 35 undergraduate students.

LOCATION: Poland
HEAD: Metropolitan Sawa (born 1938, elected 1998)
Title: Metropolitan of Warsaw and All Poland
Residence: Warsaw, Poland
MEMBERSHIP: 570,000

III. A. 13. The Orthodox Church of Albania

Christianity arrived in Albania before the 4th century from two directions. The Ghegs in the north of the country became Latin Christians, while the Byzantine tradition was predominant among the Tosk people in the south. But following the Turkish conquest in the 15th century, the majority of Albanians became Moslem. During Turkish occupation, the remaining Orthodox population in Albania came under the jurisdiction of the Patriarchate of Constantinople.

Albania became an independent nation after the Balkan wars in 1912-1913, and almost immediately a movement for the independence of the Albanian Orthodox Church sprang up. After 1918 this movement was led by Fr. Fan Noli, an Albanian Orthodox priest from the United States. In 1922 an Orthodox Congress meeting at Berat unilaterally proclaimed the autocephaly of the Albanian Orthodox Church. The Greek bishops then fled the country. In 1926 Constantinople offered an agreement that would have led to autocephaly, but the Albanian government rejected it. In 1929, Bishop John Bessarion, with the participation of a Serbian Orthodox bishop, ordained two additional Albanian Orthodox bishops. A synod of bishops was thus formed in Tirana and the church again declared itself autocephalous.

In reaction to this, Constantinople deposed the Albanian bishops, and the Albanian government in turn expelled the representative of

Constantinople in the country. Thus a de facto schism was created. But Constantinople recognized the autocephalous status of the Albanian Orthodox Church and regularized the situation on April 12, 1937.

During the interwar period, aside from the Archbishopric of Tirana, there were Orthodox dioceses in Berat, Argyrokastro, and Korytsa. Greek was still widely used in the liturgy, but a process of translation of the texts into Albanian began in 1930. An Orthodox seminary was founded at Korytsa in 1937.

The communist revolution of 1945 marked the beginning of savage persecution of all religious groups in Albania. By this time the population was approximately 22% Orthodox and 10% Catholic. A number of influential Orthodox clergy were executed, and in 1949 Archbishop Christopher Kissi of Tirana was deposed. By 1951 all the Orthodox bishops had been replaced by men acceptable to the regime.

The Albanian government eventually took much stronger measures against religion than other governments in Eastern Europe. In 1967 the communist regime announced that all religious edifices in Albania, including 2,169 churches, mosques, monasteries and other institutions, were being closed and that all religious practices were illegal. In the same year, Orthodox Archbishop Damianos of Tirana was sent to prison where he died in 1973.

When the communist government in Albania began to disintegrate in 1990, the long period of religious persecution came to an end. Since no Albanian Orthodox bishops had survived, in January 1991 the Ecumenical Patriarchate, which had granted autocephalous status to the Albanian Church, appointed Metropolitan Anastasios of Androusis, a Professor at the University of Athens, as Patriarchal Exarch in Albania. It was his task to oversee the process of the canonical reconstruction of the autocephalous Albanian Orthodox Church. On June 24, 1992, the Holy Synod of the Ecumenical Patriarchate elected Anastasios as Archbishop of Tirana and All Albania and named three other bishops (also Greek nationals) for the remaining Orthodox dioceses in the country. Although the government did not recognize the appointment of the other three bishops, Anastasios was enthroned the following August. In July 1996 the Ecumenical Patriarchate proceeded to the ordination of the three other bishops it had named for Albania. But the government refused to allow them to enter the country and insisted that ethnic Albanians be appointed to those positions.

The position of Archbishop Anastasios as head of the Albanian Orthodox Church was threatened in late 1994. In October President Berisha stated that the Archbishop had only been appointed temporarily, and the government proposed a new draft constitution which required that the heads of large religious communities be Albanian citizens who were born in the country and who had resided there permanently for at least 20 years. But when the referendum on the new constitution was held on November 6th, it was defeated by 60% of the vote. By December relations between the Orthodox Church and the state had improved, but the position of the Archbishop still seemed uncertain. Tension between the Greek and Abanian governments over the status of the Greek minority in the country complicated the position of the Archbishop, who is an ethnic Greek. The 1989 census indicated that there are just under 60,000 Greeks in Albania, but the great majority of the Orthodox in the country are ethnic Albanians.

The impasse over the appointment of new Albanian Orthodox bishops was resolved in 1998. With the mutual consent of the Ecumenical Patriarchate, the Orthodox Church of Albania and the Albanian government, two of the previously ordained bishops resigned their offices, and one of them (Metropolitan Ignatios of Berat) was enthroned on July 18th. On the same day, Archbishop Anastasios and Metropolitan Ignatios met in extraordinary session with two representatives of the Ecumenical Patriarchate and elected two new ethnic Albanian bishops. Archimandrite John Pelushi (43 years old) was elected Metropolitan of Korça, and Fr. Kosma Qirjo (77 years old) was elected Bishop of Apollonia. Thus a full Holy Synod of the Albanian Orthodox Church was formed.

In the first six years since the church was reestablished, 70 new churches have been built, 63 reconstructed, and 100 repaired, as compared to the original 324 churches confiscated by the communist regime. In March 1992 the Resurrection of Christ Theological Academy was opened in an abandoned hotel in Durrës, where about 60 young men began to study for the priesthood. The seminary moved into newly constructed quarters at St. Vlash Monastery in Durrës in late 1996. When the communist government fell there were only 22 surviving Orthodox priests in the country. By early 1998, only five of those 22 had survived, and 92 new priests had been ordained. But there is still a severe shortage of priests. A monthly official church periodical, *Ngjallia* ("Resurrection"), began publication in October 1992, and in 1997 an Orthodox radio station with the same name began broadcasting.

In North America there are two separate Albanian Orthodox jurisdictions. The Albanian Orthodox Archdiocese in America, which makes up a distinct ethnic diocese within the Orthodox Church in America [see III.A.15] and has 13 parishes, is currently administered by Metropolitan Theodosius. The diocesan chancery is at 519 East Broadway, South Boston, Massachusetts 02127.

In addition, the Albanian Orthodox Diocese in America, which has two parishes, is under the spiritual care of the Greek Orthodox Archdiocese of America [see III.C.4].

LOCATION: Albania, small diaspora
HEAD: Metropolitan Anastasios (born 1929, elected 1992)
Title: Archbishop of Tirana and All Albania
Residence: Tirana, Albania
MEMBERSHIP: 160,000

III. A. 14. The Orthodox Church in the Czech and Slovak Republics

At the time of its founding as an independent state after World War I, Czechoslovakia was a preponderantly Catholic nation. But soon after independence, a number of Catholic priests and faithful decided to become Orthodox. The elected leader of the movement, Fr. Matej Pavlik, was ordained a bishop in 1921 by a Serbian Orthodox bishop in Belgrade, and assumed the name Gorazd. But the larger part of this group soon split away and formed a Protestant church. At this point the Orthodox group numbered about 40,000. Their number soon increased when some Byzantine Catholics in Transcarpathia became Orthodox.

Subsequent developments led to divisions within the Orthodox community in the country. In 1923 the Patriarchate of Constantinople granted the Czechoslovak church autonomous status and sent Metropolitan Sabbazd to look after the Orthodox faithful there. And in 1930 the Serbian Patriarchate sent a bishop of its own to Transcarpathia. Most Orthodox Czechoslovaks, however, remained within Bishop Gorazd's jurisdiction.

During World War II, this church was virtually annihilated by the Nazis, who executed Bishop Gorazd and his close associates in 1942. All the priests were sent to German labor camps.

In the 1931 census, there were 145,583 Orthodox in the country, with 117,897 of them in Transcarpathia. The annexation of that region by the Soviet Union in 1945 reduced the number of Orthodox in Czechoslovakia to about 40,000. In 1946 the Czechoslovak Orthodox placed themselves under the protection of Russian Patriarch Aleksy I and asked him to send them a bishop. All the Orthodox in the country were now united under a single hierarchy.

In 1950 the Byzantine Catholics in Slovakia were absorbed into the Czechoslovak Orthodox Church [see Slovak Catholic Church, IV.D.8]. This brought about 200,000 new members into the church, which in the same year was reorganized into four dioceses. But most of these new members were lost again when the Byzantine Catholic Church in Slovakia was allowed to resume functioning during the "Prague Spring" of 1968. Church buildings, however, were left in the hands of the Orthodox.

On December 9, 1951, the Patriarchate of Moscow granted autocephalous status to the Orthodox Church of Czechoslovakia. The Patriarchate of Constantinople did not recognize Moscow's authority to do this, and issued its own *Tomos* of autocephaly for this church on September 8, 1998.

In its first act of the kind, the Czechoslovak Church canonized Bishop Gorazd in September 1987 because of the central role he played in the formation of the Orthodox Church in that country and his martyrdom for the faith.

The collapse of the communist government in 1989, and the subsequent division of Czechoslovakia into independent Czech and Slovak states on January 1, 1993, required modifications in the structure of this Orthodox church. In November 1992 the Holy Synod decided to divide into two metropolitan provinces, with two dioceses in each of the new republics. In this arrangement, Metropolitan Nicholas of Prešov became head of the Orthodox Church in Slovakia. But the united Holy Synod continues to meet periodically as before, under the presidency of Metropolitan Dorotheos of Prague.

In Slovakia the government has returned most former Greek Catholic churches that were confiscated and given to the Orthodox in 1950 to their earlier owners. It was reported in March 1993 that 135 of the 170 Orthodox churches in Slovakia had been returned to the Greek Catholics. Since that time more than 50 new Orthodox churches have been built. According to the 1991 Slovak census, the Orthodox made up 0.6% of the population, or about 34,000 people concentrated in the easternmost sections of the country.

Candidates for the priesthood are educated at a seminary in Prešov that is supervised by the Holy Synod. It was integrated into

Safarik University, based in Košice, in 1990. In January 1997 the university was divided into two parts, and a new Prešov University was created from the faculties located in that city. Today the Orthodox Theological Faculty of the University of Prešov offers courses of study for seminarians, teachers of religion and ethics, and other pastoral workers in the Orthodox Church in the Czech Republic and Slovakia, as well as continuing education for priests. It also maintains a detached department in Olomouc, Czech Republic, to provide part-time training for Orthodox faithful in that country.

LOCATION: The Czech Republic and Slovakia
HEAD: Metropolitan Dorotheos (born 1913, elected 1964)
Title: Metropolitan of Prague and Archbishop of the Czech and
    Slovak Republics
Residence: Prague, Czech Republic
MEMBERSHIP: 55,000

III. A. 15. The Orthodox Church in America

Orthodoxy arrived in North America when a band of Russian Orthodox missionaries from Valaam monastery reached Alaska in 1794. At that time, Alaska was a Russian imperial territory. A first church was built on Kodiak Island, and a number of Alaskan natives were baptized. In 1840 a diocese was erected for Kamchatka, the Kurile and Aleutian Islands, with its see at Sitka. The first bishop was Innocent Veniaminov, who was later to become the Metropolitan of Moscow. By 1867, when Alaska was sold to the United States, the Russian mission was flourishing among the natives and the Bible and the Orthodox liturgy had been translated into several Alaskan native languages.

The headquarters of the diocese was transferred from Sitka to San Francisco in 1872. By the time Bishop Tikhon (Belavin) was appointed to North America in 1898, there had been much growth of the Orthodox population on the East Coast due to the arrival of new immigrants. Given this new situation, the diocesan see was moved to New York in 1905. Tikhon had consecrated an auxiliary bishop for Alaska in 1903 and an auxiliary for the Arab parishes in 1904 with residence in Brooklyn, New York. In 1905 Bishop Tikhon was elevated to the rank of Archbishop. After leaving America in 1907, he served several dioceses and was elected Patriarch of Moscow and All Russia in 1917. He died under house arrest in 1925 and was canonized as a confessor by the Russian Orthodox Church in 1989.

A significant number of Eastern Catholics joined the Russian Orthodox Church in America in the late 19th century. This in part was the result of the disapproval of the presence of married Greek Catholic priests in their dioceses by some Roman Catholic bishops. Archbishop John Ireland of St. Paul, for instance, refused to accept Fr. Alexis Tóth (1854-1909) as pastor of the Ruthenian Catholic parish in Minneapolis because he was a widower. As a result, Tóth and his parishioners entered into the Russian Orthodox Church in 1891. He eventually founded 17 Orthodox parishes in the USA for erstwhile Ruthenian Catholics. Tóth would be canonized as a saint by the Orthodox Church in America in 1994.

A separate Greek Orthodox Archdiocese dependent on the church of Greece was established in North America in 1921. It was later transferred to the Ecumenical Patriarchate. This marked the end of Orthodox unity on the continent, and the way was cleared for the subsequent foundation of other American Orthodox jurisdictions for various ethnic groups dependent on their mother churches overseas.

Following the Bolshevik Revolution in Russia in 1917, there was a large influx of Russian immigrants into America. Many of these Russian Orthodox were intensely aware of the persecution of their mother church by the communist regime. For this reason, in April 1924 the North American Diocese declared itself a temporarily self-governing church while retaining spiritual communion with the Church of Russia.

In 1935, an agreement was reached with the Russian Orthodox Church Outside Russia [see III.D.2], which had broken with the Moscow Patriarchate, according to which the North American "Metropolia" would be considered one of its districts, but would remain independent in practice.

But by 1946 it had become clear that the Russian Orthodox Church Outside Russia lacked canonical legitimacy in the eyes of most Orthodox churches. Therefore, the Metropolia decided to again recognize the Patriarch of Moscow as its spiritual head on the condition that their church retain complete administrative autonomy.

In 1970, the Moscow Patriarchate granted autocephalous status to the Metropolia, which adopted the name the Orthodox Church in America (it is also known simply as "the OCA"). Those parishes in America that wished to remain directly under Moscow's supervision were allowed to do so [see III.A.5]. This action provoked an exchange of letters between Moscow and Constantinople in which the Ecumenical Patriarchate challenged Moscow's authority to grant autocephalous status to its daughter church. The autocephaly of the OCA was subsequently recognized, however, by the Orthodox churches of Bulgaria, Georgia, Poland, and Czechoslovakia.

This dispute has still not been resolved. However, there have been significant contacts between the OCA and the Ecumenical Patriarchate. OCA delegations visited Istanbul in 1990 and 1991, and another encounter took place during Patriarch Dimitrios' visit to the United States in July 1991. Metropolitan Theodosius himself led a delegation to the Patriarchate in December 1992. They were received by Patriarch Bartholomew and had meetings with the Synodical Commission for Inter-Orthodox Affairs. Both sides expressed a commitment to Orthodox canonical unity and order in America. A further step in this direction was taken when almost all the Orthodox bishops in the United States and Canada met in Ligonier, Pennsylvania, from November 30 to December 2, 1994. The assembled bishops rejected the use of the term diaspora to describe the centuries-long Orthodox presence in America, and resolved to take concrete steps towards co-ordinating their activities and working towards Orthodox unity on the continent. Subsequently, the Ecumenical Patriarchate rejected the Ligonier statement.

In practice, the OCA is in communion with the rest of the Ortho-dox churches, and its bishops take part in the Standing Conference of Canonical Orthodox Bishops in America. But the OCA has not been able to participate in pan-Orthodox activities such as the interna-tional theological dialogues with other Christian communions be-cause it lacks the necessary unanimous recognition of its status as autocephalous or autonomous by the other Orthodox churches.

Three other Orthodox jurisdictions of different ethnic back-grounds have come into full canonical union with the OCA, giving it a multi-ethnic character. These are an Albanian Diocese with 13 par-ishes, a Bulgarian Diocese with 16 parishes, and a Romanian Diocese with 59 parishes.

There are six monastic communities under the direct jurisdiction of the Primate. The largest of these are New Skete Monastery (12 monks) with the affiliated Monastery of Our Lady of the Sign (12 nuns) in Cambridge, New York, and St. Tikhon's Monastery (10 monks) in South Canaan, Pennsylvania. Thirteen other OCA monas-tic communities in North America fall under the jurisdiction of the local dioceses.

At present the OCA administers three theological schools. St. Herman's Orthodox Theological Seminary in Kodiak, Alaska, was founded in 1973 for the training of Alaska Native clergy and church workers. St. Tikhon's Seminary at South Canaan, Pennsylvania, was founded in 1937 and is affiliated with St. Tikhon's Monastery. The largest and best known school is St. Vladimir's Orthodox Theological Seminary in Crestwood, New York, also established in 1938. In De-cember 1994 the Orthodox Church in America was given use of the Church of St. Catherine in Moscow as its official representation to the Russian Orthodox Church.

In the United States, there are 12 dioceses and 623 parishes, missions, and institutions. The ethnic dioceses extend into Canada, which also has one non-ethnic archdiocese presided over by Bishop Seraphim (PO Box 179, Spencerville, Ontario K0E 1X0). Altogether there are 91 Canadian parishes. The OCA has a Mexican Exarchate with nine parishes and missions, and there are five parishes in South America. In addition, there are three parishes in Australia under the OCA's canonical protection, two in Sydney and another near Brisbane.

LOCATION: North America
HEAD: Metropolitan Theodosius (born 1933, elected 1977)
Title: Archbishop of Washington, Metropolitan of All America and Canada
Residence: Syosset, New York, USA
MEMBERSHIP: 1,000,000
WEB SITE: http://www.oca.org

III. B. THE AUTONOMOUS ORTHODOX CHURCHES

There are five Orthodox churches which, although functioning independently on a day-to-day basis, are canonically dependent on an autocephalous Orthodox church. In practice this means that the head of an autonomous church must be confirmed in office by the Holy Synod of its mother autocephalous church. The Orthodox churches of Finland and Estonia are dependent on the Ecumenical Patriarchate, and Mount Sinai is dependent on the Patriarchate of Jerusalem. In addition, the Moscow Patriarchate has granted autonomous status to its Orthodox daughter churches in Japan and China, but these actions have not been recognized by the Ecumenical Patriarchate.

III. B. 1. The Orthodox Church of Mount Sinai

Given its importance as the site where, according to the Book of Exodus, Moses received the Books of the Law from God, Mount Sinai has been frequented by Christian pilgrims since ancient times. By the third century, Christian anchorites had begun to live in the area, and by the fourth century one or more communities of monks had been formed.

Because the area had become unstable and the monks vulnerable to attack, the Emperor Justinian decided to fortify the monastery in 528. He also settled 200 families from Egypt and Trebizond in the area to protect and serve the monastic community.

At first the monastery had a highly international character, with Slavic, Arab, Latin, Armenian, Ethiopian and Syrian monks, as well as Greeks. Perhaps the best known monk of the monastery was St. John Climacus, who was abbot in the 7th century. By that time, the area had been conquered by the Moslem Arabs. Islamic governments were generally tolerant, but on several occasions wild tribes ravaged the monastery, requiring the monks to temporarily close it and take refuge in Cairo or Alexandria. During this period, monks of other nationalities abandoned the monastery to the Greeks.

St. Catherine's monastery, as it has been known since the 9th century, was originally part of the Patriarchate of Jerusalem, within the diocese of Pharan. After the bishop of Pharan was deposed for monotheletism in 681, the see was transferred to the monastery itself, the abbot becoming the bishop of Pharan. With the subsequent union of the diocese of Raitho with the monastery, all the Christians in the Sinai peninsula came under the jurisdiction of the Abbot-Archbishop.

In 1575 the Patriarchate of Constantinople granted Mount Sinai autonomous status. This was reaffirmed in 1782. The only remaining link with the Jerusalem Patriarchate is that the abbot, who is elected by an assembly of senior monks, must be ordained a bishop by the

Jerusalem Patriarch, who is also commemorated in the monastery's liturgy.

The monastery's library is renowned for its great antiquity and its manuscripts. It was here in 1859 that Tischendorf found the *Codex Sinaiticus* of the Bible. Today it contains about 4,000 manuscripts. Some of the world's most ancient icons are also found in the monastery, which was already outside the Byzantine Empire during the iconoclast controversy when most icons in the empire were destroyed.

Currently the monastery, in addition to the library, has a guest house and a hospital for the local population. The monks also administer a school in Cairo. The monastery has historically had many dependent churches and monasteries (*metochia*) in other countries. At present there are one in Cairo (where the Abbot often resides), seven in Greece, three in Cyprus, one in Lebanon and one in Istanbul, Turkey.

Today, in addition to the 20 or so monks in the monastic community, this church includes a few hundred Bedouins and fishermen who live in the Sinai. There was an agreement between the Greek and Egyptian governments in 1984 that allowed the monastery to receive up to 50 new Greek monks.

Since the Israeli invasion in 1967, perhaps the greatest problem facing the community has been maintaining an authentic monastic lifestyle while dealing with a massive influx of tourists. This problem has continued after the area's return to Egyptian administration.

LOCATION: Sinai peninsula, Egypt
HEAD: Archbishop Damianos (born 1935, elected 1973)
Title: Abbot of St. Catherine's Monastery, Archbishop of Sinai, Pharan, and Raitho
Residence: Cairo, Egypt
MEMBERSHIP: 900

III. B. 2. The Orthodox Church of Finland

Although it appears that the earliest Christians in Finland were Byzantines, most of the country received the Christian faith in the Latin tradition through the activity of Swedish missionaries. The easternmost Finnish province of Karelia, however, was evangelized by Byzantine monks from the ancient monastery of Valamo ("Valaam" in Russian) located on an island in Lake Ladoga.

In the 13th century Finland was a battleground between Catholic Sweden and Orthodox Russia. Eventually Sweden gained control of most of Finland, but Karelia came under Russian control.

But in 1617 Karelia was also taken over by Sweden, which had in the meantime adopted the Lutheran faith. The Swedes persecuted the Orthodox for a time, but conditions improved in the later part of the century.

Karelia was again occupied by Russia in 1721, and in 1809 the Tsar conquered all of Finland, which then became an autonomous Grand Duchy within the Russian Empire. Later in the 19th century Orthodox Karelians began to assert their national identity. The liturgy and many Orthodox theological and spiritual works were translated into Finnish, which remains the liturgical language of this church.

In 1917 Finland gained independence from Russia, and in 1918 the Orthodox in Finland declared themselves an autonomous church in relation to Moscow. Patriarch Tikhon of Moscow recognized this status in 1921. In 1923 the Finnish Orthodox Church was received by the Patriarchate of Constantinople as an autonomous church.

The 1939-1940 Winter War between Finland and the Soviet Union, and the subsequent annexation of most of Karelia by the USSR, resulted in the loss of 90% of the property belonging to the Finnish Orthodox Church. Most Orthodox Finns were evacuated to other parts of Finland and began new lives scattered across the country.

In 1957 the Moscow Patriarchate recognized the Finnish Orthodox Church's autonomy under the Ecumenical Patriarchate. In 1980 the General Assembly of the Finnish Orthodox Church voted to seek autocephalous status from the Ecumenical Patriarchate, but no action has been taken on this proposal.

There is a long history of Finnish Orthodox monasticism in Karelia, but the monasteries had to be evacuated during the Russo-Finnish War as the Soviets gained control of the area. The famous Valamo Monastery was refounded at Heinävesi in central Finland under the name New Valamo. The community also included monks from other Karelian monasteries. The last of the original monks from Valamo died in 1981. Lintula Convent was also refounded near New Valamo. Today these two monasteries are important centers of Finnish Orthodox spiritual life.

The disintegration of the Soviet state facilitated the development of better relations between the Finnish and Russian Orthodox churches. In 1994 six pastoral teams, each headed by a priest, were sent by the Finnish church to provide Christmas and Holy Week services in Orthodox parishes in the Russian section of Karelia. In September 1994 Russian Patriarch Aleksy II visited Finland and thanked the local Orthodox church for giving hospitality to the Valamo community. The Finnish church is now assisting in the restoration of the original Valamo monastery in Russia.

A Finnish Orthodox Seminary was founded at Sortavala in Karelia in 1918, just after Finland became independent. After the city was annexed by the Soviets in 1940, the seminary moved to Helsinki. It was transferred to Humaljärvi in 1957, and to Kuopio four years later. It was officially closed on July 31, 1988, to make way for the establishment of a Department of Orthodox Theology at the University of Joensuu, which began functioning in the fall of 1988.

When a new Archbishop of Finland is chosen, his election must be confirmed by the Ecumenical Patriarchate. Finnish Orthodox representatives now take part in all pan-Orthodox activities alongside delegates of the autocephalous Orthodox churches.

The government of Finland recognizes the Finnish Orthodox Church as the second national church, after the predominant Evangelical Lutheran Church. This is the only Orthodox church that uses the western dates for Easter and fixed feasts. A demographic shift was taking place in the 1990s, with the Orthodox population moving steadily towards Helsinki and the more heavily populated southern region of the country. Currently there are about 50 churches and 100 chapels within a total of 25 parishes in Finland.

LOCATION: Finland
HEAD: Archbishop John (born 1923, elected 1987)
Title: Archbishop of Karelia and All Finland
Residence: Kuopio, Finland
MEMBERSHIP: 57,000
WEB SITE: http://www.ort.fi

III. B. 3. The Orthodox Church of Japan

This church began in 1861 with the arrival in Japan of a young Russian missionary priest-monk named Nicholas Kassathin. Before his death in 1912, he had baptized some 20,000 Japanese into the Orthodox faith and had translated the New Testament and many liturgical books into Japanese. Because of his central role in the foundation of the Orthodox Church in Japan, he was canonized in 1970.

Orthodoxy in Japan quickly became an indigenous phenomenon, which enabled it to survive periods of hostility between Japan and Russia. This process was completed with the installation of Bishop Theodosius as the first native Japanese Metropolitan in 1972.

As a result of canonical problems with the Russian Orthodox Church in the period following the Bolshevik Revolution, the Orthodox Church in Japan placed itself under the jurisdiction of the American Metropolia [see the OCA, III.A.15] from 1945 to 1970. When the Orthodox Church in America was declared autocephalous by the Moscow Patriarchate in 1970, the OCA returned the Japanese Orthodox Church to the jurisdiction of Moscow, and Moscow simultaneously declared the Japanese church autonomous. Consequently, the election of the head of the Japanese Orthodox Church must now be confirmed by the Moscow Patriarchate. The autonomy of the Japanese church has not been recognized by the Ecumenical Patriarchate and most other Orthodox churches. Nevertheless, Metropolitan Theodosius met with Ecumenical Patriarch Bartholomew I when he visited Japan in April 1995.

At present there are three dioceses with 30 priests and five deacons serving approximately 150 worshiping communities. Most of the parishes are located on the northern island of Hokkaido. All the clergy are now of Japanese origin and are trained at the church's seminary in Tokyo.

LOCATION: Japan
HEAD: Metropolitan Theodosius (born 1935, elected 1972)
Title: Archbishop of Tokyo, Metropolitan of All Japan
Residence: Tokyo, Japan
MEMBERSHIP: 30,000

III. B. 4. The Orthodox Church of China

The origins of Chinese Orthodoxy can be traced back to 1686, when the Chinese Emperor hired a group of Russian Cossacks as his personal bodyguard. Their descendants were eventually completely absorbed into Chinese culture but remained Orthodox in faith and formed the nucleus of an Orthodox community in China.

The Russian Orthodox Church began missionary activity in China at the end of the 19th century. By 1914 there were about 5,000 Chinese Orthodox, including Chinese priests and a seminary in Peking.

After the 1917 Russian revolution, Russian émigrés swelled the Orthodox population in China. In 1939 there were five bishops in the country and an Orthodox University at Harbin. By 1949 there were 100,000 faithful, 60 parishes, 200 priests, two monasteries and a seminary in Manchuria, as well as 150 parishes and 200,000 faithful in the rest of China.

After the communist revolution in China, most of the Russian clergy and faithful were either repatriated to the Soviet Union or fled to the West. By 1955, there were only 30 Russian priests left.

The Moscow Patriarchate granted autonomous status to the Chinese Orthodox Church in 1956 and recalled its Russian hierarchy. At that time there were about 20,000 faithful with one bishop in Shanghai and one in Peking. Today there is only one functioning church, in Harbin.

In 1996 the Ecumenical Patriarchate established a metropolitanate in Hong Kong with jurisdiction over all of China as well as India, the Philippines, Singapore and Indonesia. But in February 1997 the Russian Orthodox Holy Synod reaffirmed its links to the Chinese Orthodox Church and stated that, pending the election of a primate, the maintenance of Orthodoxy in the country remained the responsibility of the Moscow Patriarchate.

III. B. 5. The Estonian Apostolic Orthodox Church

The Estonians came under Swedish control in the late 16th century, and soon thereafter they adopted the Lutheranism of their rulers. Peter the Great conquered the region for Russia in the early 18th century. Under Russian rule, especially in the 19th century, a significant number of ethnic Estonians became Orthodox, and there was an influx of ethnic Russians into the province. Thus a sizable Orthodox community was established in Estonia.

After the overthrow of the Tsar in 1917, Estonia proclaimed its independence. This was recognized by the Soviets in 1920. In view of Estonian independence and the persecution of the Russian Orthodox Church, Bishop Alexander of Tallinn asked the Patriarchate of Constantinople to receive his church into its jurisdiction. On July 7, 1923, Patriarch Meletios IV of Constantinople issued a *Tomos* accepting the Estonian Church and granting it autonomous status. He named Bishop Alexander Metropolitan of Tallinn and All Estonia. By 1940 this church had over 210,000 faithful, three bishops, 156 parishes, 131 priests, 19 deacons, two monasteries, and a theological seminary. The majority of the faithful were ethnic Estonians.

In 1940 the Soviet Union annexed Estonia. The Germans occupied the country during World War II, and the Soviets returned in 1944. Metropolitan Alexander then went into exile in Stockholm, Sweden, with 23 of his clergy. The church based in Stockholm remained attached to the Ecumenical Patriarchate and served about 10,000 Estonian Orthodox exiles in various countries. After Metropolitan Alexander died in 1953, the Ecumenical Patriarchate consecrated a new Estonian Orthodox bishop, Juri Valbe, to oversee the Estonian Church based in Stockholm. After his death in 1961, these Estonian parishes were placed under local bishops of the Ecumenical Patriarchate.

The Orthodox Church in Estonia itself had been incorporated into the Moscow Patriarchate after the Soviet annexation. In 1978, at the request of the Russian Orthodox Church, the Ecumenical Patriarchate declared inoperative the 1923 *Tomos* that had established the autonomous Estonian church. Due to demographic shifts, Russians made up the majority of the Orthodox population of Estonia by the end of Soviet rule.

Following the breakup of the Soviet Union and the renewed independence of Estonia in 1991, a dispute developed within the Orthodox community between those who wished to remain linked to the Moscow Patriarchate and those who sought the re-establishment of the autonomous Orthodox church under the Ecumenical Patriarchate [see the Orthodox Church of Russia, III.A.V]. Lengthy negotiations between Moscow and Constantinople failed to produce an agreement. On February 20, 1996, the Holy Synod of the Patriarchate of Constantinople formally reactivated the 1923 *Tomos* that had established the autonomous church under its jurisdiction and appointed Archbishop John of Finland as *locum tenens* to head the church pending the election of a primate. The Moscow Patriarchate reacted swiftly and strongly to this move, breaking relations with the Ecumenical Patriarchate and removing the name of the Ecumenical Patriarch from the diptychs of the liturgy.

In April 1996 delegations from the two sides met in Zurich, Switzerland, and reached an agreement in principle. On May 16 both Holy Synods formally adopted the recommendations made at the Zurich meeting. The agreement provided for parallel jurisdictions in Estonia, and allowed individual parishes and clergy to join either the Estonian autonomous church under Constantinople or the diocese that would remain dependent on Moscow. For its part, Constantinople agreed to a four-month suspension of its February 20th decision to re-establish the Estonian autonomous church. Moscow agreed to lift the penalties that had been imposed on clergy who had joined the autonomous church. Both Patriarchates agreed to work together with the Estonian government, so that all Estonian Orthodox might enjoy the same rights, including rights to property. As a result of this agreement, full communion was restored between Moscow and Constantinople, and the name of Ecumenical Patriarch Bartholomew was again included in the diptychs in Moscow.

Of the 84 Orthodox parishes in Estonia, 50 with about 7,000 members joined the new autonomous church under Constantinople. Another 30 parishes with anywhere between 50,000 and 100,000 members, as well as the monastic community at Pjukhtitsa, opted to remain within the Russian Orthodox diocese of Tallinn.

III. C. CANONICAL CHURCHES UNDER CONSTANTINOPLE

These are churches which, because of special circumstances or political turmoil in their countries of origin, have been received under the canonical protection of the Ecumenical Patriarchate. The Patriarchate provides these churches with Holy Chrism and confirms the election of their bishops.

III. C. 1. The American Carpatho-Russian Orthodox Greek Catholic Diocese of the USA

This church exists only in the United States and is made up of descendants of Ruthenian Catholic [see Ruthenian Catholic Church, IV.D.3] immigrants from a section of the Austro-Hungarian Empire known as Subcarpathia or Transcarpathia, now in western Ukraine and eastern Slovakia.

When they immigrated to the United States in the 19th century, these Ruthenian Catholics were often accompanied by their own married priests. The presence of married Catholic priests within their dioceses met with the disapproval of some Roman Catholic bishops.

Heeding a request from the Catholic hierarchy of the United States, the Vatican issued a decree, *Cum Data Fuerit*, in 1929. It stated that newly ordained and newly arrived eastern priests in North America were henceforth to be celibate in spite of the terms of union with Rome that had guaranteed Ruthenian Catholics the right to retain married clergy. This gave rise to widespread dismay in the Eastern Catholic community.

In 1937 a meeting was held in Pittsburgh, Pennsylvania, of disaffected Ruthenian Catholics under the leadership of Fr. Orestes Chornock. The meeting decided to petition Patriarch Benjamin I of Constantinople to received the group into the Orthodox Church and to ordain Fr. Chornock as its first bishop, consolidating them into a distinct diocese. Constantinople approved the request, and Fr. Chornock was ordained to the episcopate at the Ecumenical Patriarchate in 1938. The new diocese was placed under the spiritual supervision of the Greek Orthodox Archdiocese.

A seminary was founded in New York City soon after the establishment of the diocese. After several transfers, in 1951 it was permanently moved to Johnstown, Pennsylvania, and named Christ the Savior Seminary. The diocese, headquartered at 312 Garfield Street in Johnstown, currently has 75 parishes and six missions.

LOCATION: The United States
HEAD: Metropolitan Nicholas of Amissos (born 1936, elected 1985)
Residence: Johnstown, Pennsylvania, USA
MEMBERSHIP: 50,000

III. C. 2. The Ukrainian Orthodox Church of the USA and Diaspora

Beginning in the 19th century, large numbers of Ukrainian Orthodox immigrants arrived in the United States. There were also several waves of conversions of Ukrainian Greek Catholics to Orthodoxy. In 1919, with nationalist feelings intensified by events in Ukraine, some of these groups in the United States organized an autonomous Ukrainian Orthodox Church. In December 1923 the recently established Ukrainian Autocephalous Orthodox Church [see III.D.3] sent Metropolitan John Teodorovich to assume leadership of a combined American-Canadian diocese. He arrived in the United States in 1924.

Metropolitan John was a good administrator who had much success in consolidating a number of Ukrainian Orthodox parishes into his new jurisdiction in the United States and Canada. But there were serious questions about the validity of his consecration as a bishop, given the method by which the bishops of his mother church had been ordained.

Meanwhile, another Ukrainian Orthodox jurisdiction was emerging, the Ukrainian Orthodox Church of America. It was formed as a result of the concerns of some Ukrainian Greek Catholics in the 1920s over the ownership of parish property and the Vatican's imposition of clerical celibacy among Eastern Catholic clergy in North America. These Ukrainian Catholics wanted to become Orthodox. But they wished to join a jurisdiction recognized by the other Orthodox churches and shared the concerns of others about the validity of Metropolitan John Teodorovich's consecration. Therefore, on April 9, 1929, a meeting of 15 clergy and 24 laymen took place at St Mary's Ukrainian Catholic Church in Allentown, Pennsylvania. They decided in principle to form a distinct Ukrainian Orthodox diocese. A second meeting took place in New York in July 1931, where the group nominated Fr. Joseph Zuk as its bishop. He was ordained as the first head of the new diocese in September 1932, but died soon thereafter, in 1934. In 1937 the diocese was received into the jurisdiction of the Patriarchate of Constantinople when Zuk's successor, Fr. Bohdan Shpylka, was ordained a bishop in New York City by Archbishop Athenagoras of America, the future Ecumenical Patriarch. At one point during his tenure, there were 45 missions and parishes within the diocese.

In 1949, Metropolitan Teodorovich was re-consecrated by canonical Orthodox bishops, which ended questions about the validity of his consecration. At this point a number of parishes of the Ukrainian Orthodox Church of America joined his jurisdiction, which then became the largest Ukrainian Orthodox church in the United States.

But the church was still not recognized as canonical by the other Orthodox churches.

Metropolitan Teodorovich died in 1971 and was succeeded by Metropolitan Mstyslav, who in 1990 was elected Patriarch of the Ukrainian Autocephalous Orthodox Church in Kiev. His death in 1993 was followed by serious divisions among the Orthodox in Ukraine, but the Ukrainian Orthodox in the United States avoided taking sides in the dispute.

On March 12, 1995, the entire Ukrainian Orthodox hierarchy outside Ukraine that had not already done so was received into the jurisdiction of the Ecumenical Patriarchate, including the Ukrainian Orthodox Church in the United States. It is estimated that in total this group has about 150,000 faithful and 200 parishes, mostly in the United States, but also in Brazil, Western Europe and elsewhere. The Ukrainian Orthodox in Canada had been received under the jurisdiction of the Ecumenical Patriarchate in 1990 [see III.C.6].

The reception of the Ukrainian Orthodox Church of the USA into the jurisdiction of the Ecumenical Patriarchate removed the remaining obstacles to full unity with the Ukrainian Orthodox Church of America. This was accomplished in November 1996. Bishop Vsevolod, the head of the Ukrainian Orthodox Church of America, became a bishop with geographical responsibilities based in Chicago, Illinois.

Sadly, however, this unity was threatened almost as soon as it was achieved. In 1996 a Metropolitan of the Ukrainian Autocephalous Orthodox Church issued a *Tomos* establishing a parish in Cleveland, Ohio, and ordained a local priest a bishop under the title Metropolitan Stephan. In 1998 four of the church's parishes were received into the jurisdiction of the Ukrainian Orthodox Church-Kiev Patriarchate in Ukraine [see III.D.3]. The priests of these parishes had been suspended and wished to establish links with the Ukrainian Patriarchate in spite of its non-canonical character. The bishops of the Ukrainian Orthodox Church in the Diaspora vigorously protested these actions by the Ukrainian Orthodox Church-Kiev Patriarchate when they met together in Winnipeg in June 1998.

The Ukrainian Orthodox Church in the United States has a total of 115 parishes, two monasteries and five missions. The Ukrainian Orthodox in Great Britain are under the care of Bishop Ioan Derevjanka whose offices are at 1A Newton Avenue, Acton, London W3 8AJ. The President of the Ukrainian Orthodox Consistory of Australia and New Zealand is Very Rev. Mykola Serdiuk, 21 Timbury Street, Moorooka, Queensland 4105.

LOCATION: The United States, diaspora
HEAD: Metropolitan Constantine of Irinopolis (born 1936, elected 1995)
Residence: South Bound Brook, New Jersey, USA
WEB SITE: http://www.uocofusa.org

III. C. 3. The Russian Orthodox Archdiocese in Western Europe

After the Bolshevik Revolution in Russia in 1917, many Russian Orthodox faithful and clergy found themselves in exile outside the Soviet Union. A group of Russian Orthodox bishops met in Constantinople in 1920 to form an autonomous church that would reestablish relations with the Moscow Patriarchate as soon as conditions allowed. This provided the nucleus of what would become the Russian Orthodox Church Outside Russia [see III.D.2].

This Synod of bishops, which took a strongly anti-communist political position, was condemned by Patriarch Tikhon, who in 1921 appointed Metropolitan Evlogius as his legitimate representative in Western Europe, based in Paris. In 1927 the Synod suspended Metropolitan Evlogius and broke communion with him. This effectively split the Russian émigré community in Europe between those loyal to the Synod in exile and those loyal to the Patriarchate through Evlogius.

In 1928 Metropolitan Sergius (then patriarchal *locum tenens*) called on all Russian bishops to refrain from political activity and to recognize the Soviet regime. Evlogius initially accepted this, but in 1930 he took part in an Anglican prayer service in London for persecuted Christians in the Soviet Union. In response, Metropolitan Sergius removed Evlogius from office and appointed another bishop for patriarchal parishes in Western Europe.

Most Russian Orthodox bishops and faithful of this jurisdiction remained loyal to Evlogius, however, and considered Metropolitan Sergius' call for acceptance of the Soviet regime unacceptable. Evlogius then petitioned the Ecumenical Patriarchate's assistance, and in 1931 Patriarch Photius II received Evlogius and his followers under the jurisdiction of Constantinople. Since that time the Russian Archdiocese has become a multi-cultural jurisdiction, now composed of about 60 parishes served by 58 priests and deacons, and four monastic communities. Centered in France where it is the largest Orthodox group, the Archdiocese also has communities in Belgium, the Netherlands, Germany, Norway, Sweden, and Italy.

Relations with the Russian Orthodox Church have improved since the collapse of the Soviet Union. For the first time since it was received into the jurisdiction of the Ecumenical Patriarchate in 1931, an official delegation from the Archdiocese visited the Moscow Patriarchate in November 1994. This was followed by a historic visit of Archbishop Sergius to the Russian Orthodox Church in May 1995.

The best-known institution of this archdiocese is St. Sergius Orthodox Theological Institute in Paris. It was founded by Metropolitan Evlogius in 1925 and is recognized worldwide as an intellectual center of Orthodox theology.

LOCATION: Western Europe
HEAD: Archbishop Sergius Konovalov (born 1941, elected 1993)
Title: Russian Orthodox Archbishop of Western Europe

Residence: Paris, France
MEMBERSHIP: about 100,000

III. C. 4. The Albanian Orthodox Diocese of America

After the establishment of a communist government in Albania after World War II and the destruction of the Albanian Orthodox
Church [see III.A.13] in 1967, Albanian Orthodox in the diaspora,
located mainly in the United States, found themselves without a
mother church. The majority eventually formed the Albanian Orthodox Archdiocese in America, which joined the Orthodox Church in
America [see III.A.15].

But a small group preferred to come directly under the jurisdic-
tion of the Patriarchate of Constantinople and formed this Albanian
Orthodox Diocese of America. At present, its two parishes (one in
Chicago and one in South Boston, Massachusetts) are headed by a
vicar priest who is directly responsible to Archbishop Spyridon of the
Greek Orthodox Archdiocese of America.

LOCATION: The United States
HEAD: Rev. Ilia Katre, Vicar General
Residence: 6455 Silver Dawn Lane
Las Vegas, Nevada 89118
MEMBERSHIP: 5,100

III. C. 5. The Belarusan Council of Orthodox Churches
in North America

This is a group of four Belarusan Orthodox [see III.D.4] parishes
in the United States and one in Canada that have placed themselves
under the jurisdiction of the Ecumenical Patriarchate. They do not
have a bishop of their own but are under the care of an administra-

tor. He is directly responsible to Archbishop Spyridon of the Greek Orthodox Archdiocese of America.

LOCATION: The United States and Canada
HEAD: Very Rev. Sviatoslaw Kous, Administrator
Residence: 284 Whitehead Avenue
South River, New Jersey 08882 USA

III. C. 6. The Ukrainian Orthodox Church of Canada

In 1918 a group of Ukrainian Greek Catholics in Canada, fearing that as Catholics their Ukrainian identity could not be preserved, decided to become Orthodox. Since the situation of Orthodox in Canada was confused because of the effects of the Bolshevik revolution in Russia, it was some time before the group found a permanent jurisdiction to which it could belong. But in late 1919, the group was received into communion with the self-proclaimed Ukrainian Autocephalous Orthodox Church [see III.D.3 below]. Metropolitan John Teodorovich, who had been ordained uncanonically in Ukraine, became the first head of a new American-Canadian diocese in 1924. Although the Canadian church accepted Teodorovich as its bishop, it always remained a separate entity administered from Winnipeg.

This original group of former Greek Catholics was strengthened when Orthodox from Ukraine later began to arrive in Canada in large numbers. It was to become the largest Orthodox community in Canada, having some 50 parishes by 1940.

In 1947 the Ukrainian Orthodox in Canada replaced Metropolitan John with Archbishop Mstyslav Skrypnyk of the Ukrainian autocephalous church who had recently arrived from Europe. He resigned in 1950 and transferred to the church in the United States. Relations were established with the Ukrainian Autocephalous Church Abroad, then based in Western Europe.

By 1955 the Ukrainian Orthodox Church in Canada had 270 parishes and 76 priests. In 1960 St. Andrew's Institute in Winnipeg (founded in 1945) was moved to a new location and affiliated with the University of Manitoba. By that time the church had some 140,000 members.

New efforts to regularize this church's canonical status began in the late 1980s and culminated in the official reception of the Ukrainian Greek Orthodox Church of Canada into the jurisdiction of the Ecumenical Patriarchate of Constantinople on April 1, 1990. There are bishops in Winnipeg, Saskatoon and Edmonton.

Although there have been some attempts to use English in the liturgy, the church consistory has repeatedly confirmed Ukrainian as the official liturgical language. St. Andrew's Institute remains the only Orthodox theological school in the country. Today there are some 200 places of worship in Canada served by about 100 priests.

LOCATION: Canada
HEAD: Metropolitan Wasyly (born 1909, elected 1985)
Title: Metropolitan of Winnipeg and All Canada
Residence: 174 Seven Oaks
Winnipeg, Manitoba R2V 0K8
MEMBERSHIP: 120,000
WEB SITE: http://uocc.ca

III. D. ORTHODOX CHURCHES OF IRREGULAR STATUS

The canonical status of each of the churches in this group is questioned in some way by Orthodoxy as a whole. This is not to put them all on the same level, as some are considered simply uncanonical, while others are in full schism and out of communion with the Orthodox Church.

III. D. 1. The Old Believers

The Old Believers, also known as Old Ritualists, came into existence as the result of a schism within the Russian Orthodox Church in the 17th century. The Russian Church had adopted certain liturgical usages that differed from those of the Greeks. Patriarch Nikon (1605-1681) introduced changes intended to make Russian practices conform to Greek usage. This was offensive to some Russian Orthodox who believed that it was legitimate for the Russian Church to adopt its own traditions. Opposition coalesced around a priest named Avvakum, who was burnt at the stake in 1682. His followers became known as Old Believers, or those who followed the old rituals before the reform.

The Old Believers, who at one time may have composed 10% of the Russian population, were harshly persecuted under the tsars. Many fled into Asia in the 18th century and others were forcefully exiled from European Russia. Many communities lived in almost complete isolation for centuries. Since no Orthodox bishop had joined the Old Believers, the group was deprived of a hierarchy. This, along with the fact that the communities were spread over vast areas, caused them to split into as many as 12 groups, each with its own characteristics. But the Old Believers managed to preserve traditional Russian iconography at a time when the official church supported more modern art forms.

The two most important groups are known as "Popovtsy," who have retained priests and sacraments, and "Bezpopovtsy," who reject them. The priestless communities are scattered throughout the far north from Karelia to the Urals. In 1847 the former Orthodox Metropolitan Ambrosios of Sarajevo (Bosnia) embraced the Old Believers and consecrated two bishops for those who remained loyal to the priesthood and sacraments. This gave rise to the hierarchy of the largest priestly group.

It was only after May 3, 1905, when Tsar Nicholas II issued the Edict of Toleration, that Old Believers were allowed to function freely in Russia. The situation of this community since the Bolshevik Revolution of 1917 is poorly known, but there were attempts to overcome the schism. Metropolitan Sergius and the Holy Synod took unsuccessful measures to heal the rift in 1929. Meetings took place in the period following World War II which culminated in the solemn lifting of the anathemas in 1971. So far, however, full communion between Old Believers and the Russian Orthodox Church has not been re-established.

The largest priestly group of Old Believers today is known as the "Bielaia Krinitsia" Church, a reference to the village in western Ukraine where one of their largest communities is located. The church headquarters was established there in tsarist times because it was then on the Austrian side of the border. They canonized Metropolitan Ambrosios — from whom their ordinations derive — in 1997. The church is currently headed by Metropolitan Alimpyj of Moscow and All Russia (born 1929, elected 1988), with headquarters in Moscow. It has about 120 parishes in Russia with four additional bishops in Kostroma, Siberia, Ukraine, and Moldova. A seminary was opened in Moscow in 1996. The Bielaia Krinitsia Church is in full communion with a group of Old Ritualist Orthodox in Romania headed by Metropolitan Leonty, whose headquarters is in Braila, Romania.

The other significant group of priestly Old Believers is much smaller, and is headed by Archbishop Aristarch of Novozybkov, Moscow, and All Russia, with headquarters in Novozybkov. They obtained a valid hierarchy during the turmoil of the 1920s and now have about 50 parishes. There are additional bishops in Kamyshin, Kursk, the Urals and Burjatia, as well as in Georgia and Belarus.

The Old Believers are believed to have substantially declined in numbers after the 1917 Soviet revolution. They have now achieved legal recognition, and churches have been reopening at a rapid rate, creating an acute shortage of clergy. Reliable figures concerning membership are not available, but estimates run between 2,000,000 and 2,500,000 faithful.

The hierarch for the United States, Canada and Australia is Bishop Sofrony (elected 1996), based in Gervais, Oregon. There are five Old Believer parishes in the United States, and about 500 members in Canada. In Australia contact Mr. Moisey Ovchinnikoff at the Old Orthodox Church of Holy Nativity, 20 Norval Street, Auburn NSW 2144.

III. D. 2. The Russian Orthodox Church Outside Russia

Following the Bolshevik Revolution of 1917, over a million Russians found themselves in exile scattered in many countries. Many of these had fled Russia after the defeat of the White armies that had attempted to destroy the new Soviet regime, and a significant number of clergy came with them.

In 1920 there was a meeting of over 20 Russian Orthodox bishops in Constantinople. They decided temporarily to create an autonomous church for the émigré Russians, intending to re-establish canonical links with the Moscow Patriarchate when conditions permitted. A synod of bishops was established under the presidency of Anthony Khrapovitsky, the exiled Metropolitan of Kiev. At the invitation of the Serbian Orthodox Church, they established their headquarters at Karlovci, Yugoslavia.

The monarchist political views of this group became clear when in 1921 the Synod formally called for the restoration of the Romanov dynasty in Russia. (The Synod would canonize Tsar Nicholas II and his family in 1982.) Patriarch Tikhon denounced the Synod for its support of the monarchy in May 1922. In 1928, after the Karlovci Synod flatly refused to accept the call of Metropolitan Sergius (patriarchal *locum tenens*) for all Russian bishops to refrain from political activity, Sergius ordered that the Synod be dissolved. In 1934

Sergius and the Russian Orthodox Synod in Moscow formally suspended all the bishops of the Karlovci Synod pending an ecclesiastical trial which, in fact, has never taken place.

Most of the bishops of the Synod either did not survive World War II or were reconciled individually to the Moscow Patriarchate. But the group was reinforced after the war by Orthodox bishops who had ministered in the Nazi-occupied regions of the Soviet Union and who subsequently fled the country. The headquarters of the Synod had been moved from Karlovci to Munich during the war, and in 1950 it was moved to the United States.

There have been a number of appeals from the Moscow Patriarchate for this group to return to canonical communion with it, but so far to no avail. In 1974 Patriarch Pimen sent a message to the Synod's Sobor of Bishops, Clergy, and Laity, in which he invited them only to recognize the validity of the Moscow Patriarchate and allow intercommunion with it. Moscow no longer requested that they also support the Soviet State. Until now, however, the Synod has continued to deny the ecclesial nature of the Moscow Patriarchate, as well as such churches as the Orthodox Church in America who are in full communion with it. The local council of the Russian Orthodox Church that was held in Zagorsk in June 1988 on the occasion of the millennium of the Baptism of Rus issued an appeal for the canonical unity of all Russian Orthodox and expressed the hope that a dialogue for this purpose might soon begin.

After the fall of the communist government and the dissolution of the Soviet Union, the Russian Orthodox Church Outside Russia began to establish itself in its homeland. It now has about 100 worshiping communities in Russia and the other countries of the Commonwealth of Independent States. Currently four bishops oversee these parishes. Two of them broke with Metropolitan Vitaly in New York in April 1994, founded their own temporary administration called the "Free Orthodox Church of Russia," and ordained three additional bishops. They were reconciled in November 1994, and the ordination of the three new bishops was declared invalid, but some tensions remain.

In the mid-1990s proposals for a reconciliation with the Moscow Patriarchate were causing lively debate. The synod of bishops of the Russian Orthodox Church Outside Russia continued to insist that there could be no agreement unless the Moscow Patriarchate renounce its "apostasies" of "Sergianism" (the way it describes the church's *modus vivendi* with the Soviet government) and ecumenism, which it characterizes as a "repudiation of the purity of Orthodoxy."

Altogether the Russian Orthodox Church Outside Russia has over 400 parishes, monasteries and convents in 40 countries around the world. There are 133 worshiping communities in the United States, and 22 in Canada. There are several monasteries, the most important of which is Holy Trinity Monastery in Jordanville, New York, which has 38 monks. There are five communities in the United Kingdom under the spiritual guidance of Bishop Mark, who resides in Munich, Germany. Archbishop Hilarion Kapral presides over the 21 parishes in the Australian Diocese, including three in New Zealand (18 Chelmsford Avenue, Croydon, NSW 2132). There are also two monasteries, one for men near Cooma, New South Wales, and another for women near Campbelltown, New South Wales.

LOCATION: Worldwide and recently in Russia
HEAD: Metropolitan Vitaly (born 1910, elected 1986)
Title: Primate of the Russian Orthodox Church Outside Russia
Residence: New York, New York, USA
MEMBERSHIP: 150,000
WEB SITE: http://www.synod.org

III. D. 3. The Ukrainian Orthodox Church-Kiev Patriarchate and the Ukrainian Autocephalous Orthodox Church

Although the church in Kiev survived the Mongol destruction of the city in 1240, its Metropolitans soon began to reside in the new principality of Moscow. This situation continued until 1448, when Kiev, then under Polish-Lithuanian domination, was established as a distinct metropolitanate under the jurisdiction of Constantinople. Soon thereafter, in 1461, the bishops of Moscow ceased using the title of Kiev and began to style themselves as Metropolitans of Moscow. Moscow later gathered strength and eventually gained control of Kiev. The Orthodox Metropolitanate of Kiev was consequently transferred from the jurisdiction of Constantinople to that of Moscow in 1686, an act which the Patriarchate of Constantinople has never recognized.

The Orthodox in Ukraine remained part of the Russian Orthodox Church until Ukraine declared its independence in the chaotic situation following World War I and the Russian revolution. The government of this new republic passed a law allowing for the establishment of an autocephalous Ukrainian Orthodox Church in 1919. Meanwhile, a spontaneous movement in favor of ending ties with the Russian church was gaining ground among the Ukrainian Orthodox faithful.

All this led to the proclamation of Ukrainian autocephaly at a church council in 1921. Since no Orthodox bishop would take part in this action, the council decided to ordain its leader, Archpriest Vasyl Lypkivsky, as Metropolitan of Kiev and All Ukraine through the laying-on-of-hands by the priests and laypeople present. Because of the highly unorthodox method it used to obtain a hierarchy, and because of its disregard for some established canonical principles, this church was never recognized by any other Orthodox church. Nevertheless, by early 1924 the new church had 30 bishops and approximately 1,500 priests and deacons serving in nearly 1,100 parishes in the Ukrainian

Soviet Socialist Republic, with possibly as many as six million members. Strong lay participation in this church's administration caused it to become known as the "sobornopravna" or "conciliar" church.

When Ukraine was absorbed into the Soviet Union, the new authorities at first viewed the Ukrainian Orthodox Church in a positive way, but by the late 1920s, they saw it as a dangerous expression of Ukrainian nationalism. Under government pressure, it declared itself dissolved and integrated into the Moscow Patriarchate in 1930.

However, during the German occupation of Ukraine during World War II, the Ukrainian Orthodox Church was briefly re-established by bishops who had been validly ordained by Polish Orthodox bishops. Thus it has subsequently claimed to be within the traditional apostolic succession, a fact still disputed by some Orthodox churches. In any case, it was suppressed again when the Soviets regained control of the area. The situation remained unchanged until the advent of greater religious freedom in the last days of the Soviet Union.

In these new conditions, a Ukrainian Orthodox council met in Kiev in June 1990 and elected the exiled Metropolitan Mstyslav of the United States as Patriarch. He returned to Ukraine in October 1990 to preside over the reemergence of this church in its homeland.

The situation became more complicated after May 21, 1992, when the Moscow Patriarchate deposed Metropolitan Filaret of Kíev and reduced him to the lay state on June 11. He had been accused of trying to separate his church from Moscow. Filaret then joined forces with the autocephalous Ukrainian Orthodox Church and even took the title of *locum tenens* of Patriarch Mstyslav who had returned to the United States. Filaret enjoyed the support of the Ukrainian government in his efforts to form an autocephalous Orthodox church. All this happened, however, without the knowledge of Patriarch Mstyslav, who broke all ties with Filaret in November.

This provoked a split within the autocephalous church between those loyal to Mstyslav and those linked to Filaret, who now call themselves "The Ukrainian Orthodox Church-Kiev Patriarchate."

After the death of Patriarch Mstyslav on June 11, 1993, each of these groups elected its own head. On September 7, 1993, the Ukrainian Autocephalous Orthodox Church elected 77-year-old Rev. Volodymyr Jarema as Patriarch. He took the name Dimitry I. On October 21, 1993, the Ukrainian Orthodox Church-Kiev Patriarchate elected Rev. Vasyl Romaniuk, 67, as Patriarch Volodymyr I. He died in 1995 and was succeeded by Filaret, who was enthroned as Patriarch on October 22, 1995. He was subsequently excommunicated by a Bishops' Council of the Moscow Patriarchate in February 1997.

As a result, there are three separate Orthodox jurisdictions in Ukraine. The Ukrainian Orthodox Church still linked to the Moscow Patriarchate (headed by Metropolitan Volodymyr Sabodan) is the largest with 7,541 parishes according to Ukrainian government statistics released in March 1998. Its headquarters is at the Monastery of the Caves (Pecherska Lavra) in Kiev. Next is the Ukrainian Orthodox Church-Kiev Patriarchate headed by Patriarch Filaret I, which has 21 dioceses, 14 monasteries, four seminaries, and 1,977 parishes. It is based at St. Volodymyr Church in Kiev. The Ukrainian Autocephalous Orthodox Church is the smallest, with 1,085 parishes, mostly in western Ukraine. In late 1996 the bishops' council of the autocephalous church deposed Patriarch Dimitry because of alleged financial improprieties, provoking a split of his church into two factions.

The Ukrainian Orthodox Church has a significant presence in the diaspora, all of which is now under the jurisdiction of the Patriarchate of Constantinople [see the Ukrainian Orthodox Church of the USA and Diaspora, III.C.2, and The Ukrainian Orthodox Church in Canada, III.C.6].

III. D. 4. The Belarusan Autocephalous Orthodox Church

Belarus (formerly known as Byelorussia or "White Russia") was for many centuries a part of the Russian Empire and later the Soviet Union. When united to Russia, this region's mostly Orthodox population was part of the Russian Orthodox Church.

When Moscow's authority was weakened because of the chaos that followed the 1917 revolution, unsuccessful attempts were made in 1922 and 1927 to establish an autocephalous Belarusan Orthodox Church. Under Nazi occupation during the Second World War, the Germans supported both the revival of religious practice and the creation of separate Orthodox churches in order to weaken the allegiance of local populations to Moscow. Thus a group of Belarusan bishops was able to declare the Belarusan Orthodox Church autocephalous in 1942. By 1944 there were ten hierarchs in nine eparchies. But the Soviets put an end to this status when they reoccupied the area.

These bishops then emigrated to the West, and most of them joined the Russian Orthodox Church Outside Russia. But in 1949, a group of Belarusan bishops in exile declared themselves autocephalous. This group exists only in the diaspora and has not been recognized by any Orthodox church. The autocephalous church has not re-established itself in Belarus following that country's independence in 1991.

After the death of Archbishop Andrei Kryt in the late 1970s, there was a split in the Belarusan Orthodox community, which now includes 12 parishes worldwide. The two groups are led by Archbishop Mikalay Maciukevich (524 St. Clarens Avenue, Toronto, Ontario M6H 3W7, Canada), who has one parish in Canada, one in Australia, and five in the United States; and Metropolitan Iziaslau Brucki (401 Atlantic Avenue, Brooklyn, New York 11217-1702 USA), who has two parishes in Australia and three in England. The community in Australia may be reached through Fr. Alexander Kzilakozsky, 42 Thornton

Drive, St. Albans VIC 3021. Total membership in the church is estimated at 140,000.

There are also four Belarusan Orthodox parishes in the United
States and one in Canada under the jurisdiction of the Ecumenical
Patriarchate [see III.C.5].

III. D. 5. The Macedonian Orthodox Church

Macedonia, an important geopolitical center of the Balkans since
ancient times, has for centuries been a focal point of territorial rivalries involving Turkey, Serbia, Bulgaria, and Greece.

While Macedonia was under Ottoman administration, the Orthodox church there was part of the Patriarchate of Constantinople.
When Turkish rule was ended following the Balkan Wars of 1912-
1913, southern Macedonia became part of Greece. But northern
Macedonia, inhabited by Slavs who called themselves Macedonians
because of the name of the area in which they lived, was incorporated into the newly formed kingdom of Yugoslavia. By agreement
with the Ecumenical Patriarchate, the Orthodox in this northern area
were integrated into the Serbian Patriarchate and reorganized into
three dioceses.

When the communists took power in Yugoslavia following World
War II, they decided to reorganize Yugoslavia on a federal basis and
provided for the creation of a separate Macedonian Republic. The
communists supported the aspirations of some Macedonians who
wished to assert their separate identity, in order to gain their backing
for the new government.

During the same period, the government supported efforts by
some Orthodox in the Macedonian Republic to establish a separate
Macedonian Orthodox Church. In October 1958 an Ecclesiastical and
National Council of 220 priests and laity was held in Ohrid that declared the restoration of the ancient Archbishopric of Ohrid and the

autonomy of the Macedonian Orthodox Church. It also elected three new bishops for the three dioceses of the church. This was considered an irregular election, as only one bishop was present. But the new church declared itself in canonical unity with the Serbian Orthodox Church in the person of the Serbian Patriarch. In June 1959 the Serbian Holy Synod accepted this *fait accompli*, and the next month the three bishops-elect were consecrated by Serbian Orthodox bishops.

In the autumn of 1966, the Macedonian Orthodox Church formally petitioned the Serbian Patriarchate for autocephalous status. But when it met in May 1967, the Serbian episcopate rejected this request.

Nevertheless, the Macedonians went forward and held a council in Ohrid from July 17 to 19, 1967. On July 19, acting on a resolution of the council, the Holy Synod of the Church of Macedonia proclaimed the autocephaly of the Orthodox Church in the Republic of Macedonia. The Metropolitan was given the new title of "Archbishop of Ohrid and Macedonia." All this was openly supported by the state authorities, who gave the new Metropolitan state honors and attended his installation ceremonies.

In September 1967 the Serbian Orthodox Synod declared the Macedonian Orthodox Church to be a schismatic religious organization and broke off all liturgical and canonical links with its hierarchy, although not with its faithful. This decision has been supported by other Orthodox churches, as none has recognized the legitimacy of the Macedonian church.

The disintegration of Yugoslavia led to Macedonia's declaration of independence in 1991. But its name has been disputed by Greece and consequently it has not been recognized by most of the countries of the world.

In December 1991 Archbishop Gavril resigned his post as head of the church, possibly because of tensions within the hierarchy concerning the church's canonical status. But he was persuaded to withdraw his resignation after the Holy Synod assured him of its confidence. Serbian Patriarch Pavle received a delegation of Macedonian Orthodox bishops in mid-1992 to discuss the church's status, but so far these contacts have not led to a restoration of canonical communion. The present government of the Former Yugoslav Republic of Macedonia strongly supports the church's autocephaly. But Patriarch Bartholomew of Constantinople has declared that such status cannot be recognized because of the clear political factors involved.

At the time of the declaration of autocephaly in 1967, the Macedonian Orthodox Church included some 334 priests ministering in approximately 400 parishes. Monasticism has experienced a serious decline. In 1992 it was reported that there were a total of ten religious sisters associated with communities in Bitola and Prilep, while a young religious community of men had been founded at the ancient monastery of St. Naum on Lake Ohrid. About two thirds of the population of Macedonia is Orthodox.

Macedonian Orthodox bishops resident in Skopje, the republic's capital, have responsibility for their church's parishes in the diaspora. Archbishop Mikhail of Ohrid is responsible for the 17 parishes in the United States and five in Canada. Bishop Petar oversees the 21 parishes and two monasteries in Australia. The diocesan secretary is Fr. Grigor Kifelinov, 642 Plenty Road, Preston, Victoria 3072.

LOCATION: Former Yugoslav Republic of Macedonia, diaspora in
    North America and Australia
HEAD: Archbishop Mihail (born 1912, elected 1993)
Title: Archbishop of Ohrid and Macedonia
Residence: Skopje, Former Yugoslav Republic of Macedonia
MEMBERSHIP: 1,200,000

III. D. 6. The Old Calendar Orthodox Churches

After World War I various Orthodox churches, beginning with the Patriarchate of Constantinople, began to abandon the Julian calendar for some purposes and adopt the Gregorian calendar (known as New Julian in the East), which is 13 days ahead of the Julian. At present most Orthodox churches (with the exception of Jerusalem, Russia, Serbia, and Mount Athos) use the new calendar for fixed feasts but the Julian calendar for Easter and movable feasts dependent upon it. A similar diversity exists among Eastern Catholics where, for instance, the great majority of Ukrainian Greek Catholics use the Julian calendar.

When this reform was introduced in the Church of Greece in 1924 by the Holy Synod with support from the government, strong opposition immediately arose, mainly among the lower clergy and laity. The group claimed that such a decision could only be taken by an ecumenical council with the involvement of all the Orthodox churches. While the calendar question was the issue at hand, the opposition saw the adoption of the new calendar as only one result of the fledgling ecumenical movement and the influence of other churches which, in their view, compromised the purity of the Orthodox faith.

In May 1935 three bishops of the Church of Greece returned to the Old Calendar and assumed leadership of the movement. They quickly consecrated four additional bishops. One of the three bishops and two of the new ones returned to the Church of Greece. The Holy Synod of the Church of Greece immediately deposed the other four bishops, deprived them of episcopal rank, and sentenced them to terms of exile in distant monasteries. The Holy Synod also asked the government to either use effective means to suppress the opposition or agree to a restoration of the Julian calendar. The authorities refused to take decisive action, however, in part because most of those opposed to the reforms supported the monarchy which was weak at the time. The four deposed bishops quietly returned to Athens a few months later.

Those opposed to the new calendar became known as the Old Calendarists, or The Church of True Orthodox Christians of Greece. In the early years they were led by Metropolitan Chrysostomos of Florina. Soon the community was plagued by divisions, usually over the question of the validity of the sacraments of the Orthodox Church of Greece. A smaller group insisted that there was no such grace in the sacraments of the official church. After the death of Chrysostomos in 1955, the Old Calendarists were left without bishops. But in 1960 new bishops were consecrated for them by bishops of the Russian Orthodox Church Outside Russia. New divisions occurred in the 1970s, causing the bishops to split in 1979 into two hostile synods led by Archbishop Auxentios of Gardikia and Metropolitan Kallistos of Corinth. Kallistos retired in 1983 and was succeeded by Metropolitan Antonios of Megara. In 1984 Auxentios' synod split, the dissidents being led by Metropolitan Gerontios of Piraeus. Later that year Metropolitan Antonios' synod dissolved itself and joined with the synod of Metropolitan Gerontios, thus aligning with those who rejected the validity of the sacraments of the Church of Greece. They elected Archbishop Chrysostomos II as head of the synod. At this point Metropolitan Cyprian of Oropos and Fili and Giovanni of Sardinia remained the only Old Calendar bishops to recognize the sacraments of the Church of Greece. They ordained new bishops in 1985, and were joined in their stand by the Old Calendar Church in Romania and Bulgaria. Archbishop Auxentios died in 1994, and a new head of his synod of bishops had not been elected by mid-1998.

At present the synod headed by Archbishop Chrysostomos II is the largest group of Old Calendarists in Greece. The second largest group is led by Metropolitan Cyprian. The synod formerly led by Archbishop Auxentios has greatly reduced in size in Greece, but has a strong presence outside the country, especially in the United States.

In addition, a small ultra-extremist minority known as "Matthewites" has about 40 priests in Greece and a strong monastic tradition centered on the convent of the Entrance of the Theotokos at Keratea (300 nuns) and Transfiguration Monastery (60 monks). Their several tens of thousands of faithful firmly believe that they are the only Orthodox left in the world.

In spite of these divisions, the Greek Old Calendarists think of themselves as a single movement. Although they were actively persecuted in Greece, especially during the 1950s, today they are allowed to function with greater freedom. They claim to have hundreds of thousands of faithful, over 200 priests serving about 120 parishes, including 38 in the Athens area alone, where there are also almost 100 Old Calendar monastic communities. Their churches are recognizable by the absence of electric lighting and pews, and certain practices including traditional Byzantine chant and frequent all-night vigils.

In North America, there are 27 parishes in the Holy Orthodox Church in North America that belong to the synod of the late Archbishop Auxentios, centered on Holy Transfiguration monastery in Brookline, Massachusetts. The presiding hierarch is Bishop Ephraim (850 South Street, Roslindale, Massachusetts 02130). Twelve parishes are linked to the synod of Archbishop Chrysostomos II through Metropolitan Pavlos (22-68 26th Street, Astoria, New York 11105). Nine parishes associated with Metropolitan Cyprian, including the Center for Traditionalist Orthodox Studies in Etna, California, are under the jurisdiction of Archbishop Chrysostomos (St. Gregory Palamas Monastery, PO Box 378, Etna, California 96027). The Matthewites have four parishes and two chapels under the direction of Bishop Chrysostomos (8906 Hazelton, Redford, Michigan 48239).

In May 1998 St. Irene Chrysovalantou monastery, an important Old Calendar center of the synod of Archbishop Chrysostomos in Astoria, Queens, New York, was received by the Ecumenical Patriarchate as a stavropegial monastery along with two other monasteries and six parishes associated with it. Its two founders were re-consecrated bishops at the Ecumenical Patriarchate and were given the titles Metropolitan Paisios of Tyana and Bishop Vikentios of Apameia. The monastery and its dependencies continue to use the Julian calendar.

A parallel Old Calendar movement sprang up in Romania after Patriarch Miron Cristea introduced the Gregorian calendar in 1924. Opposition centered around the abbot of Pokrov Skete in Moldavia, Hieromonk Glicherie. By 1936 he had built 40 churches, most of them in Moldavia. The Romanian government took strong measures against the movement so that by the eve of World War II, all the Old Calendar churches had been closed. But after the war Glicherie resumed his efforts and by 1950 nearly all these churches had been reopened.

The communists allowed the movement to continue, although they subjected it to periodic persecutions. In 1955 a retired Romanian Orthodox bishop, Metropolitan Galaction Cordun, joined the Old Calendarists and began ordaining priests for them. He also single-handedly ordained three new bishops, thus establishing a continuing hierarchy. The community has not experienced the divisions that have troubled the Old Calendar Church in Greece.

Today the Romanian Old Calendar Church claims to have 500,000 believers. In 1998 there were a total of six bishops, 119 priests, 30 deacons, 218 monks, 427 nuns, 110 parishes and 13 large monastic communities (six for men and seven for women) in the country. The first hierarch, Metropolitan Vlasie (elected 1992), resides at Holy Transfiguration Monastery at Slatioara, the spiritual and administrative center of the church.

An Old Calendar Orthodox Church also exists in Bulgaria, where the Patriarchate adopted the new calendar in the 1960s. The Bulgarian Old Calendarists are headed by Bishop Photius of Triaditsa (born 1956, consecrated 1993), and have become a rather vibrant community after the fall of communism. In total there are 19 priests, three deacons, 17 parishes, nine chapels, one convent with 25 nuns and one monastery with 20 monks in Bulgaria. The administrative center of the church is in Sofia.

The Old Calendar Orthodox churches of Romania and Bulgaria, the moderate Old Calendar group in Greece under Metropolitan Cyprian, and the Russian Orthodox Church Outside Russia are all in full communion with one another.

IV. THE CATHOLIC EASTERN CHURCHES

The split between the Latin and Byzantine churches, which had been symbolized by the mutual excommunications of the bishops of Rome and Constantinople in 1054, became definitive in the minds of the common people in the east after the Crusades and the sacking of Constantinople by the Latins in 1204. Attempts at reunion took place at the Second Council of Lyons in 1274 and at the Council of Ferrara-Florence in 1439, but neither was successful.

Subsequently, a Roman Catholic theology of the Church continued to develop which vigorously emphasized the necessity of the direct jurisdiction of the Pope over all the local churches. This implied that churches not under the Pope's jurisdiction could be considered objects of missionary activity for the purpose of bringing them into communion with the Catholic Church. At the same time, the notion of "rite" developed, according to which groups of eastern Christians who came into union with Rome would be absorbed into the single Church, but allowed to maintain their own liturgical tradition and canonical discipline.

This missionary activity, which was sometimes carried out with the support of Catholic governments of countries with Orthodox minorities, was directed towards all the eastern churches. Eventually segments of virtually all of these churches came into union with Rome. It should be recognized, however, that not all these unions were the result of the activity of Catholic missionaries. The Bulgarian Byzantine Catholic Church, for example, was the direct result of a spontaneous movement of Orthodox towards Rome. And the Maronites in Lebanon claim never to have been out of communion with the Roman Church.

Inevitably, these unions resulted in a process of latinization, or the adoption of certain practices and attitudes proper to the Latin

Church, to a certain degree, depending on the circumstances of the group. As a result, these churches sometimes lost contact with their spiritual roots. The monastic tradition, so central to Orthodox spirituality, died out in most of the Eastern Catholic churches, although religious life often continued in the form of congregations modeled on Latin apostolic communities. Since the Second Vatican Council, efforts have been made to reverse this process.

All of these churches come under the jurisdiction of the Pope through the Congregation for the Oriental Churches, one of the offices of the Roman Curia. It was created in 1862 as part of the *Propaganda Fide* (which oversaw the church's missionary activity), and was made an autonomous Congregation by Benedict XV in 1917. It has the same role with regard to bishops, clergy, religious, and the faithful in the Eastern Catholic churches that other offices of the Curia have in relation to the Latin church.

The Oriental Congregation also oversees the prestigious Pontifical Oriental Institute in Rome, which is under the direction of the Jesuits and has one of the best libraries for eastern Christian studies in the world.

It should be mentioned that in the past the Eastern Catholic churches were often referred to as "Uniate" churches. Since the term is now considered derogatory, it is no longer used.

Most Orthodox view these churches as an obstacle in the way of reconciliation between the Catholic and Orthodox churches. They feel that their very existence constitutes a denial by Catholics of the ecclesial reality of the Orthodox Church, and that these unions grew from efforts to split local Orthodox communities. They tend to consider Eastern Catholics either as Orthodox whose presence in the Catholic Church is an abnormal situation brought about by coercive measures, or even as Roman Catholics pretending to be Orthodox for the purpose of proselytism.

One of the documents of the Second Vatican Council, *Orientalium Ecclesiarum*, dealt with the Eastern Catholic churches. It affirmed their equality with the Latin church and called upon Eastern Catholics to rediscover their authentic traditions. It also affirmed that Eastern Catholics have a special vocation to foster ecumenical relations with the Orthodox.

The ecclesial life of the Eastern Catholic churches is governed in accordance with the *Code of Canons of the Eastern Churches*, which was promulgated by Pope John Paul II on October 18, 1990, and began to have the force of law on October 1, 1991. According to the new Oriental Code, the Eastern Catholic churches fall into four categories: (1) Patriarchal (the Chaldean, Armenian, Coptic, Syrian, Maronite, and Melkite churches), (2) Major Archepiscopal (Ukrainian and Syro-Malabar Catholic churches), (3) Metropolitan *sui iuris* (the Ethiopian, Syro-Malankara, Romanian and American Ruthenian churches), and (4) other churches *sui iuris* (Bulgarian, Greek, Hungarian, Italo-Albanian, and Slovak churches, as well as a diocese covering all of former Yugoslavia). The Belarusan, Albanian, Georgian and Russian Eastern Catholic churches have no hierarchy.

Each Eastern Catholic patriarchal church has the right to choose its own Patriarch. He is elected by the Synod of Bishops and is immediately proclaimed and enthroned. He subsequently requests ecclesiastical communion from the Pope. The synods of patriarchal churches also elect bishops for dioceses within the patriarchal territory from a list of candidates that have been approved by the Holy See. If the one elected has not been previously approved, he must obtain the consent of the Pope before ordination as bishop. A Major Archbishop is elected in the same manner as a Patriarch, but his election must be confirmed by the Roman Pontiff before he can be enthroned. Metropolitans are named by the Pope on the basis of a list of at least three candidates submitted by the church's council of bishops.

In the following presentation, the Eastern Catholic churches are grouped according to their provenance. It begins with those that have no direct non-Catholic counterpart, and then considers the Eastern

Catholic churches that correspond to the Assyrian Church of the East, the Oriental Orthodox, and, finally, the Orthodox churches.

The Congregation for the Oriental Churches
Achille Cardinal Silvestrini, Prefect
(born 1923, ordained bishop 1979, Cardinal 1988, Prefect 1991)
Archbishop Miroslav Stefan Marusyn, Secretary
Via della Conciliazione, 34
00120 Vatican City State

IV. A. CHURCHES WITH NO DIRECT COUNTERPART

These are two Eastern Catholic churches which, because of unique historical circumstances, do not have an immediate counterpart among the other eastern churches.

IV. A. 1. The Maronite Catholic Church

The Maronites of Lebanon trace their origin back to the late 4th century when a group of disciples gathered around the charismatic figure of St. Maron. They later founded a monastery located midway between Aleppo and Antioch. In the 5th century the monastery vigorously supported the christological doctrine of the Council of Chalcedon.

By the 8th century, the monks had moved with their band of followers into the remote mountains of Lebanon, where they existed in relative isolation for centuries. It was also during this period that they began to develop a distinct identity as a church and to elect a bishop as their head, who took the title of Patriarch of Antioch and All the East.

The Maronites came into contact with the Latin Church in the 12th century, when the Latin crusader principality of Antioch was founded. In 1182 the entire Maronite nation formally confirmed its union with Rome. But there is a strong tradition among the Maronites that their church never lacked communion with the Holy See.

Patriarch Jeremias II Al-Amshitti (1199-1230) became the first Maronite Patriarch to visit Rome when he attended the Fourth Lateran Council in 1215. This marked the beginning of close relations with the Holy See and a continuing latinizing tendency. The 16th century saw the conquest of the Maronite homeland by the Turks and the beginning of long centuries of Ottoman domination.

A major reforming synod took place at Mount Lebanon in 1736. It drafted an almost complete Code of Canons for the Maronite Church, created a regular diocesan structure for the first time, and established the main lines of Maronite ecclesial life that endure to this day.

By the 19th century the western powers, especially France, began to offer protection to the Maronites within the Ottoman Empire. A massacre of thousands of Maronites in 1860 provoked the French to intervene with military forces. After World War I both Lebanon and Syria came under French control.

When France granted Lebanon full independence in 1944, it attempted to guarantee the safety of the Maronite community by leaving behind a constitution guaranteeing that the president would always be a Maronite. The civil war that erupted in Lebanon in 1975 revealed, however, that the community's future remained precarious. Many thousands of Maronites left Lebanon to make new lives for themselves in the West.

The Maronite Patriarchs have resided at Bkerke, about 25 miles from Beirut, since 1790. Today there are ten dioceses in Lebanon with about 770 parishes, and seven other jurisdictions in the Middle East. This is the largest church in Lebanon, making up about 37% of the Christians and 17% of the overall population.

There is a Maronite Patriarchal Seminary at Ghazir and a diocesan seminary at Karm Sadde, near Tripoli. Advanced theological education is provided at the University of the Holy Spirit at Kaslik. A Maronite College was founded in Rome in 1584.

The Maronite liturgy is of West Syrian origin, but it has been influenced by the East Syrian and Latin traditions. The Eucharist is essentially a variation of the Syriac liturgy of St. James. Originally celebrated in Syriac, the liturgy has been for the most part in Arabic since the Arab invasions.

The steady emigration of Maronites from Lebanon in recent years has produced flourishing communities in the diaspora. In the United States, there are two dioceses with a total of 57 parishes and 102 priests serving about 55,000 faithful. The diocese of St. Maron of Brooklyn is presided over by Bishop Hector Doueihi (294 Howard Avenue, Staten Island, New York), and Bishop John Chedid heads the new diocese of Our Lady of Lebanon of Los Angeles (333 South San Vicente Boulevard, Los Angeles, California, 90048), founded in 1994. In Canada, the diocese of St. Maron of Montreal, headed by Bishop Joseph Khoury (12475 Grenet Street, Montreal, Quebec H4J 2K4) has 12 parishes for about 80,000 faithful. Bishop Joseph Hitti oversees the diocese of St. Maron of Sydney (105 The Boulevard, PO Box 385, Strathfield, NSW 2135 Australia), which has nine parishes for an estimated 150,000 Maronites in Australia.

LOCATION: Lebanon, Syria, Cyprus, Egypt, Brazil, USA, Canada, Australia

HEAD: Patriarch Nasrallah Cardinal Sfeir (born 1920, elected 1986, cardinal 1994)

Title: Patriarch of Antioch of the Maronites

Residence: Bkerke, Lebanon

MEMBERSHIP: 3,222,000

WEB SITE: http://www.bkerke.org.lb

IV. A. 2. The Italo-Albanian Catholic Church

Southern Italy and Sicily had a strong connection with Greece in antiquity and for many centuries there was a large Greek-speaking population there. In the early centuries of the Christian era, although most of the Christians were of the Byzantine tradition, the area was included in the Roman Patriarchate, and a gradual but incomplete process of latinization began.

During the 8th century, Byzantine Emperor Leo III removed the region from papal jurisdiction and placed it within the Patriarchate of Constantinople. There followed a strong revival of the Byzantine tradition in the area. But the Norman conquest in the early 11th century resulted in its return to the Latin Patriarchate. By this time the local Byzantine church was flourishing, and there were hundreds of monasteries along the coasts of southern Italy. The Normans, however, discouraged Byzantine usages in their lands, and the Greek bishops were replaced by Latin ones. This marked the beginning of a process which led to the almost total absorption of the Byzantine faithful into the Latin Church.

This decline was reversed in the 15th century with the arrival of two large groups of Albanian immigrants who had fled their country following its conquest by the Turks. Those from the northern part of Albania, where the Latin rite was prevalent, were quickly absorbed into the local population. But those from the Orthodox south of the country remained loyal to their Byzantine heritage. At first they met with little understanding from the local Latin bishops. Although in the 16th century Popes intervened in favor of the Byzantines — in 1595 an ordaining bishop was appointed for them — the community continued to decline.

The situation began to improve in the 18th century. In 1742 Pope Benedict XIV published the bull *Etsi Pastoralis* which was intended to buttress the position of the Italo-Albanians in relation to the Latins. It paved the way for more progressive legislation — and recognition of the equality of the Byzantine rite with the Latin — in the next century.

Italo-Albanian seminaries were founded in 1732 in Calabria and in 1734 in Palermo. Seminarians in advanced theological studies in Rome reside at the Greek College (founded in 1577).

Today there are two dioceses of equal rank for the Italo-Albanians: the diocese of Lungro (in Calabria) was founded in 1919, has 27 parishes, and has jurisdiction over continental Italy; the diocese of Piana degli Albanesi, founded in 1937, covers all of Sicily and has 15 parishes. Alongside these two dioceses is the monastery of Santa Maria di Grottaferrata, just a few miles from Rome, which, having been founded in 1004, is the only remnant of the once-flourishing Italo-Greek monastic tradition. In 1937 the monastery was given the status of territorial abbey, according to which the abbot exercises jurisdiction over the monks and local faithful similar to that of a diocesan bishop.

The Italo-Albanians have no parishes in the English-speaking world, but the identity of the small immigrant communities in these areas has been preserved through such groups as the Italo-Albanian Byzantine Rite Society of Our Lady of Grace based in Staten Island, New York.

LOCATION: Southern Italy, small diaspora
MEMBERSHIP: 64,000

IV. B. FROM THE ASSYRIAN CHURCH OF THE EAST

IV. B. 1. The Chaldean Catholic Church

As early as the 13th century, Catholic missionaries — primarily Dominicans and Franciscans — had been active among the faithful of the Assyrian Church of the East. This resulted in a series of individual conversions of bishops and brief unions, but no permanent community was formed.

In the mid-15th century a tradition of hereditary patriarchal succession (passing from uncle to nephew) took effect in the Assyrian church. As a result, one family dominated the church, and untrained minors were being elected to the patriarchal throne.

When such a patriarch was elected in 1552, a group of Assyrian bishops refused to accept him and decided to seek union with Rome. They elected the reluctant abbot of a monastery, Yuhannan Sulaka, as their own patriarch and sent him to Rome to arrange a union with the Catholic Church. In early 1553 Pope Julius III proclaimed him Patriarch Simon VIII "of the Chaldeans" and ordained him a bishop in St. Peter's Basilica on April 9, 1553.

The new Patriarch returned to his homeland in late 1553 and began to initiate a series of reforms. But opposition, led by the rival Assyrian Patriarch, was strong. Simon was soon captured by the pasha of Amadya, tortured and executed in January 1555. Eventually Sulaka's group returned to the Assyrian Church of the East, but for over 200 years, there was much turmoil and changing of sides as the pro- and anti-Catholic parties struggled with one another. The situation finally stabilized only on July 5, 1830, when Pope Pius VIII confirmed Metropolitan John Hormizdas as head of all Chaldean Catholics, with the title of Patriarch of Babylon of the Chaldeans, with his see in Mosul.

The Chaldean Catholics suffered heavily from massacres during World War I (1918) when four bishops, many priests, and about 70,000 faithful died.

The location of the Patriarchate shifted back and forth among several places over the centuries, but gained a measure of stability after it was set up at Mosul in 1830. In 1950 it moved to its present location in Baghdad after substantial migration of Chaldean Catholics from northern Iraq to the capital city.

The Chaldean Catholic Church's relationship with the Assyrian Church of the East has improved dramatically since the signing of a joint christological agreement between the Pope and the Assyrian Patriarch in Rome in November 1994. In August 1997 the Holy Synods of the two churches formally instituted a commission for dialogue to discuss pastoral cooperation at all levels [see Assyrian Church of the East, I].

Chaldean candidates for the priesthood study at St. Peter's Patriarchal Seminary in Baghdad. It no longer grants advanced degrees. There are centers offering courses in theology for the laity in Baghdad and Mosul. A proposal to set up a Catholic university in Iraq is being considered.

Today the largest concentration of these Catholics remains in Baghdad, Iraq. There are ten Chaldean dioceses in Iraq, four in Iran, and four others in the Middle East. The Chaldean (or East Syrian) liturgy is in use, with the addition of a number of Latin customs. The liturgical language is Syriac.

The approximately 65,000 Chaldeans in the United States have 12 parishes in the diocese of St. Thomas the Apostle of Detroit of the Chaldeans, under the leadership of Bishop Ibrahim Ibrahim (25585 Berg Road, Southfield, Michigan 48034). In other areas of the diaspora, Chaldeans are under spiritual supervision of the local Latin ordinaries. In Australia the Catholic Chaldean Chaplain is Fr. Emmanuel Khoshaba. He resides at 39 Major Road, Fawkner, Victoria 3060.

LOCATION: Iraq, Iran, Syria, Lebanon, Turkey, Israel, Egypt, France, USA
HEAD: Patriarch Raphael I Bidawid (born 1922, elected 1989)
Title: Patriarch of Babylon of the Chaldeans
Residence: Baghdad, Iraq
MEMBERSHIP: 304,000

IV. B. 2. The Syro-Malabar Catholic Church

Members of this church are direct descendants of the Thomas Christians that the Portuguese encountered in 1498 while exploring the Malabar coast of India (now the state of Kerala). As mentioned above [see I: Thomas Christians], they were in full communion with the Assyrian Church in Persia. But they greeted the Portuguese as fellow Christians and as representatives of the Church of Rome, whose special status they had continued to acknowledge despite centuries of isolation.

In general, however, the Portuguese did not accept the legitimacy of local Malabar traditions, and they began to impose Latin usages upon the Thomas Christians. At a synod held at Diamper in 1599 under the presidency of the Portuguese Archbishop of Goa, a number of such latinizations were adopted, including the appointment of Portuguese bishops, changes in the Eucharistic liturgy, the use of Roman vestments, the requirement of clerical celibacy, and the setting up of the Inquisition. This provoked widespread discontent, which finally culminated in a decision by most Thomas Christians in 1653 to break with Rome. In response, Pope Alexander VII sent Carmelite friars to Malabar to deal with the situation. By 1662 the majority of the dissidents had returned to communion with the Catholic Church.

European Carmelites would continue to serve as bishops in the Syro-Malabar Church until 1896, when the Holy See established three Vicariates Apostolic for the Thomas Christians (Trichur, Ernakulam and Changanacherry), under the guidance of indigenous Syro-Malabar bishops. A fourth Vicariate Apostolic (Kottayam) was established in 1911. In 1923 Pope Pius XI set up a full-fledged Syro-Malabar Catholic hierarchy.

This new autonomy coincided with a strong revival of the church. While in 1876 there were approximately 200,000 Syro-Malabar Catholics, this number had more than doubled by 1931. By 1960 there were nearly one and one half million faithful, and today they

number almost four million. Vocations to the priesthood and religious life have been very strong. In November 1994 there were 27,869
religious in the Syro-Malabar Church, in addition to 20,022 Syro-
Malabar religious who belonged to Latin communities. There are 16
different congregations of women religious, five of pontifical right.
Major seminaries exist at Alwaye (interritual), Kottayam, Satna, Bangalore, and Ujjain.

In 1934 Pope Pius XI initiated a process of liturgical reform that
sought to restore the oriental nature of the heavily latinized Syro-
Malabar rite. A restored eucharistic liturgy, drawing on the original
East Syrian sources, was approved by Pius XII in 1957 and introduced in 1962. Despite a reaffirmation of the main lines of the 1962
rite by the Oriental Congregation in 1985, however, there has been
strong resistance to this reform. The majority of Syro-Malabar dioceses still use a rite that in externals is hardly distinguishable from
the Latin Mass. In January 1996 Pope John Paul II presided over the
opening of a special synod of bishops of the Syro-Malabar Church in
Rome which was to attempt to overcome factional disputes that have
centered on the proposed liturgical reforms. In 1998 Pope John Paul
II gave the Syro-Malabar bishops full authority in liturgical matters
in a further effort to facilitate a resolution of the dispute.

Relations between the Syro-Malabar Catholic Church and the
Latin Church in India have often been marked by tension, particularly regarding the question of the establishment of Syro-Malabar
jurisdictions in other parts of India to care for the many Malabars
who have emigrated there. Only in 1977 did the Holy See begin to
establish Syro-Malabar dioceses in parts of India where Latin dioceses already existed.

Until recently there was no single head of the Syro-Malabar
Catholic Church, but two metropolitan dioceses (Ernakulam and
Changanacherry) of equal rank. But on December 16, 1992, Pope
John Paul II raised the Syro-Malabar Church to Major Archepiscopal
rank and appointed Cardinal Antony Padiyara of Ernakulam-Anga-

maly as the first Major Archbishop. He retired in 1996, and as of mid-1998 a successor had not been chosen. Archbishop Varkey Vithayathil was named apostolic administrator of the church *sede vacante et ad nutum Sanctae Sedis*.

There are six organized Syro-Malabar Catholic communities in the United States and one in Canada.

LOCATION: India, especially Kerala State
HEAD: [Archbishop Varkey Vithayathil, Apostolic Administrator]
Title: Major Archbishop of Ernakulam-Angamaly
Residence: Ernakulam, India
MEMBERSHIP: 3,886,000

IV. C. FROM THE ORIENTAL ORTHODOX CHURCHES

IV. C. 1. The Armenian Catholic Church

The Latin Crusaders established close contacts with the Armenian Apostolic Church in the 12th century when they passed through the Armenian kingdom in Cilicia on their way to the Holy Land. An alliance between the Crusaders and the Armenian King contributed to the establishment of a union between the two churches in Cilicia in 1198. This union, which was not accepted by Armenians outside Cilicia, ended with the conquest of the Armenian kingdom by the Tatars in 1375.

A decree of reunion with the Armenian Apostolic Church, *Exultate Deo*, was published at the Council of Florence on November 22, 1439. Although it had no immediate results, the document provided the doctrinal basis for the establishment of an Armenian Catholic church much later.

Catholic missionary activity among the Armenians had begun early, led initially by the Friars of Union, a now-defunct Armenian community related to the Dominicans, founded in 1320. With the passage of time, scattered but growing Armenian Catholic communities began to ask for a proper ecclesial structure and their own patriarch. In 1742 Pope Benedict XIV confirmed a former Armenian Apostolic bishop, Abraham Ardzivian (1679-1749), as Patriarch of Cilicia of the Armenians, based in Lebanon, and with religious authority over the Armenian Catholics in the southern provinces of the Ottoman Empire. In the north, they continued to be under the spiritual care of the Latin Vicar Apostolic in Constantinople. The new patriarch took the name Abraham Pierre I, and all his successors have likewise taken the name Pierre in their ecclesiastical title.

The Ottoman millet system, which provided for the administrative autonomy of minorities under the direction of their religious leaders, had placed all Armenian Catholics under the civil jurisdiction of the Armenian Apostolic Patriarch in Constantinople. This resulted in serious difficulties and even persecution of Armenian Catholics until 1829 when, under French pressure, the Ottoman government gave them the right to be organized civilly as a separate millet, with an Archbishop of their own in Constantinople. In 1846 he was vested with civil authority as well. The anomaly of having an Archbishop with both civil and religious authority in the Ottoman capital and an exclusively spiritual Patriarch in Lebanon was resolved in 1867 when Pope Pius IX united the two sees and moved the patriarchal residence to Constantinople.

The vicious persecution of Armenians in Turkey at the end of World War I decimated the Armenian Catholic community in that country: seven bishops, 130 priests, 47 nuns and as many as 100,000 faithful died. Since the community in Turkey had been drastically reduced in size, an Armenian Catholic synod in Rome in 1928 decided to transfer the Patriarchate back to Lebanon (Beirut), and to make Constantinople (now Istanbul) an Archdiocese.

There were also a number of Armenian Catholic communities in the section of historic Armenia which came under Russian control in

1828. Pius IX established the diocese of Artvin for all Armenian Catholics in the Russian Empire in 1850. But tsarist opposition to eastern Catholicism resulted in the abandonment of the Artvin diocese within 40 years. In 1912 the Armenian Catholics in the Empire were placed under the Latin bishop of distant Tiraspol. The Armenian Catholic Church was entirely suppressed under communism, and it was only with the independence of Armenia in 1991 that communities of Armenian Catholics began to resurface. On July 13, 1991, the Holy See established an Ordinariat for Armenian Catholics in Eastern Europe based in Gyumri, Armenia.

In November 1992 a meeting of the Armenian Catholic synod of bishops took place in Rome to consider the church's needs in the new situation. In June 1997 they met again in Rome to continue the preparation of a new particular law of the Armenian Catholic Church.

An important example of Armenian Catholic religious life is provided by the Mechitarist Fathers, founded in Constantinople in 1701. The community transferred to the island of San Lazzaro, Venice, in 1717. In 1811 a second foundation of Mechitarists was set up in Vienna. These two communities have long served the entire Armenian nation through their scholarship both in Europe and the Middle East.

A brotherhood of priests at Bzoummar, Lebanon, has an extensive library and a seminary that dates back to 1771. For higher theological studies, an Armenian College was founded in Rome in 1883.

Today the largest concentrations of Armenian Catholics are in Beirut, Lebanon, and Aleppo, Syria. The church has seven dioceses in the Middle East: two in Syria and one each in Lebanon, Iraq, Iran, Egypt and Turkey.

Armenian Catholics in Britain, Australia, and New Zealand are under the spiritual supervision of the local Latin ordinaries. The Armenian Catholic Chaplain for Australia is Msgr. Serge Ouzounian, who resides at 41 Station Street, Ferntree Gully, VIC 3156. In the United States and Canada, the 35,000 Armenian Catholics form an apostolic exarchate of eight parishes under the direction of Bishop Hovhannes Tertsakian (110 East 12th Street, New York, New York 10003).

> LOCATION: Lebanon, Syria, Iraq, Turkey, Egypt, Iran, diaspora
> HEAD: Patriarch Jean Pierre XVIII Kasparian (born 1927, elected 1982)
> Title: Patriarch of Cilicia of the Armenians
> Residence: Beirut, Lebanon
> MEMBERSHIP: 344,000

IV. C. 2. The Coptic Catholic Church

A formal union between the Catholic and Coptic Orthodox churches [see II.B] took place with the signing of the document *Cantate Domino* by a Coptic delegation at the Council of Florence on February 4, 1442. But, because this act was not supported in Egypt, it had no concrete results.

Catholic missionaries were first active among the Copts in the 17th century, with the Franciscans in the lead. A Capuchin mission was founded in Cairo in 1630, and in 1675 the Jesuits began missionary activity in Egypt. During the same century a number of lengthy but fruitless theological exchanges took place between Rome and the Coptic Church.

In 1741 a Coptic bishop in Jerusalem, Amba Athanasius, became a Catholic. Pope Benedict XIV appointed him Vicar Apostolic of the small community of Egyptian Coptic Catholics, which at that time numbered no more than 2,000. Although Athanasius eventually returned to the Coptic Orthodox Church, a line of Catholic Vicars Apostolic continued after him.

In 1824, under the mistaken impression that the Ottoman viceroy wished it to do so, the Holy See erected a Patriarchate for Coptic Catholics, but it existed only on paper. The Ottoman authorities permitted the Coptic Catholics to begin building their own churches only in 1829.

In 1895 Leo XIII re-established the Patriarchate and in 1899 he appointed Bishop Cyril Makarios as Patriarch Cyril II "of Alexandria of the Copts." As Patriarchal Vicar Bishop Cyril had presided over a Catholic Coptic synod in 1898 which introduced a number of Latin practices. He became embroiled in controversy and felt compelled to resign in 1908. The office remained vacant until 1947, when a new Patriarch was finally elected.

The offices of the Patriarchate are located in Cairo, but the largest concentration of Coptic Catholics has always been in upper Egypt. In recent times there has been some migration to other parts of the country.

Most candidates for the priesthood are trained at St. Leo's Patriarchal Seminary in Maadi, a suburb of Cairo. There are also minor seminaries at Maadi, Tahta and Alexandria. More than 100 Coptic Catholic parishes administer primary schools, and some have secondary schools as well. The church maintains a hospital in Assiut, a number of medical dispensaries and clinics, and several orphanages.

There are no Coptic Catholic monasteries to rival the Coptic Orthodox monastic tradition, but there are religious orders modeled on western apostolic communities involved in educational, medical, and charitable activities.

In 1990 Coptic Catholic sources estimated that there were about 10,000 faithful in the diaspora under the care of local Latin bishops. There are a total of six parishes located in Paris (France), Montréal (Canada), Brooklyn and Los Angeles (USA), and Sydney and Melbourne (Australia).

LOCATION: Egypt, small diaspora
HEAD: Patriarch Stephanos II Ghattas (born 1920, elected 1986)
Title: Patriarch of Alexandria of the Copts
Residence: Cairo, Egypt
MEMBERSHIP: 197,000

IV. C. 3. The Ethiopian Catholic Church

Catholic missionaries arrived in Ethiopia in the 14th century, and Pope Eugenius IV sent a letter to the Ethiopian Emperor on August 28, 1439, inviting him to unity with the Catholic Church, but such efforts were unsuccessful. In the 16th century, Islamic attacks, culminating in 1531, threatened the very existence of Christian Ethiopia. The Emperor appealed for assistance to the Portuguese, who sent sufficient military support from Goa to defeat the Islamic armies definitively in 1543.

The Portuguese in Ethiopia were accompanied by Jesuit missionaries, who began an effort to bring the Ethiopian Orthodox Church [see II.C] into union with Rome. They focused their activity on the political elite of the country including the Emperor himself. Largely through the efforts of Fr. Peter Paez, Emperor Susenyos converted and declared Catholicism the state religion in 1622. The following year Pope Gregory XV appointed another Portuguese Jesuit, Affonso Mendez, as Patriarch of the Ethiopian Church. A formal union was declared when Mendez arrived in the country in 1626. But this union was to last only ten years. Mendez imposed a series of latinizations on the Ethiopian liturgy, customs, and discipline, which Susenyos then tried to enforce with cruelty and bloodshed. This led to a violent public reaction. Susenyos died in 1632. In 1636 his successor expelled Mendez, dissolved the union, and either expelled or executed the Catholic missionaries. The country was closed to Catholic missionary activity for the next 200 years.

In 1839 limited activity was resumed by the Lazarists and Capuchins, but public hostility was still very strong. It was only with the accession of King Menelik II to the throne in 1889 that Catholic missionaries could again work freely in the country. Catholic missionary activity expanded in Ethiopia during the Italian occupation from 1935 to 1941, as it had earlier in Eritrea which had been under Italian control since 1889.

The present ecclesiastical structure of the Ethiopian Catholic Church dates from 1961, when a metropolitan see was established at Addis Ababa with suffragan dioceses in Asmara and Adigrat. The largest concentrations of Ethiopian-rite Catholics are in Addis Ababa and Asmara. After the independence of Eritrea on May 24, 1993, about half the faithful found themselves within that new country. Two new dioceses were created in Eritrea in 1995, at Keren and Barentu, from territory taken from the diocese of Asmara.

The Ethiopian Catholic Church maintains seminaries in Addis Ababa and Adigrat in Ethiopia, and in Asmara and Keren in Eritrea. In 1919 Pope Benedict XV founded an Ethiopian College within the Vatican walls and restored St. Stephen's Church directly behind St. Peter's Basilica for the use of the college.

Paulos Cardinal Tzadua, who as Archbishop of Addis Ababa had headed the Ethiopian Catholic Church since 1977, resigned his office on September 11, 1998. On the same day, Pope John Paul II named Bishop Berhane-Yesus Demerew Souraphiel as Apostolic Administrator *sede vacante* pending the nomination of a new Archbishop.

LOCATION: Ethiopia and Eritrea
HEAD: [Bishop Berhane-Yesus Demerew Souraphiel, Apostolic Administrator]
Title: Archbishop of Addis Ababa of the Ethiopians
Residence: Addis Ababa, Ethiopia
MEMBERSHIP: 203,000

IV. C. 4. The Syrian Catholic Church

During the Crusades there were many examples of warm relations between Catholic and Syrian Orthodox bishops. Some Syrian bishops seemed favorable to union with Rome, but no concrete results were achieved. There was also a decree of union between Syrian Orthodox and Rome at the Council of Florence (*Multa et Admirabilia* of November 30, 1444), but this also came to nothing.

Jesuit and Capuchin missionaries began to work among the Syrian Orthodox faithful at Aleppo in 1626. So many Syrians were received into communion with Rome that in 1662, when the Patriarchate had fallen vacant, the Catholic party was able to elect one of its own, Andrew Akhidjan, as Patriarch. This provoked a split in the community, and after Akhidjan's death in 1677 two opposed patriarchs were elected, an uncle and nephew, representing the two parties. But when the Catholic Patriarch died in 1702, this brief line of Syrian Catholic Patriarchs died out with him.

The Ottoman government supported the Oriental Orthodox against the Catholics, and throughout the 18th century the Catholic Syrians underwent much suffering and persecution. There were long periods when no Syrian Catholic bishops were functioning, and the community was forced underground.

In 1782 the Syrian Orthodox Holy Synod elected Metropolitan Michael Jarweh of Aleppo as Patriarch. Shortly after he was enthroned, he declared himself Catholic, took refuge in Lebanon and built the still-extant monastery of Our Lady at Sharfeh. After Jarweh there has been an unbroken succession of Syrian Catholic Patriarchs.

In 1829 the Turkish government granted legal recognition to the Syrian Catholic Church, and the residence of the Patriarch was established at Aleppo in 1831. Catholic missionary activity resumed. Because the Christian community at Aleppo had been severely persecuted, the Patriarchate was moved to Mardin (now in southern Turkey) in 1850.

Steady Syrian Catholic expansion at the expense of the Syrian Orthodox was ended by the persecutions and massacres that took place during World War I. In the early 1920s the Patriarchal residence was moved to Beirut, to which many Syrian Catholics had fled.

The Syrian Catholic Patriarch always takes the name Ignatius in addition to another name. Although Syrian Catholic priests were bound to celibacy at the Synod of Sharfeh in 1888, there are now a number of married priests. A patriarchal seminary and printing house are located at Sharfeh Monastery in Lebanon.

The largest concentrations of Syrian Catholics are found in Syria, Lebanon, and Iraq. The common language is Arabic, although Syriac is still spoken in a few villages in eastern Syria and northern Iraq.

A diocese for Syrian Catholics in the United States and Canada, Our Lady of Deliverance of Newark, was founded in 1996. The first bishop is Joseph Younan (502 Palisade Avenue, Union City, New Jersey 07087). The new jurisdiction included seven parishes in the United States and two in Canada. The Chaplain for Australia is Msgr. Michael Berbari, 60 Kingsland Road, Beralla 2141.

LOCATION: Lebanon, Syria, Iraq, diaspora
HEAD: Patriarch Ignatius Moussa I Daoud (born 1930, elected 1998)
Title: Patriarch of Antioch of the Syrians
Residence: Beirut, Lebanon
MEMBERSHIP: 129,000

IV. C. 5. The Syro-Malankara Catholic Church

During the 18th century there were no less than four formal attempts to reconcile the Catholic and Malankara Orthodox Syrian Churches [see II.E], all of which failed.

In 1926, a group of five Malankara Orthodox Syrian bishops who were opposed to the jurisdiction of the Syrian Orthodox Patriarch in India commissioned one of their own number, Mar Ivanios, to open negotiations with Rome with a view to reconciliation. They asked only that their liturgy be preserved and that the bishops be allowed to retain their dioceses. After discussions, Rome required only that the bishops make a profession of faith and that their baptisms and ordinations be proven valid in each case.

In the event, only two of the five bishops accepted the new arrangement with Rome, including Mar Ivanios, who had founded the first monastic communities for men and women in the Malankara Orthodox Syrian Church. These two bishops, a priest, a deacon and a layman were received into the Catholic Church together on September 20, 1930. Later in the 1930s two more bishops, from among those who had favored the jurisdiction of the Syrian Patriarch in India, were received into communion with Rome.

This triggered a significant movement of faithful into the new Syro-Malankara Catholic Church. By 1950 there were some 65,588 faithful, in 1960 112,478, and in 1970 183,490. There are now three dioceses for over 325,000 faithful, all in Kerala State, India.

The Syro-Malankara Catholic Church plays an important role in the educational field in Kerala: in addition to Mar Ivanios College in Trivandrum, the church administers 270 schools and six colleges. It also has 13 hospitals.

St. Mary's Malankara Major Seminary was founded at Trivandrum in 1983. The foundation stone was blessed by Pope John Paul II in 1986, and the present building was completed in 1989. Theology courses began in 1992. The seminary currently has about 160 students and 30 teaching staff.

This church has also promoted the ecumenical movement in India. The diocese of Tiruvalla owns the St. Ephrem Ecumenical Research Institute in Kottayam, which brings together Catholics and Orthodox of the St. Thomas tradition to study their common liturgical heritage and patrimony. Mar Baselios, the new head of the Syro-Malankara Church, has been a member of the dialogue between the Catholic Church and the two Oriental Orthodox jurisdictions in India since 1988.

An interesting development in this church was the foundation of Kurisumala Ashram in 1958. This is a monastic community based on a strict Cistercian interpretation of the Benedictine monastic rule, the observance of the West Syrian liturgical tradition, and forms of asceticism in use among Hindu ascetics. It has become a spiritual center for Christians and Hindus alike.

There are twelve Syro-Malankara Catholic worshiping communities in the United States and Canada, and five in Germany.

LOCATION: Kerala State, India
HEAD: Archbishop Cyril Mar Baselios Malancharuvil (born 1935, appointed 1995)
Title: Metropolitan of Trivandrum of the Syro-Malankarese
Residence: Trivandrum, Kerala State, India
MEMBERSHIP: 327,000

IV. D. FROM THE ORTHODOX CHURCH

These Eastern Catholic churches adhere to the Byzantine liturgical, spiritual and theological traditions of Eastern Orthodoxy, from which they derive. Because of the Greek origin of that tradition, most of these churches prefer to call themselves "Greek Catholic," which was their legal name in the Austrian Empire, the Ottoman Empire, and other states of Eastern Europe. Although this term has largely fallen out of use in the United States, where many parishes are called "Byzantine Catholic," the older term "Greek Catholic" is still used in the homeland of most of these churches. The two terms are used here interchangeably.

IV. D. 1. The Melkite Catholic Church

The word "Melkite" comes from the Syriac and Arabic words for "King," and was originally used to refer to those within the ancient Patriarchates of Alexandria, Antioch and Jerusalem [see III.A.2-4] who accepted the christological faith professed by the Byzantine

Emperor after the Council of Chalcedon (451). Today, however, the term more often refers to Byzantine Catholics associated with those three Patriarchates.

Jesuits, Capuchins and Carmelites began missionary activity in the Orthodox Patriarchate of Antioch in the mid-17th century. While there were some conversions, the missionaries were primarily concerned with forming a pro-Catholic party within the Patriarchate itself. By the early 18th century, the Antiochene church had become polarized, with the pro-Catholic party centered in Damascus and the anti-Catholic party in its rival city, Aleppo.

Patriarch Athanasios III Debbas, who died on August 5, 1724, had designated as his successor a Cypriot monk named Sylvester. His candidacy was supported by the Aleppo party and the Patriarch of Constantinople. But on September 20, 1724, the Damascus party elected as Patriarch a strongly pro-Catholic man who took the name Cyril VI. A week later, the Patriarch of Constantinople ordained Sylvester as Patriarch of Antioch. The Ottoman government recognized Sylvester, while Cyril was deposed and excommunicated by Constantinople and compelled to seek refuge in Lebanon. Pope Benedict XIII recognized Cyril's election as Patriarch of Antioch in 1729. Thus the schism was formalized, and the Catholic segment of the patriarchate eventually became known as the Melkite Greek Catholic Church.

In the beginning this new Catholic community was limited to what is now Syria and Lebanon. But Melkite Catholics later began to immigrate to Palestine, where Melkite communities had long existed, and especially to Egypt after that country rebelled against Turkish control. In view of the new demographic situation, the Melkite Catholic Patriarch was given the additional titles of Patriarch of Jerusalem and Alexandria in 1838.

At first the Ottoman government was very hostile to this new church and took strong measures against it. But conditions improved with the passage of time. In 1848 the government formally recognized the Melkite Catholic Church, and the Patriarchate itself moved to Damascus from Holy Savior Monastery near Sidon, Lebanon, where it had been established by Cyril VI after he fled there. This was followed by a period of growth, enhanced by the popular perception of the Melkite church as a focus of Arab resistance against the Turks. The Orthodox Patriarchate of Antioch, on the other hand, was viewed by many as dependent upon Constantinople and therefore upon the Ottoman government.

In the 19th century the Melkite church experienced tensions in its relationship with Rome because many Melkites felt that their Byzantine identity was being overwhelmed by the Latin tradition. This uneasiness was symbolized at Vatican I when Melkite Patriarch Gregory II Youssef left Rome before the council fathers voted on the constitution *Pastor Aeternus*, which defined papal infallibility and universal jurisdiction. At Rome's request, the Patriarch later assented to the document, but he only did so with the clause, "all rights, privileges and prerogatives of the Patriarchs of the Eastern Churches being respected" added to the formula.

At the Second Vatican Council, Melkite Patriarch Maximos IV Sayegh spoke forcefully against the latinization of the Eastern Catholic churches, and urged a greater receptivity to the eastern Christian traditions, especially in the area of ecclesiology. Today the Melkite bishops, including Patriarch Maximos IV, support the idea that, in the event of a reconciliation between the Orthodox and Catholic churches, their church should be reintegrated into the Orthodox Patriarchate of Antioch. A bilateral commission for dialogue between the Melkites and Antiochene Orthodox was established in 1995, and both sides expressed the firm intention to heal the schism of 1724 [see the Patriarchate of Antioch, III.A.3].

St. Anne's Seminary in Jerusalem, under the direction of the White Fathers (now called the Missionaries of Africa), was the main seminary for the Melkite church until it was closed in 1967 because of the political situation. There are now three major seminaries in the

Melkite church: the patriarchal seminary of St. Anne in Raboué, Lebanon; Holy Savior Seminary in Beit Sahour, Israel, for dioceses in Israel, Jordan, the West Bank and Gaza; and St. Gregory the Theologian Seminary in Newton, Massachusetts, USA, for the United States and other English-speaking countries. The Melkite Paulist Fathers direct an important theological institute at Harissa and administer a well-known publishing house.

After the Maronites, the Melkite Catholic Church is the largest and most prosperous Catholic community in the Middle East. The majority of its faithful live in Syria, Lebanon, Israel, the West Bank, and Jordan.

Significant emigration from the Middle East in recent years has created flourishing Melkite communities in the West. Bishop John Adel Elya presides over the Diocese of Newton of the Melkites in the United States (19 Dartmouth Street, West Newton, Massachusetts 02165) with 38 parishes and 28,000 members. In Canada, the diocese of Saint-Sauveur de Montréal, under the guidance of Bishop Sleiman Hajjar (34 Maplewood, Outremont, Quebec H2V 2M1), has 12 parishes and 43,000 faithful. Bishop Issam Darwish heads the diocese of St. Michael's of Sydney in Australia (25 Golden Grove Street, Darlington, NSW 2008), which has nine parishes for 45,000 Melkite Catholics. There is also a parish in London.

LOCATION: Syria, Lebanon, Israel, Egypt, Jordan, the West Bank, the Americas, Europe, Australia
HEAD: Patriarch Maximos V Hakkim (born 1908, elected 1967)
Title: Melkite Greek Catholic Patriarch of Antioch and All the East, of Alexandria and of Jerusalem
Residence: Damascus, Syria
MEMBERSHIP: 1,190,000

IV. D. 2. The Ukrainian Catholic Church

The Ukrainians received the Christian faith from the Byzantines, and their church was originally linked to the Patriarchate of Constantinople. By the 14th century most Ukrainians were under the political control of Catholic Lithuania. Metropolitan Isidore of Kiev attended the Council of Florence and agreed to the 1439 act of union between Catholics and Orthodox. Although many Ukrainians within Lithuania initially accepted this union, within a few decades they had rejected it.

In 1569, when Lithuania and Poland united to form a single commonwealth, most of Ukraine passed to Poland. By this time Protestantism was expanding rapidly in the Ukrainian lands, and the Jesuits had begun to work for a local union between Catholics and Orthodox as a way of reducing Protestant influence. Soon many Orthodox also began to view such a union favorably as a way of improving the situation of the Ukrainian clergy and of preserving their Byzantine traditions at a time when Latin Polish Catholicism was expanding.

These developments culminated in a synod of Orthodox bishops at Brest in 1595-1596 which proclaimed a union between Rome and the Metropolitan province of Kiev. This event sparked a violent conflict between those who accepted the union and those who opposed it. The dioceses of the far western province of Galicia, which lie at the heart of what is now the Ukrainian Catholic Church, adhered to the union much later (Przemysl in 1692 and Lviv in 1700). By the 18th century, two-thirds of the Orthodox in western Ukraine had become Greek Catholic.

But as Orthodox Russia expanded its control into Ukraine, the union was gradually suppressed. In 1839, Tsar Nicholas I abolished it in all areas under Russian rule with the exception of the eparchy of Kholm (in Polish territory), which was itself integrated into the Russian Orthodox Church in 1875. Thus by the end of the 19th century Greek Catholicism had virtually disappeared from the empire.

But the Ukrainian Catholic Church survived in Galicia, which had come under Austrian rule in 1772 and passed to Poland at the end of World War I. The church flourished under the energetic leadership of Metropolitan Andrew Sheptytsky, who was Archbishop of Lviv from 1900 to 1944. The situation changed dramatically, however, at the beginning of World War II, when most of Galicia was annexed by the Soviet Union.

The new Soviet administration acted decisively to liquidate the Ukrainian Catholic Church. In April 1945 all its bishops were arrested, and the following year they were sentenced to long terms of forced labor. In March 1946 a "synod" was held at Lviv which officially dissolved the union and integrated the Ukrainian Catholic Church into the Russian Orthodox Church. Those who resisted were arrested, including over 1,400 priests and 800 nuns. Metropolitan Joseph Slipyj, the head of the church, was sent to prison in Siberia. He was released in 1963 and exiled to Rome. In the same year he was given the title Major Archbishop of Lviv of the Ukrainians. He was made a cardinal in 1965 and died in 1984.

Although the exact role played by the Moscow Patriarchate in the suppression has not been clearly established, the events of 1946 poisoned the atmosphere between Ukrainian Catholics and Orthodox. All this came to the surface in the late 1980s when the new religious freedom inaugurated by Soviet President Michael Gorbachev enabled the Ukrainian Catholic Church to emerge from the catacombs.

On December 1, 1989, Ukrainian Catholic communities were given the right to register with the government. With the support of the local authorities, Ukrainian Catholics gradually began to take possession of their former churches. All this marked the beginning of a strong Ukrainian Catholic resurgence in the region. As this was happening, the Moscow Patriarchate protested that violence had been used in repossessing some churches (a claim the Catholics denied), and that Ukrainian Catholics were attempting to expand at the expense of the Orthodox. The situation was complicated by the strong presence of the Ukrainian Autocephalous Orthodox Church in western Ukraine [see III.D.3]. While many property disputes are still unresolved, for the most part a peaceful *modus vivendi* had been worked out by the mid-1990s.

In the meantime, the Ukrainian Catholic Church has resumed a normal ecclesial life. On March 30, 1991, Myroslav Ivan Cardinal Lubachivsky, the exiled head of the church, was able to leave Rome and take up residence in Lviv. In May 1992 Ukrainian Catholic bishops from all over the world convened for a synod in Lviv for the first time in many decades. In August 1992 the remains of Joseph Cardinal Slipyj were translated from Rome to Lviv where he was buried next to Metropolitan Andrew Sheptytsky. In July 1993 four new dioceses were created in Ukraine from the territory of Lviv, Ivano-Frankivsk, and the Ukrainian section of the diocese of Przemysl of the Ukrainians, Poland. By late 1997 the church had 2,363 parishes, 11 bishops, 1,526 priests, 590 monks, 729 nuns, and 1,298 seminarians. In April 1996 an Archepiscopal Exarchate of Kiev-Vyshhorod was established to provide pastoral care for the faithful in central and eastern Ukraine. Ukrainian Catholic officials in Lviv believe that there are as many as six million faithful of their church scattered throughout the country. Seminaries have been set up in Lviv, Ivano-Frankivsk Ternopil, and Drohobych. In September 1994 the Lviv Theological Academy, which had been closed down by the Soviets in 1946, was reopened.

After the re-establishment of the church in Ukraine, the synod of bishops began meeting there regularly. The first General Council of the Ukrainian Greek Catholic Church was held in Lviv in October 1996. Composed of 40 bishops along with six clergy and six lay delegates from each eparchy, such General Councils were expected to be held annually until the year 2000. Due to the ill health of Cardinal Lubachivsky, one of his auxiliary bishops, Lubomyr Husar, was named Administrator of the Ukrainian Greek Catholic Church by the General Council in 1996.

Ukrainian Catholics also have a significant presence in Poland. When the Soviet Union annexed most of Galicia during World War II, about 1,300,000 Ukrainians remained in Poland. In 1946 the new Polish communist authorities deported most of these Ukrainians to the Soviet Union and suppressed the Ukrainian Catholic Church. Approximately 145,000 Ukrainian Catholics dispersed around the country were able to worship openly only in the Latin rite. Only in 1957 were pastoral centers opened to serve them. In 1989 Pope John Paul II appointed a Ukrainian bishop as auxiliary to the Polish Primate. Bishop Ivan Martyniak was appointed bishop of Przemysl of the Byzantine-Ukrainian rite on January 16, 1991, thus providing Byzantine Catholics in Poland with their first diocesan bishop since the war. In the general reshaping of Polish ecclesiastical structures that took place in 1992, Przemysl was made a suffragan of the Archdiocese of Warsaw and removed from the metropolitan province of Lviv to which it had belonged since 1818. It was later made immediately subject to the Holy See. In 1996 Pope John Paul II elevated the Przemysl diocese to the rank of metropolitan see, and changed its name to Przemysl-Warsaw. At the same time, he created a new Ukrainian Catholic diocese of Wrocław-Gdańsk, making it a suffragan of the new metropolitan see of Przemyśl-Warsaw. There are now about 85,000 Ukrainian Catholics in Poland.

There is a large diaspora of Ukrainian Catholics. In the United States there are four dioceses and 209 parishes for 121,000 members. The Metropolitan is Archbishop Stephen Sulyk of Philadelphia of the Ukrainians (827 North Franklin Street, Philadelphia, Pennsylvania 19123). In Canada there are five dioceses and 395 parishes with 174,000 faithful. The Metropolitan is Archbishop Michael Bzdel of Winnipeg of the Ukrainians (233 Scotia Street, Winnipeg, Manitoba R2V 1V7). The eight parishes serving an estimated 38,000 Ukrainian Catholics in Australia have been placed under the pastoral care of Most Rev. Peter Stasiuk, Bishop of Sts. Peter and Paul of Melbourne (35 Canning Street, North Melbourne, Victoria 3051). There is an

Apostolic Exarchate for Ukrainian Catholics in Great Britain, headed by Bishop Michael Kuchmiak (22 Binney Street, London W1Y 1YN), with 14 parishes and about 17,000 members.

In the diaspora there are major Ukrainian seminaries in Washington, DC; Stamford, Connecticut; Ottawa, Canada; and Curitiba, Brazil. In addition, the Pontifical Ukrainian College of St. Josaphat has existed in Rome since 1897.

> LOCATION: Ukraine, Poland, United States, Canada,
> Brazil, Argentina, Australia, Western Europe
> HEAD: Myroslav Ivan Cardinal Lubachivsky
>   (born 1914, elected 1984, cardinal 1985)
> Title: Major Archbishop of Lviv of the Ukrainians
> Residence: Lviv, Ukraine
> MEMBERSHIP: 5,182,000
> WEB SITE: http://www.ugkc.lviv.ua

IV. D. 3. The Ruthenian Catholic Church

The motherland of the Ruthenian Catholic Church is now in extreme western Ukraine southwest of the Carpathian mountains. The area was known variously in the past as Carpatho-Ukraine, Carpatho-Ruthenia, Carpatho-Russia, Subcarpathia, and now as Transcarpathia. Although the ecclesiastical term "Ruthenian" was formerly used more broadly to include Ukrainians, Belarusans and Slovaks as well, it is now used by church authorities in a narrower sense to denote this specific Greek Catholic Church. In terms of ethnicity, Ruthenian Catholics prefer to be called Rusyns. They are closely related to the Ukrainians and speak a dialect of the same language. The traditional Rusyn homeland extends beyond Transcarpathia into northeast Slovakia and the Lemko region of extreme southeast Poland.

In the late 9th century, most of this area came under the control of Catholic Hungary, which much later promoted Catholic missionary work among its Orthodox population, including the Rusyns. This activity culminated in the reception of 63 of their priests into the Catholic Church on April 24, 1646, at the town of Užhorod. The Union of Užhorod affected the Orthodox population of an area which roughly corresponds to today's eastern Slovakia. In 1664 a union took place at Mukačevo which involved the Orthodox in today's Transcarpathia in Ukraine and the Hungarian diocese of Hajdúdorog. A third union, which affected the Orthodox in today's county of Maramures in Romania to the east of Mukačevo, took place in about 1713. Thus within 100 years after the 1646 Union of Užhorod, the Orthodox Church virtually ceased to exist in the region.

Early on there were jurisdictional conflicts over who would control the Ruthenian Catholic Church in this area. In spite of the desire of the Ruthenian Catholics to have their own ecclesiastical organization, for more than a century the Ruthenian bishop of Mukačevo was only the ritual vicar of the Latin bishop of Eger, and Ruthenian priests served as assistants in Latin parishes. The dispute was resolved in 1771 by Pope Clement XIV who, at the request of Empress Maria-Theresa, erected the Ruthenian eparchy of Mukačevo and made it a suffragan of the Primate of Hungary. A seminary for Ruthenian Catholics was set up at Užhorod in 1778.

After World War I, Transcarpathia became part of the new republic of Czechoslovakia. There were two Byzantine Catholic dioceses at Mukačevo and Prešov. Although in the 1920s a group of these Ruthenian Catholics returned to the Orthodox Church [see Orthodox Church in the Czech and Slovak Republics, III.A.14], Rusyn ethnic identity remained closely tied to the Ruthenian Catholic Church.

At the end of World War II, Transcarpathia, including Užhorod and Mukačevo, was annexed to the Soviet Union as part of the Ukrainian Soviet Socialist Republic. Prešov, however, remained in Czechoslovakia [see Slovak Catholic Church, IV.D.8]. The Soviet authorities soon initiated a vicious persecution of the Ruthenian Church in the newly acquired region. In 1946 the Užhorod seminary was closed, and in 1949 the Ruthenian Catholic Church was integrated into the Russian Orthodox Church. Rusyns on the other side of the Czechoslovak border were also forced to become Orthodox, while those in the Polish Lemko region were deported *en masse* in 1947 either to the Soviet Union or other parts of Poland. In all three countries, an attempt was made to wipe out any residual Rusyn national identity by declaring them all to be Orthodox and Ukrainian.

The collapse of communism throughout the region had a dramatic effect on Ruthenian Catholics. The first changes took place in Poland in the mid-1980s, where Lemko organizations began to surface and press for recognition of their rights and distinct status. In Czechoslovakia, the much-diminished Rusyn minority began in November 1989 to press for recognition within the predominantly Slovak Greek Catholic diocese of Prešov. And finally, in the Transcarpathian heartland, on January 16, 1991, the Holy See confirmed a bishop and two auxiliaries that had been functioning underground for the Ruthenian Catholic eparchy of Mukačevo. By 1997 the eparchy had 264 parishes served by 141 priests. A seminary was opened in Užhorod in 1995. New facilities were under construction.

A continuing issue for Ruthenian Catholics has been their relationship with the much larger Ukrainian Catholic Church. For the first time ever, the Mukačevo diocese finds itself functioning freely in the same country with the Ukrainian Catholic Church. Although it is not officially a part of the Ukrainian church and is still immediately subject to the Holy See, Ruthenian Catholic bishops have attended recent Ukrainian Catholic synods. The bishop of Mukačevo has made it clear, however, that he opposes integration into the Ukrainian Catholic Church and favors the promotion of the distinct ethnic and religious identity of his Rusyn people.

In 1996 Pope John Paul II established an Apostolic Exarchate for Catholics of the Byzantine rite in the Czech Republic and appointed Fr. Ivan Ljavinec, until then the syncellus of the Presov Slovak Catholic diocese, as its first bishop. One reason for the establishment of this jurisdiction — which was officially classified as belonging to the Ruthenian rite — was to regularize the situation of married Latin priests secretly ordained in Czechoslovakia under communist rule. Sixty of these priests had been accepted by the church but had been allowed to minister only as permanent deacons in the Latin rite because of their marriages. In 1997, 18 of these men were re-ordained Greek Catholic priests by Bishop Ljavinec. There are about 40,000 Eastern Catholics in the Czech Republic.

Many Ruthenian Catholics immigrated to North America in the late 19th and early 20th centuries. Because of strained relations with the Latin hierarchy and the imposition of clerical celibacy on the Eastern Catholic clergy in the United States in 1929, large numbers of these Catholics returned to the Orthodox Church. In 1982 it was estimated that out of 690,000 people of Rusyn descent in the United States, 225,000 were still Ruthenian Catholics, 95,000 belonged to the Carpatho-Russian Orthodox diocese [see III.C.1], 250,000 were in the Orthodox Church in America [see III.A.15], 20,000 were in Orthodox parishes directly under the Moscow Patriarchate, and 100,000 belonged to various other Orthodox, Ukrainian Catholic, Roman Catholic, and Protestant denominations.

In the United States today, the Ruthenians constitute a separate ecclesiastical structure with four dioceses, 243 parishes, and about 170,000 members. The Metropolitan Archdiocese of Pittsburgh is headed by Archbishop Judson Procyk (54 Riverview Avenue, Pittsburgh, Pennsylvania 15214). This church, generally known simply as Byzantine Catholic, emphasizes its American character, and celebrates liturgy in English in most parishes. Candidates for the priesthood are trained at Sts. Cyril and Methodius Seminary in Pittsburgh. In 1998 the Ruthenian Catholic metropolitanate of Pittsburgh drafted new Statutes which stated that marriage was no longer an impediment to presbyteral orders. The new law was to take effect on September 1, 1998, but implementation was delayed temporarily at the request of the Holy See.

In other areas of the diaspora, including Australia, Great Britain, and Canada, Ruthenian Catholics are not distinguished from Ukrainian Catholics.

Thus today there are three distinct Ruthenian Catholic jurisdictions: (1) the Ruthenian Byzantine Catholic Metropolitanate in the United States, a metropolitan church *sui iuris*, (2) the eparchy of Mukačevo in Ukraine, which is immediately subject to the Holy See, and (3) the Apostolic Exarchate in the Czech Republic. The relationship between the three has not been clarified. The bishop of Mukačevo is listed below as head of the church, but he has no authority over the other two jurisdictions. The membership figure includes the combined statistics for all three.

LOCATION: Ukraine, United States, Czech Republic
HEAD: Bishop Ivan Semedi (born 1921, appointed 1991)
Title: Bishop of Mukačevo of the Byzantines
Residence: Užhorod, Ukraine
MEMBERSHIP: 533,000
WEB SITE: http://www.byzcath.org

IV. D. 4. The Romanian Catholic Church

Transylvania, presently one of the three major regions of Romania along with Wallachia and Moldavia, became part of Hungary in the early 11th century. Although the principality was also home to large numbers of Hungarians and Germans, who were mostly Latin Catholics, Orthodox Romanians made up the majority of the population. Soon after the province was taken by the Turks in the 16th century, Calvinism became widespread among the Hungarians, and Lutheranism among the Germans.

In 1687, the Hapsburg Austrian Emperor Leopold I drove the Turks from Transylvania and annexed it to his empire. It was his policy to encourage the Orthodox within his realm to become Greek

Catholic. For this purpose the Jesuits began to work as missionaries among the Transylvanian Romanians in 1693. Their efforts, combined with the denial of full civil rights to the Orthodox and the spread of Protestantism in the area which caused growing concern among the Orthodox clergy, contributed to the acceptance of a union with Rome by Orthodox Metropolitan Atanasie of Transylvania in 1698. He later convoked a synod which formally concluded the agreement on September 4, 1700.

At first this union included most of the Romanian Orthodox in the province. But in 1744, the Orthodox monk Visarion led a popular uprising that sparked a widespread movement back to Orthodoxy. In spite of government efforts to enforce the union with Rome — even by military means — resistance was so strong that Empress Maria Theresa reluctantly allowed the appointment of a bishop for the Romanian Orthodox in Transylvania in 1759. In the end, about half of the Transylvanian Romanians returned to Orthodoxy.

It proved difficult for the new Greek Catholic community, known popularly as the Greek Catholic Church, to obtain in practice the religious and civil rights that had been guaranteed it when the union was concluded. Bishop Ion Inochentie Micu-Klein, head of the church from 1729 to 1751, struggled with great vigor for the rights of his church and of all Romanians within the empire. He would die in exile in Rome.

The Romanian Greek Catholic dioceses had originally been subordinate to the Latin Hungarian Primate at Esztergom. But in 1853 Pope Pius IX established a separate metropolitan province for the Greek Catholics in Transylvania. The diocese of Făgăraş-Alba Iulia was made metropolitan see, with three suffragan dioceses. Since 1737 the bishops of Făgăraş had resided at Blaj, which had become the church's administrative and cultural center.

At the end of World War I, Transylvania was united to Romania, and for the first time Greek Catholics found themselves in a predominantly Orthodox state. By 1940 there were five dioceses, over

1,500 priests (90% of whom were married), and about 1.5 million faithful. Major seminaries existed at Blaj, Oradea Mare, and Gherla. A Pontifical Romanian College in Rome received its first students in 1936.

The establishment of a communist government in Romania after World War II proved disastrous for the Romanian Greek Catholic Church. On October 1, 1948, 36 Greek Catholic priests met under government pressure at Cluj-Napoca. They voted to terminate the union with Rome and asked for reunion with the Romanian Orthodox Church. On October 21 the union was formally abolished at a ceremony at Alba Iulia. On December 1, 1948, the government passed legislation which dissolved the Greek Catholic Church and gave over most of its property to the Orthodox Church. The six Greek Catholic bishops were arrested on the night of December 29-30. Five of the six later died in prison. In 1964 the bishop of Cluj-Gherla, Juliu Hossu, was released from prison but placed under house arrest in a monastery, where he died in 1970. Pope Paul VI announced in 1973 that he had made Hossu a Cardinal *in pectore* in 1969.

After 41 years underground, the fortunes of the Greek Catholic Church in Romania changed dramatically after the Ceauşescu regime was overthrown in December 1989. On January 2, 1990, the 1948 decree which dissolved the church was abrogated. Greek Catholics began to worship openly again, and three secretly ordained bishops emerged from hiding. On March 14, 1990, Pope John Paul II reestablished the hierarchy of the church by appointing bishops for all five dioceses.

Unfortunately the reemergence of the Greek Catholic Church was accompanied by a confrontation with the Romanian Orthodox Church over the restitution of church buildings. The Catholics insisted that all property be returned as a matter of justice, while the Orthodox held that any transfer of property must take into account the present pastoral needs of both communities. As of mid-1998 this impasse had not been overcome. The Greek Catholics claim that they have received back only 97 of their 2,588 former churches, mostly in the Banat region where Orthodox Metropolitan Nicolae has been more willing to allow the return of Greek Catholic property.

Seminaries are functioning at Cluj, Baia Mare, and Oradea, and theological institutes have been set up in Blaj, Cluj and Oradea. The remains of Bishop Ion Inochentie Micu-Klein were returned to Romania and buried in Blaj in August 1997. In 1998 proceedings were initiated in Rome for the possible canonization of the Greek Catholic bishops who died during the communist persecutions. In Romania this church calls itself "The Romanian Church United with Rome."

Provincial councils of the Romanian Greek Catholic Church were held at Blaj from May 5 to 14, 1872, from May 30 to June 6, 1882, and from September 13 to 26, 1900. These councils passed legislation concerning various aspects of church life, and all were approved by the Holy See. The first session of the fourth provincial council took place at Blaj from March 17 to 21, 1997. It was to be celebrated in five sessions over a four-year period, to be concluded in 2000.

The size of the Romanian Greek Catholic Church is hotly disputed. The Greek Catholics themselves officially claim just over one million members (reflected in the figure given below) and in some publications state that they have as many as three million. A Romanian census carried out in January 1992 reported only 228,377 members, a figure the Greek Catholics firmly rejected.

The only diocese outside Romania is St. George's in Canton of the Romanians, which includes all the faithful in the United States, headed by Bishop John Michael Botean (1121 44th Street NE, Canton, Ohio 44714). The diocese has 15 parishes for 5,300 faithful. A community was recently formed in Sydney, Australia, under the pastoral care of Fr. Michael Anghel, 74 Underwood Road, Homebush 2140.

LOCATION: Romania, USA, Canada
HEAD: Metropolitan Lucian Mureşan (born 1931, appointed 1994)
Title: Archbishop of Făgăraş and Alba Iulia

Residence: Blaj, Romania
MEMBERSHIP: 1,119,000

IV. D. 5. The Greek Catholic Church

The formation of a Catholic community of the Byzantine rite in the Ottoman Empire became possible only after 1829 when Ottoman Sultan Mohammed II removed previous restrictions.

A Latin priest, Fr. John Marangos, began missionary work among the Greek Orthodox in Constantinople in 1856 and eventually formed a very small group of Byzantine Catholics. In 1878 he moved to Athens (where he died in 1885), and his work in Constantinople was continued by Fr. Polycarp Anastasiadis, a former student at the Orthodox Theological School at Halki. In the 1880s Byzantine Catholic communities were also formed in two villages in Thrace.

In 1895 the French Assumptionist Fathers began work in Constantinople where they founded a seminary and two small Byzantine Catholic parishes. These Assumptionists were distinguished above all for the valuable scholarly studies they produced on the eastern churches.

On June 11, 1911, Pope Pius X created an Ordinariate for the Greeks in the Ottoman Empire and on June 28 of that year named Fr. Isaias Papadopoulos as its first bishop. He was succeeded in 1920 by Bishop George Calavassy (died 1957). It was his task to oversee the immigration of virtually the entire Byzantine Catholic community of Constantinople to Athens, and those of the two villages in Thrace to a town in Macedonia. This was part of a general exchange of populations that took place between Greece and Turkey in the early 1920s. In 1922 Bishop Calavassy moved his offices to Athens, and in 1923 the Ordinariate was raised to the rank of Apostolic Exarchate. In 1932 the Exarchate was divided into two: Bishop Calavassy remained in Athens, while another exarch was appointed to Istanbul.

Although their presence in Greece aroused the anger of the local Orthodox hierarchy, these Greek Catholics were determined to serve their fellow countrymen by works of charity and social assistance. In 1944 they founded the Pammakaristos hospital in Athens, which has become known as one of the best in the nation.

The Greek Orthodox Church remains very hostile to the very idea of the existence of this church, which it views as a gratuitous creation of the Catholic Church in Orthodox territory. It is still illegal in Greece for Catholic priests to dress in a way typical of Orthodox clergy. In 1975 a new bishop was appointed for the Byzantine Catholics in Greece over the strong objections of the Orthodox Archbishop of Athens.

The community remains very small. In Greece, most of the faithful live in Athens, while in Turkey one small parish exists in Istanbul, currently without a priest. There are seven priests serving the church in Greece, all of them celibate and originally of the Latin rite.

LOCATION: Greece and Turkey
HEAD: Bishop Anarghyros Printesis (born 1937, appointed 1975)
Title: Apostolic Exarch for Catholics of the Byzantine Rite in Greece
Residence: Athens, Greece
MEMBERSHIP: 2,345

IV. D. 6. Greek Catholics in Former Yugoslavia

The first Greek Catholics in what would later be Yugoslavia were Serbians living in Hungarian-controlled Croatia in the early 17th century. In 1611 they were given a bishop who served as Byzantine vicar of the Latin Bishop of Zagreb. He had his headquarters at Marcha Monastery, which became a center of efforts to bring Serbian Orthodox faithful in Croatia into communion with Rome.

After a period of tension with the local Latin bishops, the Serbs in Croatia were given their own diocesan bishop by Pope Pius VI on June 17, 1777, with his see at Križevci, near Zagreb. At first he was made suffragan to the Primate of Hungary, and later (1853) to the Latin Archbishop of Zagreb.

The diocese of Križevci was extended to embrace all the Greek Catholics in Yugoslavia when the country was founded after World War I. The diocese included five distinct groups: some ethnic Serbs in Croatia, Ruthenians who had emigrated from Slovakia around 1750, Ukrainians who emigrated from Galicia in about 1900, Slavic Macedonians in the south of the country who became Catholic through missionary activity in the 19th century, and a few Romanians in the Yugoslavian Banat.

Although they belong to the diocese of Križevci, the Greek Catholics in the Former Yugoslav Republic of Macedonia come under the jurisdiction of the Latin bishop of Skopje as their Apostolic Visitator. They number 6,100 faithful and are divided into five parishes.

The diocese of Križevci still officially includes all the Greek Catholics in the former republics of Yugoslavia. This arrangement has continued after the break-up of the country into several independent nations.

LOCATION: The republics of former Yugoslavia
HEAD: Bishop Slavomir Miklovš (born 1934, appointed 1983)
Title: Bishop of Križevci
Residence: Zagreb, Croatia
MEMBERSHIP: 49,000

IV. D. 7. The Bulgarian Catholic Church

Under Ottoman rule, Bulgarian Orthodox Christians [see III.A.8], who twice before had had their own Patriarchate, were gradually brought under the control of ethnic Greek bishops as part of a general hellenization of their ecclesial life. In 1767 they were placed directly under the jurisdiction of the Greek Patriarch of Constantinople.

In the 19th century, when a struggle to obtain ecclesiastical independence from the Ecumenical Patriarchate was gaining momentum, some influential Bulgarian Orthodox in Constantinople began to consider union with Rome as a solution to their problem. They thought that as Catholics they would be able to retrieve their national ecclesiastical traditions which they felt Constantinople had denied them.

In 1861 they sent a delegation, headed by the elderly Archimandrite Joseph Sokolsky, to Rome to negotiate with the Holy See. These talks were successful: Pope Pius IX himself ordained Sokolsky a bishop on April 8, 1861, and named him Archbishop for Bulgarian Catholics of the Byzantine rite. The following June he was recognized as such by the Ottoman government. But in June 1861, almost immediately after his return to Constantinople, Sokolsky disappeared under very mysterious circumstances, was forced to travel to Odessa on a Russian ship, and spent the remaining 18 years of his life in the Monastery of the Caves at Kiev. The exact details of this episode have never been revealed.

Nevertheless, having successfully identified itself with the Bulgarian nationalist movement, the Bulgarian Byzantine Catholic Church initially gained about 60,000 members. The Russian government, meanwhile, began to support the establishment of a separate Bulgarian Orthodox Church within the Ottoman Empire. This effort bore fruit in 1870 when a separate Bulgarian Orthodox Exarchate under the Patriarchate of Constantinople was set up. This effectively put an end to the movement towards Catholicism, and before the turn of the century, three quarters of the Bulgarian Byzantine Catholics had returned to Orthodoxy.

Most of those who remained Byzantine Catholic lived in villages in Macedonia and Thrace. Therefore in 1883 the Holy See created a new ecclesiastical organization for them. Apostolic Vicariates were established in Thessalonika for Macedonia and in Adrianople for Thrace, while an Apostolic Administrator with the title of Archbishop remained in Constantinople. The community suffered grievously during the Balkan Wars of 1912-1913, and the few surviving members fled to the new Bulgarian kingdom for safety.

Given this new situation, the Holy See reorganized the Bulgarian Byzantine Catholic Church in 1926: the previous ecclesiastical entities were abolished, and a new Apostolic Exarchate was established in Sofia. This was accomplished with the support of the Apostolic Visitator (1925-1931) and later Apostolic Delegate (1931-1934) to Bulgaria, Archbishop Angelo Roncalli, subsequently Pope John XXIII. He also supported the opening of an interritual seminary in Sofia in 1934 which was directed by the Jesuits until it was closed in 1945.

The Bulgarian Byzantine Catholic Church suffered much in the early years of communist rule: the Byzantine Catholic bishop died under mysterious circumstances in 1951 and many of its priests were imprisoned. The situation improved somewhat after the election of John XXIII. Unlike most other Byzantine Catholic churches in Eastern Europe, this church was not officially suppressed during the communist regime in Bulgaria, although it functioned with many restrictions.

Since the downfall of communism, the Byzantine Catholic Church in Bulgaria has regained some of its property. By 1998 there were a total of 20 parishes but only 5 diocesan priests, with four men studying for ordination. In addition, there were 9 religious priests and 33 women religious serving the Apostolic Exarchate.

LOCATION: Bulgaria
HEAD: Bishop Christo Proykov (born 1946, appointed 1995)
Title: Apostolic Exarch for Catholics of the Byzantine-Slav Rite in
    Bulgaria
Residence: Sofia, Bulgaria
MEMBERSHIP: 15,000

IV. D. 8. The Slovak Catholic Church

The religious history of Greek Catholics in Slovakia is closely related to that of the Ruthenians [see IV.D.3]. Indeed, for centuries their histories were intertwined, since the 1646 Union of Užhorod was virtually unanimously accepted in the territory that is now eastern Slovakia.

At the end of World War I, most Greek Catholic Ruthenians and Slovaks were included within the territory of the new Czechoslovak republic, including the dioceses of Prešov and Mukačevo. During the interwar period a significant movement back towards Orthodoxy took place among these Greek Catholics. In 1937 the Byzantine diocese of Prešov, which had been created on September 22, 1818, was removed from the jurisdiction of the Hungarian primate and made immediately subject to the Holy See.

At the end of World War II, Transcarpathia with the diocese of Mukačevo was annexed by the Soviet Union. The diocese of Prešov then included all the Greek Catholics that remained in Czechoslovakia.

In April 1950, soon after the communist takeover of Czechoslovakia, a mock "synod" was convoked at Prešov at which five priests and a number of laymen signed a document declaring that the union with Rome was dissolved and asking to be received into the jurisdiction of the Moscow Patriarchate (later the Orthodox Church of Czechoslovakia). Greek Catholic Bishop Gojdic of Prešov and his auxiliary were imprisoned. Bishop Gojdic died in prison in 1960.

This situation persisted until 1968 when, under the influence of the "Prague Spring" presided over by Alexander Dubcek, former Greek Catholic parishes were allowed to return to Catholicism if they so desired. Of 292 parishes involved, 205 voted to return to communion with Rome. This was one of the few Dubcek reforms that survived the Soviet invasion of 1968. Most of their church buildings, however, remained in the hands of the Orthodox. Under the new non-communist independent Slovak government, most of these had been returned to the Slovak Greek Catholic Church by 1993. In 1997 Pope John Paul II created an Apostolic Exarchate of Kosice, Slovakia, from territory taken from the Prešov diocese.

A Greek Catholic Theological College was founded in Prešov in 1880. It was given to the Orthodox in 1950. In 1990, after the fall of communism, the Greek Catholic theological school was revived and incorporated into the Pavol Jozef Safarik University of Kosice. On January 1, 1997, the sections of Safarik University located in Prešov, including the Greek Catholic theological faculty, were separated and became the new University of Prešov. The Greek Catholic theological faculty trains priests for the two Byzantine jurisdictions in Slovakia, as well as laymen of both the Byzantine and Latin rites.

The Prešov diocese includes a significant number of ethnic Rusyn Greek Catholics. In recent times, however, they have been absorbed into Slovak culture to a certain extent, as very few religious books are available in Rusyn, and the liturgy is almost always celebrated in either Church Slavonic or Slovak. In the 1990 census, 17,000 people in Slovakia claimed Rusyn ethnicity.

In the United States and most other areas, the Slovaks are not distinguished from the Ruthenians. They have a separate diocese, however, in Canada, at present presided over by an Apostolic Administrator, Rev. John Fetsco (Diocese of Sts. Cyril and Methodius of Toronto, PO Box 70, 223 Carlton Road, Unionville, Ontario L3R 2L8). There are eight parishes for about 20,000 Slovak Catholics in Canada.

LOCATION: Slovakia, Canada
HEAD: Bishop Ján Hirka (born 1923, appointed 1989)
Title: Bishop of Prešov of Catholics of the Byzantine Rite
Residence: Prešov, Slovakia
MEMBERSHIP: 222,000

IV. D. 9. The Hungarian Catholic Church

A significant Byzantine church was present in Hungary in the Middle Ages. Indeed, there were several Byzantine monasteries in the country in the 11th and 12th centuries, but all of them were destroyed during the 13th-century Tatar invasions.

In the 15th and 16th centuries, due to widespread population shifts caused by the Turkish invasions, communities of Orthodox Serbs, Ruthenians, Slovaks and Greeks moved into the area. Most of them eventually became Catholic but retained their Byzantine heritage. In the 18th century a number of Hungarian Protestants became Catholic and chose the Byzantine rite, again adding to the number of Byzantine Catholics in Hungary. They were placed under the jurisdiction of non-Hungarian Byzantine bishops.

Once this community of Greek Catholics was integrated into Hungarian society, some began to press for the use of the Hungarian language in the liturgy. But such a proposal was resisted by the church authorities. For this reason, the first Hungarian translation of the liturgy of John Chrysostom had to be published privately in 1795. In the 19th century several other liturgical books were published in Hungarian, but their use was still not approved by the ecclesiastical authorities.

A watershed in the history of this community took place in 1900, when a large group of Greek Catholic Hungarians went to Rome on pilgrimage for the Holy Year. They presented Pope Leo XIII with a petition asking him to approve the use of Hungarian in the liturgy and to create a distinct diocese for them. The question was discussed at length both at the Holy See and in Budapest, and finally on June 18, 1912, Pope Pius X erected the diocese of Hajdúdorog for the 162 Hungarian-speaking Greek Catholic parishes. But the use of Hungarian was limited to non-liturgical functions: the liturgy was to be celebrated in Greek and the clergy were given three years to learn it. World War I intervened, however, and the requirement to use Greek was never enforced. In the 1930s the rest of the necessary liturgical books were published in Hungarian.

On June 4, 1924, an Apostolic Exarchate was established at Miskolc for 21 Ruthenian parishes formerly in the diocese of Prešov that remained in Hungarian territory after Czechoslovakia was created. They were provided with a distinct identity because they used Slavonic in the liturgy. By the 1940s, however, they had all begun to use Hungarian, and the apostolic exarchate since that time has been administered by the bishop of Hajdúdorog.

The diocese of Hajdúdorog originally covered only eastern Hungary and the city of Budapest. In 1980 its jurisdiction was extended to all Greek Catholics in Hungary. There is a seminary at Nyíregyháza.

The rather small number of Greek Catholic Hungarians who immigrated to North America have a few parishes, all of them part of the Ruthenian dioceses in the USA and the Ukrainian dioceses in Canada.

LOCATION: Hungary
HEAD: Bishop Szilárd Keresztes (born 1932, appointed 1988)
Title: Bishop of Hajdúdorog, Apostolic Administrator of Miskolc
Residence: Nyíregyháza, Hungary
MEMBERSHIP: 282,000

IV. D. 10. Eastern Catholic Communities Without Hierarchies

a. **Russians**: From the early 19th century until 1905, Greek Catholicism was illegal in the Russian Empire. But after Tsar Nicholas II issued his edict of religious toleration, a few small communities of Greek Catholics were formed. In 1917 an Apostolic Exarchate was established for them. But this was soon followed by the communist revolution, after which the group was virtually annihilated. A second Apostolic Exarchate was set up for the few Russian Byzantine Catholics in China on May 28, 1928, based in Harbin [see Orthodox Church of China, III.B.4]. This was always an extremely small community, and today approximately 3,500 live in the diaspora. A Russian College, the "Russicum," was founded in Rome in 1929 under Jesuit supervision to train clergy to work with Russian emigrés and in Russia itself. The Apostolic Exarchates in Russia and China are still officially extant, but as of mid-1998 had not been reconstituted. There are two Russian Byzantine Catholic parishes in the United States, one in Montreal, Canada, and one in Melbourne, Australia.

b. **Belarusans**: Like their Ukrainian counterparts [see IV.D.2], Belarusan Catholics originated in the Union of Brest (1595-1596). But the Belarusan Greek Catholic Church was suppressed by the Russian imperial government along with the Ukrainian Catholic Church in the 19th century.

After World War I, a community of about 30,000 Greek Catholics emerged in areas of Belarus that had been annexed by Poland. An apostolic visitator was appointed for them in 1931, and an exarch in 1940. But after World War II, when the area was absorbed by the Soviet Union, the church was again suppressed and integrated into the Russian Orthodox Church.

Following the collapse of communism and the independence of Belarus in 1991, Belarusan Greek Catholics began to emerge once again. By early 1992 three priests and two deacons were at work and, unlike most of their Roman Catholic and Orthodox colleagues, were celebrating the liturgy in Belarusan. Although gaining legal recognition was proving difficult, at least ten parishes had applied for registration. A survey of religious affiliation undertaken by the Belarus State University in 1992 indicated that about 100,000 Belarusans identified themselves as Greek Catholic.

There are about 5,000 Belarusan Greek Catholics in the diaspora. They have a parish in Chicago, Illinois, USA, and a Religious and Cultural Center in London, England.

c. **Georgians**: Catholic missionaries began to work in the Georgian kingdom in the 13th century, setting up small Latin communities. A Latin diocese existed in Tbilisi from 1329 to 1507. In 1626 missionaries began to work specifically with Georgian Orthodox faithful [see III.A.9]. In 1845, the Russian government, which had controlled Georgia since 1801, expelled the Catholic missionaries. But in 1848 Tsar Nicholas I agreed to the creation of a Latin diocese at Tiraspol with jurisdiction over Catholics in the vast southern regions of the empire, including Georgia.

A small community of Armenian Catholics existed in Georgia since the 18th century. Because the tsars forbade their Catholic subjects to use the Byzantine rite, and the Holy See did not promote its use among the Georgians, no organized Georgian Greek Catholic Church ever existed. In 1920 it was estimated that of 40,000 Catholics in Georgia, 32,000 were Latins and the remainder of the Armenian rite. However, a small Georgian Byzantine Catholic parish has long existed in Istanbul. Currently it is without a priest. Twin male and female religious orders "of the Immaculate Conception" were founded there in 1861, but have since died out.

After Georgia became independent again in 1991, the Catholic Church was able to function more freely, and a significant Armenian Catholic community was able to resume a normal ecclesial life.

d. **Albanians**: The first community of Byzantine Catholic Albanians was a small mission along the coast of Epirus that existed from 1628 to 1765. A second group was established in about 1900 by a former Albanian Orthodox priest, Fr. George Germanos. By 1912 his community numbered about 120 and was centered in the village of Elbasan. In 1938 monks from the Italo-Albanian monastery at Grottaferrata came to assist them. An Apostolic Administration of Southern Albania was set up for the community in 1939, and was temporarily placed under the pastoral care of the Apostolic Delegate in Albania, Archbishop Leone Giovanni Nigris. By 1945 it had about 400 members, but in that year Archbishop Nigris was expelled from the country. The group vanished after 1967 when Albania was declared an atheist state. In 1996 Hil Kabashi was appointed the first bishop of the Apostolic Administration since 1945, but its faithful, which number just over 2,000, are almost entirely of the Latin rite. In 1998 there were no parishes or priests for the handful of Byzantine Catholic faithful.

Appendix I

Catholic-Orthodox Relations in Post-Communist Europe: Ghosts from the Past and Challenges for the Future

In December 1991, Pope John Paul II convened a special Synod of Bishops of Europe. Although fraternal delegates from other churches and ecclesial communities were invited to participate, the Orthodox churches were almost completely absent. To explain why this was so, the Ecumenical Patriarchate sent Metropolitan Spyridon of Italy to the Synod.

In his speech in the presence of the Pope, the Metropolitan said that the Orthodox absence was due to the tensions that existed between Catholics and Orthodox in Eastern and Central Europe. He listed two main reasons for this: first, that the rebirth of so-called "uniate" churches in that region had been accompanied by acts of violence, and, secondly, that the setting up of parallel Catholic ecclesiastical structures in those countries exceeded what was required to care for the local Catholic populations. The Metropolitan continued:

> The impression is now widespread among the Orthodox that [the Catholic Church] is distancing itself from the Second Vatican Council, and that the territories of countries which have been Orthodox for centuries, now liberated from the communist regimes, are being considered by their Roman Catholic brothers as «terra missionis».[1]

The bishop warned that the situation was so bad that the theological dialogue might be suspended or even completely broken off.

Similar concerns had been expressed by the Holy Synod of the Moscow Patriarchate the previous October when it responded nega-

---

[1] "Prospettive della Chiesa Ortodossa," *L'Osservatore Romano*, December 4, 1991, page 4.

tively to the papal invitation.[2] And two months later, in February 1992, the Holy Synod of the Church of Greece issued a strongly worded statement charging Pope John Paul II with being deceitful and dishonest in his relations with the Orthodox. The Greek bishops also accused the Holy See of using the Byzantine Catholic churches to extend its influence in Orthodox countries and called upon the Greek government to break off diplomatic relations with the Vatican.[3]

It is quite clear, then, that Catholic-Orthodox relations are going through a difficult period. The fall of communism in Eastern and Central Europe, while obviously a good thing, has caused old problems to resurface and has created serious difficulties for the international commission for dialogue between the two churches.

To gain a better understanding of these problems, I would like to look back into the history of Catholic-Orthodox relations, with special emphasis on the origins of the policy of uniatism and the formation of the Byzantine Catholic churches, and the Orthodox reaction to this policy. I will then try to show the way in which this history affects the present situation, and examine the approach the international commission has taken to the problem. And finally, I will try to identify some of the challenges that the Catholic and Orthodox churches face in view of their contemporary ecumenical relationship.

Historical Background

The year 1054 has traditionally been identified as the date of the schism between East and West. But more recent scholarship has tended to view the separation between Latins and Byzantines more as what Yves Congar has described as a "mutual estrangement" — a gradual isolation and loss of the ability to understand one another. The excommunications of 1054 were a high point in that process, but

---

[2] Italian text in *Adista* news service, October 21-23, 1991, pp. 3-4.

[3] Dimitri Salachas, "Il papa: né sincero né fraterno," *Il regno-attualità* (June 1992) 132-135.

certainly ordinary Italians or Greeks were initially unaffected by it. It was only much later, in the wake of the Crusades, which saw the sacking of Constantinople by the Latin Crusaders in 1204 and the replacement of the Greek hierarchy with a Latin one in the Holy Land, that the rift progressively became embedded in the collective consciousness of both communions.

In 1274 at the Second Council of Lyons and in 1439 at the Council of Ferrara-Florence, bishops and theologians of the two churches thrashed out their differences and eventually agreed on a formula for reunion. But the conciliar agreements were not accepted in the East, and the two churches lapsed into a period of almost total isolation from one another — and a *de facto* refusal to even recognize each other as churches — that would endure for centuries.

This new situation, in which it was perceived that dialogue between the hierarchies of the two churches had proven useless, set the scene for the development of a new Catholic policy towards the Orthodox East. What this policy would be was greatly affected by other developments within the Latin Church at that time, such as the fragmentation of the West and the emergence of the nation states, and especially the shock of the Protestant Reformation. The Council of Trent was called to consider the need for new ecclesial structures and reform. A strong centralizing tendency ensued, which vigorously emphasized uniformity and obedience to the authority of the papacy as essential for authentic ecclesial life.[4] Within this context, it became possible to speak of reconciliation with the Orthodox only as a "return" to Roman obedience. And it provided a theological justification for the sending of Catholic missionaries to work among the "dissidents" for the purpose of bringing them back to Catholic unity. A corollary to this policy was the simultaneous development of the notion of "rite." The emphasis on unity remained. But it now became

---

[4] Emmanuel Lanne, "The Connection between the Post-Tridentine Concept of Primacy and the Emerging of the Uniate Churches," *Wort und Wahrheit* Supplementary Issue Number 4 (December 1978) 99-108.

possible for groups of separated eastern Christians who came into union with Rome to be absorbed into the single Church, while being allowed to maintain their own liturgical tradition and elements of their own canonical discipline.[5] It is this new policy towards the Orthodox East that is now called uniatism.

So this was the dominant outlook when significant concrete unions with sections of some Orthodox churches began to take place. And the initial results were impressive. In 1595 the Union of Brest achieved union with the entire Orthodox Metropolitan Province of Kiev. This covered a vast area that is now the western half of Ukraine and Belarus. In 1646 the Union of Užhorod was the first of a series of reconciliations with Orthodox dioceses that would eventually include all of the Ruthenians under Hungarian rule. In 1700 there was a union with most of the Romanian Orthodox in Transylvania, then a Hungarian province. And in 1724 there was a schism in the Greek Patriarchate of Antioch between pro- and anti-Catholic parties which led to the formation of the Melkite Catholic Church.[6]

By the early 19th century, the situation had stabilized somewhat. The vast majority of Catholic and Orthodox Byzantine Christians in the world lived within one of three great empires: the Russian, Austro-Hungarian, and Ottoman. The Russian Orthodox czars vigorously opposed Eastern Catholicism and suppressed it within their domain. Thus most of what is now Ukraine and Belarus had become Orthodox once again when the Russians conquered the area. In the Ottoman

---

[5] Yves Congar, *Diversity and Communion*. English translation by John Bowden (London: SCM Press, 1984) 81-82.

[6] On the Union of Brest see J. Macha, *Ecclesiastical Unification: A Theoretical Framework Together with Case Studies from the History of Latin-Byzantine Relations*, Orientalia Christiana Analecta 198 (Rome: Pontifical Oriental Institute, 1974). On the union of the Romanians in Transylvania, see K. Hitchins, "Religion and Rumanian National Consciousness in Eighteenth-Century Transylvania," *The Slavonic and East European Review* 57 (1979) 214-239. On the Melkites see S. Descy, *Introduction à l'histoire et l'ecclésiologie de l'Église melkite* (Beirut: Editions Saint Paul, 1986). English translation by K. Mortimer as *The Melkite Church* (Newton, Massachusetts: Sophia Press, 1993).

Empire, Catholic missionaries had sometimes been free to pursue their mission among the Orthodox largely because of pressure applied by the French government on the sultans. But at other times the Eastern Catholics had been severely persecuted. The great majority of Byzantine Catholics lived in the Austro-Hungarian Empire. The Austrians had actively promoted the formation of Byzantine Catholic churches, so that relatively few Orthodox remained within the Hapsburg realm.

It is very dangerous to generalize about the histories of these unions. And it should be emphasized that some of them corresponded to spontaneous pro-Catholic movements among the Orthodox, as was the case, for example, in the Union of Brest and the much smaller Bulgarian Byzantine Catholic Church.[7] And the Maronites in Lebanon claim to have never broken communion with the see of Rome.

By and large, however, these unions can be grouped into three basic categories. By far the most successful model was the one employed within the Austro-Hungarian Empire. Here whole Orthodox dioceses or ecclesiastical provinces were received into the Catholic Church. Such was the case in the Unions of Alba Iulia with the Romanians, and Užhorod with what are now called the Ruthenians. In this model, the efforts of Catholic missionaries were supported by a Catholic government that denied certain civil rights to its Orthodox subjects in order to encourage them to become Byzantine Catholic.

According to the second model, more typical of the Middle East, Catholic missionaries would work to create a sizeable pro-Catholic party within a local Orthodox church, and then try to secure the election of bishops and even a Patriarch with these views. The Catholics hoped to achieve union with entire Orthodox churches in this way, but they did not anticipate how strong the Orthodox reaction would be. In these cases, the Orthodox party then elected its own

[7] On the Bulgarian Byzantine Catholic Church, see C. Walter, "Raphael Popov, Bulgarian Uniate Bishop: Problems of Uniatism and Autocephaly," *Sobornost Incorporating Eastern Churches Review* 6 (1984) 46-60.

Patriarch, thus establishing a parallel hierarchy and splitting the church. This is what happened in the Greek Patriarchate of Antioch in 1724, and earlier in the non-Chalcedonian Syrian Orthodox Church.[8]

The third model called for Catholic missionaries to work outside the Orthodox churches, setting up Byzantine Catholic counterparts to draw Orthodox faithful away from them. The hope was that by a gradual process of attrition, the Orthodox Churches would be entirely replaced by Byzantine Catholic ones. In the end this method was not very successful and led only to the creation of very small Byzantine Catholic communities, and yet it evoked the strongest Orthodox reaction.

We can gain an insight into Orthodox feelings on this matter by examining the connection Catholic missionaries saw between their work among the Orthodox and the adoption of the Byzantine rite. A French Assumptionist patrologist, Fulbert Cayré (1884-1971) shed some light on this matter at a conference he gave at Louvain University in 1923 on "The Methods of the Oriental Apostolate."[9] Cayré was living in Constantinople where his community had set up a Byzantine-rite mission to work among the Greek Orthodox of the city.

Cayré's fundamental thesis, like the third model mentioned above, was that the promotion of Byzantine Catholicism is by far the most effective method of bringing dissident Orthodox back to Catholic unity. The efforts of Latin missionaries had born little fruit, but the conversion of large numbers of Orthodox to Catholicism could still be achieved through the method of opposing Byzantine Catholic churches to the local Orthodox ones. When they see a church of their own rite obedient to the Pope, but which nevertheless scrupulously

---

[8] Wilhelm de Vries, *Ortodossia e cattolicesimo*, trans. from German by Enzo Gatti (Brescia: Queriniana, 1983) 118.

[9] Fulbert Cayré, "Les méthodes d'apostolat oriental," *L'Union des Églises* 2 (1923) 195-198, 228-230, 260-261.

maintains all its Orthodox usages, Cayré affirmed, they will realize that they have nothing to lose in breaking with the schism:

> Here are those who can most effectively work for the Union in the East, those who can directly address the dissidents to propose that they enter into the Roman communion, those who can obtain not just a few rare individual returns [to Catholic unity], perhaps scattered over several years, as one finds in centers where Latin missionaries are working, but who can bring about numerous returns, and even bring about the return of several important groups at the same time. It is in this way, and this way only, that one can foresee ... the end of the schism. The whole question of the union, therefore, boils down to the formation of an instructed, pious and zealous Eastern Catholic clergy.[10]

Cayré went on to describe the indirect role that Latin missionaries could play in those regions by undertaking works of charity, especially by setting up Catholic schools for Orthodox students, which would be like "nurseries" for new Catholics.

I do not mean to present this outlook as the only one that existed in the Catholic Church at the time. Already the seeds of a new attitude were being planted by such Catholic churchmen as Dom Lambert Beaudoin, the founder of the Benedictine monastery now at Chevetogne.[11] Nevertheless, the way of thinking Cayré presented at Louvain was predominant and enjoyed official support. And it goes a long way towards explaining the very strong Orthodox reaction to the policy of uniatism, especially among the Greeks.

And the reaction was very strong indeed. In fact, there is some evidence that the official denial of the validity of Catholic baptism by some Orthodox churches can be seen as pastoral responses to the threat they saw in uniatism. The Union of Brest took place in 1595, and in 1620 the Holy Synod of the Russian Orthodox Church decreed

---

[10] Ibid., 198.

[11] On this see Etienne Fouilloux, "Dom Lambert entre l'unionisme et l'oecuménisme," *Unité des chrétiens* 29 (January 1978) 11-13.

that Catholics should be rebaptized. The Melkite schism in the Greek Orthodox Patriarchate of Antioch took place in 1724, and in 1755 Patriarch Cyril V of Constantinople issued an encyclical requiring the same.[12] By denying the validity of Catholic baptism, the Orthodox hierarchy hoped to counter the Byzantine Catholic claim that for Orthodox to enter into communion with Rome was a small matter entailing only minimal changes in their traditional ecclesial life.

In addition, there has always been a strong Orthodox feeling that Byzantine Catholic clergy are deceptive, that they attempt to win over converts among the uneducated by posing as Orthodox priests. This was the position taken in the 1920s by the Orthodox Archbishop Chrysostomos of Athens in his correspondence with George Calavassy, the Byzantine Catholic bishop in the same city. The Orthodox Archbishop declared,

> Some true and authentic Greeks, our fellow citizens of Athens, loyal Latin priests, wear Latin attire, while your Frenchmen "of the Greek rite" wear the attire of Orthodox priests! What confusion, what a monstrous mixture! But why do you not tell the truth? You do not differ in anything from the other subjects of the Pope of Rome, you are westerners and Latins. But for the simple Greek refugees, you pose as being "of the Greek rite," in order to show them that, in uniting with the Pope, they will keep all that they have as Orthodox, while in fact they will lose their Orthodoxy.... We do not consider the system of uniatism to be honest. It is a deceitful, hypocritical, and opportunistic system, a bridge leading to papism, which permits all the things that you and your subordinates are doing, and wish to do, in order to conceal your propagandistic aims.[13]

I believe that this background is important for understanding the origins of the current tensions. The Orthodox have always viewed the

---

[12] Raymond Janin, "La rebaptisation des Latins dans les Églises orthodoxes," *Annuaire de l'École des Législations religieuses* 3 (1952) 59-66.

[13] Letter of Archbishop Chrysostomos of Athens to Bishop George Calavassy of July 5, 1927, in Hiéromoine Pierre, *L'union de l'Orient avec Rome: Une controverse récente*. Orientalia Christiana Vol. XVIII, (Rome: Pontifical Oriental Institute, April 1930) 131.

formation of Byzantine Catholic churches as a sign of the hostile in-tentions of the Catholic Church towards them. They saw it as an at-tempt to weaken them by fomenting divisions within their communi-ties, and as an implicit denial of their ecclesial status by the Catholic Church. As André de Halleux has observed, as a result of this policy, the fault line of the schism no longer coincides with the border be-tween the Latin and Byzantine churches, but has moved east; the di-vision now lies within the Byzantine church itself.[14] On the other hand, this same policy created Byzantine Catholic churches which, in the course of the centuries, developed a distinct identity. Orthodox in origin, but in full communion with the Catholic Church, all of them underwent a certain process of latinization which distanced them from their Orthodox counterparts. The Byzantine Catholics formed a new reality in the Christian world, characterized by a strong loyalty both to the Byzantine patrimony and to the Bishop of Rome.

The Recent Past: Byzantine Catholic Churches Suppressed and Re-stored

After the dissolution of the Austro-Hungarian Empire in the wake of World War I, the largest Byzantine Catholic churches found them-selves in new countries, mostly in Poland, Romania, and Czechoslo-vakia.

But it was the territorial and political changes after World War II that proved catastrophic for these Catholic churches. The new Soviet authorities in Galicia, where the Ukrainian Catholic Church had sur-vived under Austrian and then Polish protection, acted swiftly and ruthlessly to liquidate the church. In 1945 the entire hierarchy was imprisoned, and the following year a carefully orchestrated "synod" was held in Lviv which officially dissolved the union with Rome. All the bishops and almost half the clergy were imprisoned, and the

---

[14] André de Halleux, "Uniatisme et communion: Le texte catholique-orthodoxe de Freising," *Revue théologique de Louvain* 22 (1991) 19-20.

Ukrainian Catholics were officially absorbed into the Orthodox
Church.[15]

In Romania the new communist government took similar action
against the Greek Catholic Church in Transylvania. The hierarchy
was imprisoned, all religious orders were dissolved, the churches
were handed over to the Orthodox, and all priests who resisted the
new state of affairs were banished to concentration camps.[16] The
same fate awaited the smaller Byzantine Catholic Church in Slovakia.
Altogether more than five million Byzantine Catholics were deprived
of their religious freedom and compelled to join the local Orthodox
churches.

The question of the extent to which the Orthodox collaborated
with the communists in this shameful episode has not yet been satis-
factorily answered. Certainly they appeared to eagerly participate in
the destruction of the Byzantine Catholic churches as they publicly
heaped praise on the dictatorships and welcomed these erstwhile Orthodox back into the fold. But one must also take into account the
strict state control to which the Orthodox were forced to submit and
the form of persecution they were subjected to. What is certain is that
no deviation from the official line would have been tolerated under
any circumstances. And so to distinguish what the Orthodox genu-
inely wanted to do from what the communists were forcing them to
do is very difficult indeed, especially in view of the antipathy that the
Orthodox always felt towards uniatism. It is clear that the suppression of the Byzantine Catholics by the communists for their own ne-
farious ends converged with long-held Orthodox aspirations to undo

---

[15] For an account of the suppression of the Ukrainian Catholic Church, see B.
Bociurkiw, "The Uniate Church in the Soviet Ukraine: A Case Study in Soviet Church
Policy," *Canadian Slavonic Papers* VII (Toronto: University of Toronto Press, 1965) 89-
113. Reprinted in *Ukrainian Churches Under Soviet Rule: Two Case Studies* (Cambridge, MA: Harvard University Ukrainian Studies Fund, 1984).

[16] The suppression of the Romanian Catholic Church is recounted in I. Ratiu,
"The Communist Attack on the Catholic and Orthodox Churches in Romania," *Eastern
Churches Quarterly* 8 (1949-1950) 163-197.

what they considered to be an injustice suffered long ago at the hands of the Catholic Church.

Be that as it may, the events of the 1940s convinced most Byzantine Catholics that the Orthodox Church had revealed itself as all too willing to collaborate with the forces of atheism and totalitarianism. For them, the experience of suppression only confirmed and intensified the conviction that the Orthodox Church was essentially corrupt and open to abuse by the secular authorities. This pervasive attitude of contempt would come to the surface, and clash with Orthodox sentiments about uniatism when these churches reemerged after the collapse of communism.

The fortunes of the Byzantine Catholics began to change with the accession of Mikhail Gorbachev to the post of General Secretary of the Communist Party of the Soviet Union in March 1985. As soon as its legal status was recognized, the Ukrainian Catholic Church made a dramatic recovery.[17] The process was expedited by the local Ukrainian government, which also facilitated the return of churches to the Ukrainian Catholics.

The Moscow Patriarchate protested, however, that in some cases violence was being used in the reclaiming of these churches, a charge the Catholics denied. A high-level meeting between officials of the Vatican and the Moscow Patriarchate was held in Moscow in January 1990 to discuss these problems. A document was approved which made recommendations in view of a resolution of the conflict.[18] A joint commission was set up to examine specific cases of disputed

---

[17] See B. Bociurkiw, "The Ukrainian Catholic Church in the USSR under Gorbachev," *Problems of Communism* 39 (November-December 1990) 1-19.

[18] "Recommendations for the Normalization of Relations Between Orthodox and Catholics of the Eastern Rite in the Western Ukraine," *Information Service* 71 (1989/III-IV) 131-133. Archbishop Edward Idris Cassidy, President of the Pontifical Council for Promoting Christian Unity, provided background in his "Vatican-Orthodox Reach Accord on Ukrainian Issue," *L'Osservatore Romano* [Weekly English Edition] March 5, 1990. The document was also published in *The Journal of the Moscow Patriarchate*, 1990, n. 5, pp. 8-9.

church property, but it was abandoned among mutual recriminations at its first meeting. In the meantime, the Byzantine Catholic resurgence continued, and by the end of 1991, the Orthodox presence in western Ukraine had almost vanished,[19] a process which the Moscow Patriarchate denounced as evidence of Catholic proselytism.

In Romania, one of the first acts of the National Salvation Front after the overthrow of the Ceauşescu regime in December 1989 was to annul the 1948 decree which had dissolved the Greek Catholic Church. But it did not provide for the return of the Greek Catholic church buildings to their previous owners. This set the stage for a confrontation between Greek Catholics and Orthodox which has still not been resolved.[20]

The Romanian Greek Catholics sum up their position in the phrase *restitutio in integrum*: they demand that all the property confiscated in 1948 be returned as a matter of justice, and present this as a pre-condition to any sort of dialogue with the Romanian Orthodox Church.[21] But the Orthodox insist that the demographic situation has shifted significantly in the past four decades, and that the present pastoral needs of the two communities must be taken into account. They proposed the redistribution of churches on the basis of a census and the deliberations of a joint commission. Such a census was taken in January 1992, and the outcome was announced in May.[22] But the Greek Catholics did not accept the results, according to which they were now only 1% of the population (228,377), a small fraction of the

---

[19] The only significant Orthodox presence remaining in the region was that of the Ukrainian Autocephalous Orthodox Church which is considered uncanonical by the Moscow Patriarchate and other Orthodox churches.

[20] D. Ionescu, "The Orthodox-Uniate Conflict," Report on Eastern Europe, August 2, 1991, pp. 29-34.

[21] The Greek Catholic stance was set forth by T. Langa in "Poziția noastră," *Viața creştină* n. 1 (February 1990) and n. 11 (July 1990).

[22] "Aceasta este România," *Adevărul*, May 30-31, 1991. For analysis see Michael Shafir, "Preliminary Results of the 1992 Romanian Census," *RFE/RL Research Report* 1/30 (July 24, 1992) 62-68.

1.5 million faithful they had at the time of the suppression. In fact, very few churches have been returned, and the Greek Catholics have had to begin a program of building new places of worship.

The International Commission for Dialogue

Events such as these were bound to have an effect on the work of the International Commission for Dialogue between the Catholic and Orthodox Churches. But before examining the work of the commission, it would be good to take a brief look at the sea change in attitudes between Catholics and Orthodox that began in the 1960s.

For Catholics, the convocation of the Second Vatican Council at which Orthodox observers were present marked a new beginning. A positive evaluation of the eastern tradition is found in the Council documents, especially *Unitatis Redintegratio*. Most importantly, it clearly states that the Orthodox are "churches" in the full sense of the word, and that they have valid sacraments. This would lay the foundation for the development of an ecclesiology of communion and the notion that Catholics and Orthodox are "sister churches."

This coincided with the development of what became known as the "dialogue of charity," a kind of learning to trust one another again, a process that had to take place before any fruitful theological dialogue could begin. In January 1964 Pope Paul VI and Patriarch Athenagoras of Constantinople met for the first time, in Jerusalem. On December 7, 1965 in Rome and Istanbul they simultaneously proclaimed the lifting of the mutual excommunications of 1054, declaring them "erased from the memory" of the church.[23]

All this was the prelude to the establishment of the theological commission by Pope John Paul II and Patriarch Dimitrios I of Constantinople in 1979. Its first ten years of work reflected the growing

---

[23] On the events and theological developments leading up to the dialogue, see Dimitri Salachas, "Il dialogo teologico ufficiale tra la chiesa cattolico-romana e la chiesa ortodossa: iter e documentazione," *Quaderni di O Odigos* 2/1 (1986) 7-96.

consensus between the two communions and saw the publication of three agreed statements on such issues as the relationship between the Trinity, the Church and Eucharist; the sacraments of initiation and the connection between common faith and sacramental communion; and the theology of the ordained ministry.[24]

But while all this was going on, the issue of uniatism continued to fester in the background. The largest Eastern Catholic churches were still illegal and, to a large extent, theologically frozen in the 1940s because of their isolation and persecution. And the Orthodox continued to express their strong opposition not only to the policy of uniatism, but also to the very existence of these churches. In fact, some Orthodox theologians, especially in Greece, called for the "abandonment of uniatism" by the Catholic Church before a theological dialogue could begin.[25] Once it did begin, there were objections to the presence of any Byzantines in the Catholic delegation. And even after the dialogue was in progress, some Orthodox members still called for this issue to be treated by the commission with urgency.[26]

There was a general feeling, however, that the commission was not prepared to deal with this issue. A programmatic document adopted by the preparatory commission in 1978 had called for the commission to begin with elements that the two churches held in common. Only after a solid consensus had been attained on those basic elements was it recommended that controversial points such as papal primacy and uniatism be addressed.

But the events following the revolutions of 1989 pushed this question to the forefront. The Orthodox felt threatened by what they saw

---

[24] For an overview of the commission's work see Paul McPartlan, "Towards Catholic-Orthodox Unity," *Communio* 19 (Summer 1992) 305-320.

[25] Metropolitan Chrysostomos of Peristerion, "A Problem and an Appeal: A Necessary Presupposition for the Beginning and the Success of the Theological Dialogue between the Orthodox and Roman Catholic Churches," Θεολογία 50 (1979) 856-868.

[26] Metropolitan Chrysostomos of Peristerion, "Le dialogue théologique des Eglises orthodoxe et catholique-romaine," Θεολογία 57 (1986) 329-342.

as a resurgence of uniatism and Catholic proselytism. This is why, when the sixth plenary of the dialogue met at Freising, Germany, in June 1990, the Orthodox delegates insisted that the topic already prepared for discussion be set aside and that the question of the origins of uniatism and the present status of the Byzantine Catholic churches be addressed to the exclusion of all else.

The statement issued at the end of the Freising meeting bears the hallmarks of hasty preparation.[27] Given the circumstances, this was unavoidable. Nevertheless, it made some important assertions. First, it affirmed the principle of religious freedom, and thus the right of the Byzantine Catholic churches to exist. It also rejected "uniatism," which it defined as a policy used in the past to achieve unity with the Orthodox by detaching Orthodox communities from their mother churches and uniting them with the Catholic Church. This was "a method of unity opposed to the common Tradition of our churches," and inconsistent with a sister-church ecclesiology. Thus "it would be regretful" to return to this policy, given the progress towards unity that had already been achieved.[28] Although it is provisional in nature, the Freising statement remains the only official joint statement on this problem. A few months later the Orthodox members of the commission, meeting in Istanbul, referred to it as "the only positive sign regarding the issue at hand."

At Freising the commission realized that further study was needed and set in motion an extensive examination of the issue. The result was a working document drafted by the dialogue's coordinating committee at Ariccia, near Rome, in June 1991.

---

[27] André de Halleux in his "Uniatisme et communion" cited above provides a detailed analysis of the Freising text.

[28] "Sixth Plenary Meeting of the Joint International Commission for Theological Dialogue between the Roman Catholic Church and the Orthodox Church," *Information Service* 73 (1990/II) 52-53. Quotes from number 6.

Although the Ariccia text was not intended for publication, it has nevertheless appeared in several languages.[29] Its title, "Uniatism as a Method of Union in the Past, and the Present Search for Full Communion," points to its basic thesis: while the policy of uniatism is rejected as pertaining to a past stage in relations between Catholics and Orthodox, today's search for reconciliation must continue, making use of new methods.

The document briefly treats the historical development of the Byzantine Catholic Churches and acknowledges that as a method to achieve unity between East and West uniatism failed: "...the division persists, embittered by these attempts" (n. 4). The Ariccia text also notes the subsequent development, first in the Catholic Church and then in the Orthodox Church as a reaction, of an ecclesiology in which each church viewed itself as possessing the exclusive means of salvation. Thus the conversion of others to one's own Church came to be considered necessary for salvation. This view paved the way for violations of religious freedom and even the use of force to compel Eastern Catholics to return to the church of their forefathers.

But the document also observes that this situation changed radically after the Pan-Orthodox Conferences and the Second Vatican Council. Now, neither Catholics nor Orthodox can consider themselves as Church in an exclusive sense. Consequently, the Orthodox and Catholic churches have a joint responsibility for "keeping the Church of God in faithfulness to the divine plan, especially concerning unity."

The Ariccia text affirms that the realization of unity must be a common endeavor of the two churches to attain full agreement on the content of the faith (n. 9). Once this is achieved, the Catholic and

---

[29] English: *The Journal of the Moscow Patriarchate* (1991) n. 10, pp. 60-62 (also in Russian edition); Greek: "Κρίσιμη φάση του διαλόγου Καθολικῶν καὶ Ὀρθοδόξων" *Καθολική*, July 23, 1991 (the Catholic newspaper in Athens); French: "«Le Document d'Ariccia» L'uniatisme, méthode d'union du passé, et recherche actuelle de la pleine communion," *Irénikon* 65 (1992) 491-498.

Orthodox churches will restore full communion, and the problems posed by the Eastern Catholic churches will have been eliminated. Dialogue is pointed to as the only means by which this goal can be attained. The first section of the document concludes by citing the rejection of all forms of proselytism by Pope John Paul II and Patriarch Dimitrios of Constantinople in their joint declaration of December 7, 1987.

The second section of the Ariccia document is a series of concrete recommendations suggested for the situation in Eastern Europe. The Catholic Church is encouraged to find ways in which the Byzantine Catholic churches can contribute to the process of reconciliation. The Orthodox, for their part, are called upon to accept the assurances of the Catholic Church that it does not wish to expand at the expense of the Orthodox East and that it has abandoned proselytism among the Orthodox faithful.

Again, this is a working text. It is not an official document produced by the international dialogue. It was to have been considered at the seventh plenary meeting in Lebanon in June 1992, but it had to be postponed when it was learned that eight of the fourteen Orthodox Churches would not be present. The meeting is now due to take place in June 1993 in Lebanon.

When examining the documents produced by the international commission, it is essential that one point be clearly understood. While the commission has rejected uniatism as a method for achieving unity between Catholics and Orthodox today, it has in no way called into question the existence of the Byzantine Catholic churches. This is a crucial distinction which has been lost on some commentators.[30] In these documents "uniatism" is a technical term which refers only

---

[30] For instance see Serge Keleher, "Church in the Middle: Greek-Catholics in Central and Eastern Europe," *Religion, State and Society* 20 (1992) 289-302. Keleher's definition of uniatism as "the anomalous existence of churches of the Eastern Orthodox tradition which are nevertheless attached to the western church" (p. 298) causes him to misunderstand the meaning of the Freising statement.

to a policy, a method of reconciling Catholics and Orthodox that was used in the past. The term "Uniate" is not normally used in reference to today's Byzantine Catholic churches because it is considered derogatory. By way of illustration of what the commission is doing, one could imagine that the method used in the formation of the Church of England under Henry VIII might well be rejected as inappropriate to today's relationship between Catholics and Anglicans. But such a rejection does not imply that the Church of England has no right to exist or no positive role to play.

It would not do justice to conclude this overview of current developments without also mentioning a document that was issued by the Vatican's «Pro Russia» Commission on June 1, 1992. This document, which was drafted largely in response to Orthodox concerns, is entitled "General Principles and Practical Norms for Coordinating the Evangelizing Activity and Ecumenical Commitment of the Catholic Church in Russia and in the Other Countries of the Commonwealth of Independent States (CIS)."[31]

The first section of the text has to do with general principles. The document affirms that the Catholic Church's claim to have a right to provide for the pastoral care of its own faithful should not be seen as a way of entering into competition with the Russian Orthodox Church. The ecumenical dimension of Catholic mission activity in those countries must be a pastoral priority. Indeed, because of their common heritage, "Catholics and Orthodox can bear common witness to Christ before a world which yearns for its own unity."

The «Pro Russia» document goes on to state that Catholic activities in traditionally Orthodox countries must be conducted in ways

---

[31] English translation in *Origins* 22/17 (October 8, 1992) 301-304. French: *Plamia* 85 (Christmas 1992) 39-47 and *La documentation catholique* 2056 (September 6 & 20, 1992) 786-790. A Greek translation was published in the July 21 and 28, 1992, issues of *Καθολική* (Athens). Italian: "Direttive per l'apostolato cattolico nell'ex Unione Sovietica, *La Civiltà Cattolica* 3415 (October 3, 1992) 66-75. Slightly edited versions of the document were published in both the English and French editions of *Ecumenism* [Montreal] 107 (September 1992).

that take this heritage fully into account. The Byzantine and Armenian traditions are to be held in special esteem, and Catholics should promote cooperation with the Orthodox wherever possible.

Practical directives are given in the second section. The Catholic authorities are asked to provide for an ecumenical formation for their clergy and to promote a climate of trust and peaceful cooperation. They should also ensure that no Catholic activity appear to establish "parallel structures of evangelization" over against the Orthodox. All Catholics involved in the apostolate in those countries are asked to work under the close supervision of the Catholic bishops.

The «Pro Russia» Commission also instructs Catholic authorities to inform local Orthodox bishops of all their important pastoral initiatives, especially the opening of new parishes. And in a key passage the document even states that Catholic pastors should "endeavor to cooperate with the Orthodox bishops in developing pastoral initiatives of the Orthodox Church. They should be pleased if by their contribution they can help to train good Christians" (n. 4).

Although the «Pro Russia» text is now available to the public in several languages, it is regrettable that its impact has been somewhat limited by the fact that it has not been published by an official organ of the Holy See. Nevertheless, in my view, this is the most helpful and positive set of guidelines that the Vatican has promulgated so far on the subject of Catholic-Orthodox relations. It should do much to allay Orthodox fears with regard to true Catholic intentions in the region. It is soundly based on an ecclesiology of communion and respects the ecclesial nature of the Orthodox churches, as well as the priority they enjoy in their historic homelands.

All this shows that progress has been made towards reducing the tensions between Catholics and Orthodox that flared up in the wake of the collapse of European communism that began in 1989. Nevertheless, the fact that some Orthodox churches have expressed reservations about continuing the theological dialogue, and that a question mark still hangs over its next session, indicate that we're not out of the woods yet. For the wounds of history are rarely forgotten in these regions. As an English observer of the Balkans wrote some 85 years ago, "Assuredly there is something in the spirit of the East which is singularly kindly to survivals and anachronisms. The centuries do not follow one another, they coexist. There is no lopping of withered customs, no burial of dead ideas."[32]

Challenges for the Future

So what are the prospects for significant progress towards improving relations between Catholics and Orthodox? What challenges do the two churches face on the path towards full reconciliation? I would now like to turn to some of the major issues the two churches will have to face.

First, the Orthodox. The Orthodox churches in Eastern and Central Europe are having to adjust to radical changes in their societies. In some cases these changes have triggered serious internal problems within the local churches. For example, in Bulgaria there has been a schism in the synod of bishops over the legitimacy of the election of Patriarch Maxim while the communists were in power.[33] The churches of Serbia and Georgia are preoccupied by the wars in which their faithful are involved. The Orthodox Church in the republic of Moldova has split between two rival jurisdictions dependent on Moscow and Bucharest.[34] And many of these churches have been hit hard by the catastrophic economic conditions in their countries.

Other changes are altering the shape of the Orthodox world. Perhaps the most significant of these is the decision of the Moscow

---

[32] H. N. Brailsford, *Macedonia: Its Races and Their Future* (1906), quoted by Duncan M. Perry in "The Republic of Macedonia and the Odds for Survival," *RFE/RL Research Report* 1/46 (November 20, 1992) 12.

[33] Kjell Engelbrekt, "Bulgaria's Religious Institutions under Fire," *RFE/RL Research Report* 1/38 (September 25,1992) 61-62.

[34] See *Service Orthodoxe de Presse* 175 (February 1993) 12-15.

Patriarchate to grant autonomy to the Orthodox churches in the new countries that have risen from the ashes of the Soviet Union. This rank has been granted to the Orthodox churches in Moldova, Estonia, Latvia, Belarus, and Ukraine. It is not unthinkable that this development heralds the dismemberment of the Moscow Patriarchate. But even if these new churches remain autonomous and not fully independent, they may claim the right to participate in pan-Orthodox activities, just as the autonomous Orthodox Church of Finland now does. In this case, the overall makeup of pan-Orthodox commissions would be altered decisively in a Slavic direction.

The Orthodox are also faced with the continuing problem of the canonical recognition of churches that have unilaterally asserted their administrative independence. Among these are the "Macedonian Orthodox Church" in the former Yugoslav republic and the "Ukrainian Autocephalous Orthodox Church" which does not recognize any link with the Moscow Patriarchate. In the present state of affairs, sizable numbers of Orthodox faithful are technically in a state of schism from the Orthodox Church as a whole.

All this shows that the Orthodox world is going through a period marked by the greatest transformations seen in this century. It is fortuitous at this crucial juncture that vigorous leadership is being provided by the new Patriarch of Constantinople, Bartholomew I, and that he is devoting his formidable energies to solving these internal problems. We must wish him well, because only a united and self-confident Orthodoxy will be able to engage the other churches in sustained and successful dialogue.

The Orthodox are presented with a special challenge in their relations with the Catholic Church. Many of them perceive this church as vast in size, with huge resources, and disposing of a highly efficient organizational structure. When this is coupled with their historical consciousness of being the victim of Catholic aggression, which they blame for divisions within their own ranks, many Orthodox become fearful of entering into serious dialogue with Rome. It is this fear that explains why some Orthodox still tend to blame the Vatican for such internal problems as the schism in the Bulgarian Orthodox Holy Synod or the attempt of the Macedonian Orthodox Church to gain autocephalous status. What is needed is greater trust in the expressed intentions of the Catholic Church, a trust that can only be gained by careful study of post-Vatican II developments and greater direct experience of Catholic ecclesial life. The Orthodox churches need trained individuals who know the Catholic Church firsthand and who can counter misguided stereotypes and unfounded fears.

It will also be very important for the Orthodox to try to find ways to promote a positive relationship with the Byzantine Catholic churches. The tendency to view them as artificial creations which even now exist only because they are propped up by the Vatican is very destructive and does not do justice to their centuries-long struggle for survival, sometimes even in the face of Latin Catholic hostility. While one can appreciate Orthodox feelings about the methods used in the formation of some of these churches, the most fundamental principles of religious freedom, not to speak of the Gospel, require that they be accorded the respect and, yes, even love, due to fellow Christians. Moreover, relations between Orthodox and Byzantine Catholics do not have to be hostile. In other parts of the world such as the Americas and the Middle East,[35] where relations could develop freely after Vatican II, there is often a downright friendly atmosphere between Byzantine Catholics and Orthodox. This gives reason to hope that with the passing of time, a similar situation will develop in Eastern and Central Europe.

But for this to happen, the Orthodox will need to come to terms with the role they played in the suffering that Byzantine Catholics experienced under communism. Many are scandalized by the way in which some Orthodox continue to defend the communist-inspired

---

[35] For example, on the situation in Aleppo, Syria, see Ignace Dick, "Les relations interchrétiennes à Alep: Comment est vécu l'oecuménisme dans une grande métropole syrienne?" *Proche Orient Chrétien* 39 (1989) 113-126.

"synods" of the late 1940s that sanctioned the forceful liquidation of several Byzantine Catholic churches. Only if the Orthodox squarely face up to those events will it be possible to develop a positive relationship between these two groups.

But the Catholic Church also faces daunting challenges. It can be convincingly argued that in the new situation in Eastern and Central Europe, the Catholic Church stands to gain more than any other denomination.[36] In general, Catholics display a higher religiosity than any other group in the region. They also have access to financial and other resources from fellow Catholics in the West, an advantage that the Orthodox do not have. This means that the Catholic Church is very well positioned not only to retrieve the status it held in those countries before the advent of communism, but also to expand if it wishes.

This would, however, be a foolhardy course of action. While the Catholic Church might gain a larger share of the Christians in those countries, such nations as Russia, Romania, Bulgaria and Serbia are going to remain basically Orthodox. Moreover, entering into competition with those Orthodox churches would run counter to the implications of the teachings of the Second Vatican Council and the expressed desire of Pope John Paul II, who has repeatedly stated that Catholics are not to proselytize among the Orthodox faithful.[37] The Catholic Church has opted for dialogue with the Orthodox East as the only method that corresponds to the sister church relationship that has evolved since the Second Vatican Council. It is only this method which respects the Orthodox precisely as churches and engages the legitimate ecclesial structures by which they are governed.

There are certain aspects of this commitment, however, that remain to be fleshed out. For it requires a new way of thinking on the

---

[36] Sabrina P. Ramet asserts that this is the case in "The New Church-State Configuration in Eastern Europe," *East European Politics and Societies* 5 (1991) 247.

[37] See the Pope's speech in the Orthodox Church at Bialystok, Poland, on June 5, 1991, in *Information Service* 77 (1991/II) 40.

part of those who are accustomed to providing for the needs of local Catholic churches without considering the impact such actions might have on Orthodox churches present in the same region.

It is here that the question of the establishment of Catholic diocesan structures in the former communist countries comes in. When Catholic hierarchies were re-established there, the local Russian and Romanian Orthodox churches protested strongly not only that the new structures exceeded the pastoral needs of the local Catholic faithful, but also that they had been presented with a *fait accompli*, not having been consulted in the decision-making process. Many Orthodox feared that this indicated the beginning of renewed Catholic proselytism in their countries. I believe that the reality was precisely the opposite: the setting in place of Catholic bishops with pastoral authority was intended partially as a way of stemming the enthusiasm of certain Catholic freelance groups who were intent on evangelizing the East, groups who either were not aware of the new attitudes towards the Orthodox or who simply disregarded them. The guidelines of the «Pro Russia» document hint that this is the case. Nevertheless, the time when the Catholic Church can make major decisions concerning its activity in an Orthodox country without input from the local Orthodox Church is over. If these are truly churches in the theological sense of the term, they must at least be consulted before such decisions are taken.

The role the Byzantine Catholic churches can play in relation to the Orthodox remains a difficult question. The very deep-seated Orthodox animosity towards these churches makes it difficult for them to make a positive contribution. Moreover, the Byzantine Catholics in Central and Eastern Europe are emerging from a lengthy period of isolation from the rest of the Catholic Church and are only now beginning to assimilate the new Catholic attitudes to the ecumenical movement in general and to the Orthodox in particular. It is urgent that ways be found to facilitate this process, ways that both respect the dignity of these churches and avoid patronizing attitudes. Resources need to be made available to Byzantine Catholics of those regions enabling them to send theology students to the West, for example, and to promote exchanges with the rest of the Catholic Church at every level.

But the Catholic Church has now reached a point where it must consider ways of assisting not only its own people in those regions, but the Orthodox as well. The «Pro Russia» document encourages Catholics to cooperate in Orthodox pastoral initiatives, to help the Orthodox Church re-evangelize its own people. What would have been unthinkable 25 years ago has now become official policy. But in general the concrete modes of applying this principle remain to be worked out.

Both Catholics and Orthodox in Europe, then, are presented with the challenge of learning to find new ways of relating that correspond to the increasingly explicit recognition of each other as sister churches. This will not be easy, and yet it is of the greatest importance. For at the present juncture of European history, the future development of the relationship between East and West stands at a crossroads. It is by no means clear that the countries of Eastern Europe will slavishly embrace the economic and cultural systems of the West; they might well be ill-advised to do so. But the question that remains to be answered is whether or not these countries will enter into a mutually beneficial exchange with the West or retreat into an isolationist and perhaps even fascist system that would present untold dangers for the security of the continent.

Along these lines, the greatest enigma remains Russia. The dissolution of the USSR, the collapse of the economy, the specter of hyperinflation, the presence of some 25 million Russians in the new foreign countries of the "near abroad," and a sense of national humiliation — all these things have converged to cause Russians to seriously question their nation's identity and future role in the world. The intellectual debate on this issue has crystallized around three basic groups: the "westernizers" who advocate close contacts with the

West and the evolution of Russia into a democracy on the West European model; the "isolationists" who want Russia to have only minimal contact with other countries and focus on internal problems; and the "imperialists" or "unionists" who wish to see the re-establishment of a Eurasian confederation on the territory of the old USSR.[38] This last group, which seems to be gaining in strength, is staunchly anti-democratic and anti-western in its views.[39] Thus the outcome of the current struggle between these groups could have enormous ramifications for the rest of Europe.

At the same time, there is mounting evidence of a deep thirst among the Russian people for spiritual values. A survey conducted in April and May 1992 revealed that some 74% of Russians questioned wanted to live their lives according to a set of essential values, and at least 70% wanted a more spiritual content in their lives.[40] A similar survey conducted in October 1992 showed that, while there was profound dissatisfaction with the current political situation, the institution in the country that enjoyed the highest level of confidence among the people was the church.[41]

When these facts are considered alongside the present rebirth of the Russian Orthodox Church, which is expanding rapidly in every area of church life, it is easy to see what a crucial role the church will play in determining the final direction that Russia will take. If the Russian church decides that contacts with the West are futile or even dangerous, it will tend to push Russians in the direction of the old imperialism that poses so many perils. But if the theological ex-

---

[38] Vera Tolz, "Russia: Westernizers Continue to Challenge National Patriots," *RFE/RL Research Report* 1/49 (December 11, 1992) 1-9.

[39] Igor Torbakov, "The 'Statists' and the Ideology of Russian Imperial Nationalism," *RFE/RL Research Report* 1/49 (December 11, 1992) 10-16.

[40] Mark Rhodes, "Russians' Spiritual Values," *RFE/RL Research Report* 1/41 (October 16, 1992) 64-65.

[41] Mark Rhodes, "Political Attitudes in Russia," *RFE/RL Research Report* 2/3 (January 15, 1993) 42-44.

change and other contacts produce real fruit, generating greater confidence and trust between the Orthodox and the churches of the
West, the Moscow Patriarchate could play a leading role in encouraging Russia to follow a parallel path.

The challenges, therefore, are great, and much hangs in the bal-
ance. But ultimately, whatever the political and social ramifications
of better relations between the Orthodox and Catholic churches, the
final goal of unity remains a Christian imperative that corresponds to
nothing less than the will of Christ himself. These two sister
churches, long embittered by the misunderstandings and wounds of
the past, are experiencing the rekindling of an ancient love. In doing
so, and in responding in creative ways to the challenges posed by the
process of reconciliation, the unity of our world will be strengthened,
and God will be praised.

March 18, 1993
Rome, Italy

Post Script[42]

... In its conclusion, the Freising statement affirms that "the study
of this question [the origin and present status of the Eastern Catholic
churches] will be carried forward," because it had become an obstacle to the progress of the dialogue. Therefore, the question was submitted to the full normal treatment, with three joint subcommissions
preparing draft texts, etc., over the next two years. The result was one
text that was to be considered at the seventh plenary session. After a
year-long postponement, it took place in June 1993 at the Balamand
School of Theology in Lebanon, under the auspices of the Orthodox

---

[42] The following is an excerpt from an address entitled "Balamand and Beyond:
The Eastern Catholic Churches and the Catholic-Orthodox Dialogue," given by Fr.
Roberson to the Eastern Catholic Clergy Association in Chicago, Illinois, on Septem-
ber 25, 1994. It provides an overview of events between March 1993 and mid-1994.

Patriarchate of Antioch. The draft was examined, amended and adopted on June 23.

The full title of the Balamand Document is "Uniatism, Method of Union in the Past, and the Present Search for Full Communion,"[43]and it represents a major milestone in the progress of the international Catholic-Orthodox dialogue. It hinges on two central affirmations: on one hand, "the method which has been called uniatism" is rejected because it is "opposed to the common tradition of our churches." And on the other hand, it unequivocally affirms that the Eastern Catholic churches "have the right to exist and to act in response to the spiritual needs of their faithful." Both these things had already been said, perhaps less clearly, in the Freising statement. But they are now explicitly stated in a full-fledged document of the international joint commission.

The bulk of the document is divided into two sections, the first dealing with ecclesiological principles and the second with practical recommendations. The section on ecclesiology begins by recalling the failed attempts at reunion between the Catholic and Orthodox churches (n. 7) and the subsequent attempts to achieve unity between sections of Orthodox churches and Rome. The result was that communion was broken between those communities and their mother churches. This process was complicated by "outside elements" and

---

[43] Unfortunately the English text was initially published without final changes that had been introduced into the original French. See *Information Service* 83 (1993/II) 96-99; corrections in 84 (1993/III-IV) 149. The versions published in *Origins* 23/10 (August 12, 1993) 166-169 and *One in Christ* 30 (1994) 76-82 are uncorrected. *Ecumenical Trends* published the earlier version in its September 1993 issue, but republished the entire corrected text in December 1993. The amended text is also in *Eastern Churches Journal* 1 (Winter 1993/94) 17-25. For the French original see *Service d'information* 83 (1993/II) 99-103, *Irénikon* 66 (1993) 347-356; or *La documentation catholique* 90 (1993) 711-714. For the Greek, see the Athens newspaper *Καθολική* July 20, 1993, pp. 3-4; and *Ἀπόστολος Βάρναβας*, December 1993, pp. 473-480. *Episkepsis* published the text in both its French and Greek editions, n. 496 (September 30, 1993). Italian: *Il Regno Documenti* 38 (1993) 491-493. German: *Una Sancta* 48 (1993) 256-264.

"extra-ecclesial interests," and became a source of conflict and suffering "in the first instance for Orthodox, but also for Catholics" (n. 8). Whatever the intention and authenticity of these efforts to restore the unity of Christians, the commission recognized that the reestablishment of unity between East and West was not achieved and that "the division remains, embittered by these attempts" (n. 9).

In the period that followed these unions, missionary activity developed for the purpose of bringing others "back" to one's own church. This was coupled with a growing sense in the Catholic Church of possessing the exclusive means of salvation, making such missionary activity necessary. In reaction, the Orthodox developed a similar self-understanding as the exclusive source of salvation. All this led to the practice of re-baptism in both churches and the frequent denial of religious freedom. The document also alludes to the actions of "certain civil authorities" to bring Eastern Catholics back to the church of their fathers, using "unacceptable means," an indirect but clear reference to the communist suppressions of the 1940s (n. 10).

In view of the fact that Catholics and Orthodox now consider themselves to be sister churches, Balamand states that "this form of 'missionary apostolate'... which has been called 'uniatism,' can no longer be accepted either as a method to be followed nor as a model of the unity our churches are seeking" (n. 12). This is due to the radically new perspectives achieved in the wake of the Second Vatican Council and the Pan-Orthodox Conferences. Each side now recognizes the other as having the same apostolic faith and the same sacraments. And because of this, "rebaptism must be avoided" (n. 13). Therefore, the Catholic and Orthodox churches are "responsible together for maintaining the Church of God in fidelity to the divine purpose, most especially in what concerns unity" (n. 14). The document also states that, while individual persons remain free to choose their own churches, there can be no question of efforts to bring about the conversion of people from one church to another to ensure their salvation (n. 15).

Paragraph 16 is of particular importance for Eastern Catholics. It states first of all that the attitude towards the Orthodox of all Catholics, including the Byzantines, is based on the principles enunciated by the Second Vatican Council and subsequent papal documents. And, most importantly, it states that "these [Eastern Catholic] Churches, then, should be inserted, on both local and universal levels, into the dialogue of love, in mutual respect and reciprocal trust found once again, and enter into the theological dialogue, with all its practical implications." So the Balamand Document not only recognizes the right of Eastern Catholic churches to exist and care for their own faithful; it also invites them to participate fully in the contemporary dialogue of love and truth with the Orthodox.

The second section of the document, the practical rules, is rather complex. Here it will suffice to mention a few of the more important ones. Both sides are admonished not to seek the passage of faithful from one church to another; not to use the suffering of martyrs as a way of making accusations against other Christians; to adhere to the principles of freedom of conscience and expression and to apply these principles when undertaking pastoral projects; to seek joint resolution of concrete problems through dialogue and, when possible, through local joint commissions; to avoid all physical, verbal and moral violence; to respect the liturgical celebrations of the other church; to foster the ecumenical formation of future priests (especially in what concerns the apostolic succession and valid sacraments of the other church); to strive for a common reading of the history of the two churches and their relations; to avoid recourse to civil courts to solve concrete problems and initiate fraternal dialogue instead; to avoid tendentious use of the mass media; and to honor all those who suffered persecution, regardless of church affiliation.

The document ends with an expression of the hope that since all proselytism by Catholics at the expense of the Orthodox has been excluded, the obstacles that prevented certain autocephalous Orthodox churches from attending the dialogue will have been overcome, and that the work "already so happily begun" might continue.

This last problem was a significant one at Balamand, because six of the fifteen participating Orthodox churches were not represented. These were the Patriarchates of Jerusalem, Georgia, Serbia and Bulgaria, and the churches of Greece and the Czech and Slovak Republics. Given the situation in some of those countries, it is clear that not all of them were absent as a way of expressing opposition to the dialogue. But as we will see below, some Orthodox have used these absences as a way of questioning the status of the Balamand Document as a product of the entire international commission. It would seem, however, that this question was resolved for the Orthodox at the Third Preconciliar Pan-Orthodox Conference that took place at Chambésy, Switzerland, in 1986 in the wake of the withdrawal of the Patriarchate of Jerusalem from all the theological dialogues in which the Orthodox Church was engaged. It was decided there that participation in the dialogues is a Pan-Orthodox decision, and that if a church decides not to send representatives to a particular dialogue, it will continue nevertheless.[44]

The Balamand Document, then, represents a major step forward in the dialogue between the Catholic and Orthodox churches. It has tackled head on a problem that had been festering in the background for decades and that broke out into the open after the collapse of the totalitarian governments in Eastern Europe. Given the depth of suspicion and mutual mistrust between Catholics and Orthodox in those regions, the success of the Balamand meeting is a testament to the vibrancy of the drive of these two ancient churches towards full communion. But as might be expected, the reactions to Balamand have been strong and decidedly mixed. Let us now turn to an examination of these reactions, beginning with the heads of the two

---

[44] See report in *Irénikon* 59 (1986) 512-513, based on the texts published in *Service Orthodoxe de Presse*, supplement to n. 113 (December 1986).

churches in Rome and Constantinople, and then to evaluations that have come from the local level in Greece, Romania, and Ukraine.

Reactions to Balamand

The View from the Top

Rome and Constantinople: Only a few days after the Balamand meeting ended, Metropolitan Jeremias of France headed a delegation from the Ecumenical Patriarchate to Rome to participate in the celebration of the feast of Sts. Peter and Paul. In his speech to his Orthodox guests, Pope John Paul II called Balamand a "new step" that "should help all the local Orthodox Churches and all the local Catholic Churches, both Latin and Oriental, which live together in a single region, to continue their commitment to the dialogue of charity and to begin or to pursue relations of cooperation in the area of their pastoral activity."[45] And in the message he sent to the Ecumenical Patriarch on the occasion of the feast of St. Andrew the following November, the Pope wrote that during the past year "we were able to make progress in resolving the problems that had prevented our theological dialogue from going forward. In this way the conditions were fulfilled for moving ahead more rapidly with the theological discussions already begun. In fact, it is precisely by intensifying the theological dialogue that the still necessary clarifications can be made. The Catholic Church is entirely willing to do all she can to facilitate our common journey, in obedience to the will of the Lord and for the good of the Church."[46] Although couched in highly diplomatic language, the well-connected *Irénikon* commented that this was the

---

[45] *Information Service* 84 (1993/III-IV) 145.

[46] "Theological Dialogue is Moving Ahead," *L'Osservatore Romano* [English Weekly Edition] (December 8, 1993) 9; and *Information Service* n. 85 (1994/I) 38.

equivalent of an explicit approval of Balamand.[47] No further approval of the document from the Holy See should be expected.

On the Orthodox side, Ecumenical Patriarch Bartholomew has also expressed support for the work of the international commission. In the presence of a Roman delegation at the Phanar for the celebration of the feast of St. Andrew in November 1993, the Patriarch spoke about Balamand. He called it an expression of the good intentions of both sides to overcome recent problems. His All-Holiness continued:

> The common declaration of Balamand, in renewing the condemnation of uniatism as a method of restoring unity, certainly bears witness, even if in an indirect manner, to a change of heart by the western church concerning an unacceptable method it has used in centuries past. But also, in all that is said there about the rights and pastoral needs of the ecclesial communities of eastern rite born of uniatism that are in full communion with the bishop of Rome, it becomes clear that the Orthodox tolerate an abnormal ecclesiological situation out of love for the peaceful coexistence of the disputing parties in the regions of conflict, until such time as the uniate churches finally realize where they belong.[48]

While the Ecumenical Patriarch is not exactly brimming over with enthusiasm, this is an unmistakable endorsement. He repeats the two basic theses of the Balamand Document — the renunciation of uniatism as a method of the past and the explicit affirmation of the right of the Eastern Catholic churches to exist and provide for the pastoral needs of their faithful — and makes them his own.

Both the Vatican and the Phanar, then, have expressed approval of the Balamand Document, implying that the international commission may now return to its theological agenda. But the picture is much more complicated if we look beyond Rome and Constantinople and towards countries where Byzantine Catholic minorities live in

---

[47] "Relations entre les Communions," *Irénikon* 66 (1993) 499.

[48] After the French version published in "Relations entre les Communions," *Irénikon* 66 (1993) 500-501. For another English translation of the entire text, see *Information Service* 85 (1994/I) 38-39.

countries with a strong Orthodox identity. Now let's examine reactions in Greece, Romania, and Ukraine.

The View from the Trenches

Greece: In many ways, Greece represents a special case. The country has an overwhelmingly Orthodox identity and there has never been a Byzantine Catholic community of a significant size. Out of a population of ten million, there are just under 60,000 Catholics in the country, and only about 2,300 of them belong to the Byzantine Apostolic Exarchate. And yet, the Orthodox Church of Greece has been consistently critical of the Vatican and has been especially severe in criticizing the policy of the Holy See in Eastern Europe after the fall of communism: in February 1992 the Greek Holy Synod publicly charged Pope John Paul II with being "deceitful and dishonest" in his relations with the Orthodox.[49] Because of the influential role it plays in the Greek-speaking Orthodox world, the views of this church need to be taken into account.

Although the church of Greece has participated in the international dialogue since the beginning, it has been clear that this has been undertaken with a certain reluctance. Greek representatives were present at the meeting of the Vienna subcommission in January 1990 and at Freising the following June, but they did not come to Balamand. And since the adoption of the Balamand text, the Church of Greece has been sharply critical of the document.

Ultraconservative Old Calendar groups in Greece have also taken aim at Balamand, even spreading malicious rumors that some sort of secret union was negotiated at the meeting, as in the article "The Balamand Union: A Victory of Vatican Diplomacy," that was published in English translation by an Old Calendar monastery in Cali-

---

[49] Dimitri Salachas, "Il papa: né sincero né fraterno," *Il regno-attualità* (June 1992) 132-135.

fornia.[50] It seems that such nonsense was being taken seriously by enough Orthodox to cause concern in the canonical hierarchy: Greek Orthodox Bishop Maximos of Pittsburgh, for instance, felt it necessary to issue a denial of these rumors in the strongest terms.[51]

But the opening salvo from the official church of Greece against Balamand came from the influential Metropolitan Christodoulos of Dimitrias.[52] In his diocesan publication in September 1993, the bishop insisted that there is a contradiction between condemning uniatism as a method used in the past on one hand, while affirming the right of the Byzantine Catholic churches to exist on the other. "How can the Uniates exist without uniatism?" he asks. "And if uniatism is condemned as a method of unity, how can one then justify it? And how can the Uniate churches exist in Orthodox countries without proselytism to the detriment of the Orthodox?" He believes that both the invitation to Eastern Catholics to participate in the dialogue and the pastoral recommendations will be badly received by Orthodox who have recently been subjected to violence by the uniates. He also criticizes Balamand's reference to religious freedom as a clever ruse, given the intense uniate propaganda to which Orthodox faithful are subjected. "Those who signed this document seem to live in another world," the Metropolitan mused.

But there was more to come. On December 8, 1993, the monastic community of Mount Athos sent a letter to Ecumenical Patriarch Bartholomew denouncing Balamand.[53] Their upset, however, is

---

[50] *The Balamand Union: A Victory of Vatican Diplomacy* (Etna, CA: Center for Traditionalist Orthodox Studies, St. Gregory Palamas Monastery, 1993). The original article appeared in Ὀρθόδοξος Ἐνημέρωσις n. 14 (July-September 1993), a publication of the Old Calendar Orthodox monastery of Sts. Cyprian and Justina, Fili, Greece.

[51] Bishop Maximos, "Issues in the Orthodox-Catholic Dialogue," *The Church Messenger*, May 22, 1994, pp. 4,7.

[52] "Chronique des Églises," *Irénikon* 66 (1993) 425-427.

[53] English translation: "Letter to the Patriarch of Constantinople from the Sacred Community of Mount Athos," *Orthodox Life* 44/4 (1994) 26-39. The Greek original appeared in Ὀρθόδοξος Τύπος, March 18, 1994.

caused less by the question of uniatism and more by the ecclesiological affirmations that the Catholic and Orthodox churches both possess the means of salvation. For the monks, the Orthodox Church *is*
the one, holy, catholic, and apostolic Church in an absolutely unqualified way. Their conclusion: "We are obliged never to accept union or the description of the Roman Catholic Church as a sister
church, or the Pope as the canonical bishop of Rome, or the 'church'
of Rome as having canonical apostolic succession, priesthood, and
mysteries without their expressly stated renunciation of the filioque,
the infallibility and primacy of the Pope, created grace, and the rest
of their cacodoxies."

If the Athonite letter represents an extremist position, subsequent
commentaries in official publications of the church of Greece have
not been much more positive. Beginning in mid-March 1994, the bi-
weekly newspaper of the church of Greece, Ἐκκλησιαστικὴ Ἀλήθεια, se-
rialized two lengthy critiques of Balamand, one by Professor John
Romanides and the other by a Greek member of the international
commission, Rev. Professor Theodore Zissis. Anyone who is familiar
with the work of these two men will not be surprised by the severity
of their judgments on the Balamand text.[54] But the newspaper itself
set the general tone in a box published alongside the two articles in
each issue. It states that, since the Freising Statement reflected the
Orthodox position by condemning uniatism both as a method and as
an ecclesiologically unacceptable phenomenon, the Vatican did its
best to hush up the statement by refusing to publish anything about it
in *L'Osservatore Romano*. But Balamand, according to the editors,
has been widely disseminated by the Holy See's media as a great
event because it justifies the existence of the Eastern Catholic
churches and recognizes the presence of apostolic succession and
valid sacraments in the Catholic Church.

------

[54] On Romanides, see Yannis Spiteris, *La teologia ortodossa neo-greca* (Bologna,
Italy: Edizioni Dehoniane, 1992) 281-295.

Because he is a member of the international commission and
participated in the Vienna and Freising meetings, the article by
Theodore Zissis deserves the most attention.[55] He claims, first of all,
that the absence of several Orthodox churches at the Balamand
meeting greatly diminishes the representative nature of the text,
which he claims constitutes a success for the aims of the Vatican in
the dialogue. It reversed the condemnation of uniatism found in the
Vienna and Freising statements, and, in contradiction to Orthodox
principles, recognizes the validity of Catholic sacraments. For these
reasons Zissis believes the document will not be accepted by the Orthodox. The Orthodox representatives signed "out of charm and po-
lite carelessness" a document of Roman Catholic principles, a fact
made evident by appeals in the text to the authority of John Paul II
and the designation of the Roman Catholic Church as "Catholic."

As far as Zissis is concerned, the Vienna and Freising statements
condemned not only the methods used in forming the Eastern
Catholic churches, but also their very existence. He also repeats the
canard that Vienna condemned the use of Orthodox rituals and vestments by Eastern Catholics. But none of this would ever be accepted
by the Vatican, as was shown by the fact, Zissis claims, that Cardinal
Willebrands refused to sign the Freising statement. Since Rome
would not accept the ecclesiological principles found in the statements, the Vatican developed a two-pronged policy of keeping the
dialogue going at all costs (while managing the withdrawal of the
Catholic members "responsible" for Freising), and drafting a new
document that would not only reverse Vienna and Freising by recog-
nizing the right of Eastern Catholic churches to exist, but also gain
more besides (mutual recognition of sacraments and apostolic succession).

When it comes to uniatism, Zissis takes no prisoners. He allows no
distinction between uniatism as a method of unity used in the past

[55] Theodore Zissis, "Το Νέο Κείμενο περί 'Ουνίας του Μπαλαμάντ," Ἐκκλησιαστική
Ἀλήθεια, (March 16, April 1, April 16, and May 1-16, 1994).

and the present existence of the Eastern Catholic churches. He finds unacceptable the assertion in Balamand that the formation of these churches was accompanied by suffering first for the Orthodox but also for Catholics. This, for him, is a falsification of history that equates the aggressors with their victims. What is lacking is acknowledgment of past mistakes such as the exploitation of the weakness and poverty of Orthodox communities, and seeking forgiveness for them.

But Zissis also objects to Balamand's ecclesiological presuppositions, including the characterization of the Catholic and Orthodox as sister churches, and especially the mutual recognition of apostolic succession and valid sacraments. For him, the Roman Catholic Church is not only schismatic but also heretical. And as long as there is disagreement in matters of dogma, there can be no discussion of mutual recognition of sacraments.

It is clear from all this that a visceral mistrust of the Catholic Church is still very strong in Greece. There is always the presumption that the Vatican is determined to at least weaken if not destroy the Orthodox Church and that any gestures for reconciliation are simply ploys to veil malevolent intent. And some of Zissis' assertions are demonstrably false. *L'Osservatore Romano* does not publish the texts of any agreed statements produced by the various international dialogues. If less publicity was given to the Vienna and Freising texts, it was precisely because they were provisional in nature and issued in view of a future fuller treatment by the commission. Both Freising and Balamand, in accordance with normal procedure, were published in *Information Service* of the Pontifical Council for Promoting Christian Unity, unquestionably an official organ of the Holy See.

Moreover, although the Balamand text amplifies principles that are already found in the Vienna and Freising documents, in no way does it contradict them. While Freising did acknowledge that both the origins and existence of the Byzantine Catholic churches were the topics of discussion at the meeting, it rejects uniatism only after defining it as a method of union. Indeed, from the very beginning the Catholic delegation has consistently upheld the right of the Byzantine Catholic churches to exist. And Freising specifically recognized the religious liberty of persons and communities, hardly the condemnation of the existence of Eastern Catholic churches that Zissis claims. Ultimately, his insistence that the Catholic Church do away with the Eastern Catholic churches, compelling their faithful to become either Latins or Orthodox, is a request that the Holy See use a form of coercive violence against its own faithful. This is odd, since those who make this demand would also say that the Pope should not have the authority to carry out such a program in the first place. As long as these attitudes predominate in the church of Greece, it is hard to see how that church will be able to make a positive contribution to the dialogue.

Romania: In Romania there is a significant Greek Catholic Church, but its relationship with the Romanian Orthodox Church is especially bad.[56] Although the 1948 decree that had outlawed the Greek Catholic Church was abrogated only a few days after the ouster of Nicolae Ceauşescu in December 1989, the government chose not to resolve the question of ownership of the Greek Catholic churches that had been confiscated by the government and given to the Romanian Orthodox Church. This set the stage for a very nasty confrontation between the two that has not yet been resolved. The Greek Catholic Church insists that, as a matter of justice, the government restore to it all the churches confiscated in 1948. They sum up their demand in the phrase, *restitutio in integrum*.[57] But the Orthodox contend that the demographic situation has shifted significantly in the past four decades and that the present pastoral needs of the two communities must be taken into account on the basis of a census and the

---

[56] For a slightly dated account of this situation, see D. Ionescu, "The Orthodox-Uniate Conflict," *Report on Eastern Europe*, August 2, 1991, pp. 29-34.

[57] The Greek Catholic stance was set forth by T. Langa in "Poziţia noastră," *Viaţa creştină*, n. 1 (February 1990) and n. 11 (July 1990).

deliberations of a joint commission. In January 1992 such a census was taken, but the Greek Catholics did not accept the results, according to which they numbered only 1% of the population, or 228,377 faithful, as opposed to the approximately 1.5 million they had in 1948.[58] As a result of this impasse very few Greek Catholic churches have been returned, and the two sides have indulged in a scandalous exchange of insults and polemics. All this is a sobering reminder that in some parts of the world, due mostly to the isolation imposed by communism, the improvements in Catholic-Orthodox relations in the past few decades have had no effect whatsoever.

The Romanian Orthodox and Greek Catholic churches both responded to the Balamand document in early July, in fact within three days of each other. First, during its meeting of July 6-7, 1993, the Holy Synod of the Romanian Orthodox Church formally accepted the document. It also decided that the Romanian Orthodox Church would continue to participate in the international dialogue with the Catholic Church. But this assent was conditioned upon the Catholic Church's acceptance and application of the Balamand text and its recommendations. Following the meeting of the Holy Synod, Orthodox Metropolitan Nicholas of Banat commented that Balamand's affirmation of the fraternal relationship between Catholics and Orthodox signals a radical change in perspective. If the Catholic and Orthodox churches recognize each other as sister churches, then both of them must also recognize the Eastern Catholics as sister churches. He saw the common recognition of the right of the Byzantine Catholic churches to exist as an important step forward.[59]

This was followed almost immediately, on July 8th, with a letter from Greek Catholic Bishop George Gutiu of Cluj-Gherla and Apos-

---

[58] Results in "Aceasta este România," *Adevărul*, 30-31 May 1992. For analysis see Michael Shafir, "Preliminary Results of the 1992 Romanian Census," *RFE/RL Research Report* 1/30 (July 24, 1992) 62-68.

[59] See "Relations entre les communions," *Irénikon* 66 (1993) 370-371, and *Service Orthodoxe de Presse* 188 (May 1994) 11-12.

tolic Administrator of the Metropolitan Archdiocese of Alba Iulia and Fagaras, to Pope John Paul II. The letter was published the following October.[60] Speaking for the entire Greek Catholic hierarchy, Gutiu launched a scathing attack on Balamand. He takes strong exception to the rejection of uniatism as a method of union and presents a long list of benefits that uniatism, and the Greek Catholic Church that issued from it, have brought to Romania. He presents the union of 1700 as liberation from the darkness of domination by the Orthodox "Greco-Bulgarian Church," as bringing "understanding and experience of the Gospel of Christ," as restoring the unity that existed "with the Mother Church of Rome before being separated from her because of Bulgarian domination," increasing national awareness, providing schools and culture in the national language, and providing strength to resist collaboration with communism. All this is defended as fruit of the uniatism rejected by the commission.

The Romanian Greek Catholic bishops have special problems with paragraph 31 of the Balamand text, which urges Catholics and Orthodox to resolve their disputes through fraternal dialogue and not through the civil courts. Their position is that, since it was the government that confiscated its churches in 1948, it should be the government who returns them.

But in general the search for an agreement between the two Romanian churches has proven fruitless, Gutiu tells the Pope, because "they have remained the oppressors, we the oppressed; they were collaborators with communism while we were the victims of it; they the attackers and we the defenders even up to this very day." Consequently, "The Greek Catholic Romanian Church United With Rome accepts nothing of the texts of Rhodes, Freising, Ariccia and Balamand, and declares null the signatures on those texts." Very strong words indeed. Unfortunately the letter contains a number of histori-

---

[60] Original Romanian text in *Viaţa creştină* (October 1993). French translation in *Chrétiens en Marche* (July-September 1994) 2-3. English translation in *Eastern Churches Journal* 1/2 (Summer 1994) 49-52.

cal inaccuracies. And to imply that the Orthodox do not understand or experience the Gospel of Christ flatly contradicts the teachings of the Catholic Church.[61]

Since the Romanian Orthodox Holy Synod had agreed to continue the dialogue only if the Catholic Church accepted and applied the Balamand text, this Romanian Greek Catholic response seemed to call this continuation into question. Thus at the end of March Bishop Teofan Sinaïtul, Patriarchal Vicar for Ecumenical Affairs, wrote to Cardinal Cassidy about Romanian Orthodox misgivings about the Greek Catholic position.[62] Indeed, he states that the conditions for continued participation in the dialogue set by the Holy Synod do not seem to have been met, especially in view of what he called "the silence of the Vatican on the subject of Balamand," and since Bishop Gutiu was saying even in January 1994, after a meeting of Romanian Greek Catholics in Rome, that the rejection still stood. Bishop Teofan also referred to the aggressive actions of Greek Catholic clergy and the fact that "hundreds" of priests are being formed, far beyond the needs of the community revealed by the 1992 census. Considering all this, Bishop Teofan expressed "astonishment and deep worry about the future of Catholic-Orthodox relations."

To be fair to the Greek Catholics, however, it must be said that they were reacting not only to the Balamand text itself, but also to the way it was presented by some Orthodox. *Irénikon* reports that when Metropolitan Antonie of Transylvania returned to Romania from the Balamand meeting, he published the text along with a polemical and tendentious commentary that greatly contributed to Greek Catholic intransigence. Unfortunately, this seems to be part of a trend in Ro-

---

[61] For a balanced commentary on this letter, see Serge Keleher, "Comments on the Romanian Greek-Catholic Statement," *Eastern Churches Journal* 1/2 (Summer 1994) 53-56.

[62] French version of the text in *Chrétiens en Marche* (July-September 1994) 2. The letter was also summarized in "Bucarest: l'Église roumaine dénonce les agissements des gréco-catholiques," *Service Orthodoxe de Presse* 188 (May 1994) 11-12.

manian Orthodox circles to portray the Catholic Church in highly negative terms. In his Pastoral Letter for Easter 1994, Metropolitan Antonie was still claiming that the Catholic Church did not exist until 1054 when it separated itself from Orthodoxy and that consequently it has no deep roots among the Romanian people.[63] And much worse, in 1992 the Patriarchate reintroduced a ritual for the reception of "schismatic Roman Catholics and others" into the Orthodox Church. In the ritual for the reception of Catholics, a long penitential prayer asks the Lord to free the person "from the sleep of the deceit of heresy that leads to perdition."[64] The Patriarchate has also approved the publication of a number of other shrill and misleading anti-Catholic works. When all this is taken along with the Greek Catholic attitudes towards the Orthodox, and the impasse on the property issue, it seems naive to hope for an improvement in relations between these two Romanian churches in the foreseeable future, even if Balamand gains general acceptance elsewhere.

Ukraine: The situation in Ukraine is both the most complex and, I believe, the most hopeful. This is true in spite of the fact that the reemergence of the Greek Catholic Church in that country was the epicenter of the crisis in Catholic-Orthodox relations that developed after the collapse of communism. The rebirth of this church came as a major shock to the Moscow Patriarchate, which claimed that the process had been accompanied by proselytism among, and violence against, its Orthodox faithful in western Ukraine.

But in the meantime, after the independence of Ukraine and the fragmentation of the Orthodox Church in that country into three competing jurisdictions, the situation has become much more complicated. Two of those churches are considered uncanonical by the Orthodox Church at large, and are thus unable to participate in the international dialogue with the Catholic Church. And most of the

---

[63] Antonie Plămădeală, *Cuvînt de îndemn la păstrarea credinţei ortodoxe: Pastorală la Ziua Învierii Domnului 1994* (Sibiu, 1994).

[64] "Chronique des Églises," *Irénikon* 66 (1993) 555.

Orthodox faithful in the homeland of the Ukrainian Greek Catholic Church belong to those two jurisdictions. All this may help to explain the relative silence about Balamand so far from the Orthodox in Ukraine. But an important indication of the Moscow Patriarchate's acceptance of Balamand came in the joint communiqué issued after a high-level meeting between representatives of the Vatican and the Patriarchate in Geneva last March. The two sides stated that "It is particularly important to supervise with special care the application of the *Practical Rules*" contained in the Balamand Document.[65]

For its part, the Ukrainian Greek Catholic Church has received the Balamand Document and, with a few minor reservations, has embraced it. Its remarkably open and positive approach to relations with the Orthodox is due in part to the fact that it benefits from the presence of many qualified faithful who were in the West during the long decades of persecution. This Ukrainian Catholic evaluation of Balamand has taken the form of two documents. The first was a letter that Cardinal Lubachivsky wrote to Cardinal Cassidy, the members of the commission, and the heads of other Eastern Catholic churches on August 3, 1993. And the second is the encyclical *On Christian Unity* that Cardinal Lubachivsky issued on April 7, 1994.

In his letter to Cardinal Cassidy,[66] the head of the Ukrainian Catholic Church praised the Balamand Document as the "positive fruit" of "the many prayers of good people on both sides of the dialogue." He goes on to say that the document shows that "the apprehensions of our faithful, clergy and indeed bishops regarding the work of the Joint International Commission ... have proved unfounded." The Cardinal finds some points in the ecclesiological section "particularly helpful," especially the statement that current divisions are contrary to the will of Christ, that past attempts at union with Rome were based on an authentic desire to fulfill Christ's com-

---

[65] "Biannual dialogue sessions recommended," *L'Osservatore Romano* [English Weekly Edition] (April 6, 1994) 7.

[66] Text in *Eastern Churches Journal* 1/1 (Winter 1993/94) 29-35.

mand to be united, that the divisions have caused pain for both sides, and that the principles of freedom of conscience are respected. Lubachivsky expresses his conviction that all this "will ensure that the document will be well received by Eastern Catholics."

The Cardinal has special praise for Balamand's affirmation that, as sister churches, Catholics and Orthodox profess the same apostolic faith and participate in the same sacraments and apostolic succession. But he also mentions some reservations. These center on what he sees as an inadequate assessment of the role the Orthodox churches played in the suppression of Eastern Catholics at various times in history. He is disturbed by "the apparent unwillingness or inability of the Orthodox Church to acknowledge an even partial role in individual cases of suppression of Eastern Catholic churches," and states that recent documentation about the suppression of the Ukrainian Greek Catholic Church in 1945-1946 "clearly implies more than passive acceptance of events by the Orthodox side." The Cardinal is "deeply saddened by the fact that the Orthodox seem incapable of dealing honestly with their own history."

The Cardinal writes that the years of mistrust between Orthodox and Greek Catholics will make implementation of the recommendations "particularly challenging for both Orthodox and Eastern Catholics." Nevertheless, he states that "I commit myself, my brother bishops, clergy and faithful to applying the practical rules of the Balamand Document to the best of our ability." Lubachivsky concludes his letter with the observation that a reciprocal commitment by the Orthodox in Ukraine will be difficult because of the current divisions in that community. But he assures Cardinal Cassidy that "the Ukrainian Greek-Catholic Church does not wish to exploit the internal strife within Ukrainian Orthodoxy for her own benefit."

A few months later, Cardinal Lubachivsky issued a pastoral letter *On Christian Unity* to all the faithful of his Ukrainian Greek Catholic

Church.[67] The bulk of the document is a survey of the developments in Catholic-Orthodox relations during the decades of persecution, when his church "was through no fault of her own isolated from the Church in other countries." The entire process is described in remarkably positive terms, and is, in my opinion, a major contribution to better relations between Eastern Catholics and Orthodox not only in Ukraine but in other countries as well. Although the Cardinal says that Balamand, like every document, "has its imperfections," he prefers to dwell on the positive aspects and, indeed, goes through the text and shows how the Ukrainian Greek Catholic Church intends to implement it in the concrete life of its community.

Near the end of the pastoral letter, Cardinal Lubachivsky included a paragraph that, given the profoundly anti-ecumenical attitude of some of his faithful, and even the public re-ordination of some Orthodox priests who were received into the Ukrainian Greek Catholic Church after its rebirth, is nothing short of courageous. The Cardinal states that

> the Catholic Church unequivocally recognizes all the Sacraments of the canonical Orthodox Church, without any reservation. It is absolutely forbidden to 'rebaptize' anyone who has been baptized in the Orthodox Church; likewise the Sacraments of Holy Chrismation, Holy Orders, and Matrimony conferred in the Orthodox Church may not be repeated in any way. We may not engage in any behavior which could even appear to question the full validity of Orthodox Sacraments, for this would be directly contrary to the clear teaching of the Catholic Church.

He then challenges the widespread questioning among his faithful of the validity of ordinations in the Moscow Patriarchate because of its supposed collaboration with the communist regime. Lubachivsky states,

---

[67] Text in *Сіяч / Sower* [Official Publication of the Ukrainian Catholic Diocese of Stamford] (June 26, 1994) 5-6, 15-17; and in *Eastern Churches Journal* 1/2 (Summer 1994) 7-47.

Should someone have a difficulty arising from suspicions of cooperation with the atheist, communist regime, we wish to express here our
trust that the ecclesiastical authorities of the Orthodox Church understand the seriousness of the apostolic succession and are able to take
whatever appropriate measures might be necessary.

And he concludes that "it is to be understood that the Balamand
Statement prescribes the same respect from the Orthodox regarding
the sacramental life of our Church."

This encyclical is one of the most hopeful elements in the present
situation and urgently needs to be translated into other languages,
especially Greek and Romanian. It reflects an openness, farsighted-
ness and sensitivity that is sorely lacking in most other countries of
the region.

At this point, then, some 15 months after the adoption of the
Balamand Document, the question of the reception of the text defies
generalization. On the Orthodox side, the document has been soundly
condemned in Greece while the Holy Synod of the Romanian Orthodox Church has officially adopted it. Among Eastern Catholics, the
reaction has varied from cautious acceptance with a commitment to
implement its recommendations in Ukraine to shrill denunciation in
Romania. And yet, the endorsement of the document by both Pope
John Paul II and Ecumenical Patriarch Bartholomew I gives reason
to be hopeful....

The Balamand Document is the result of a very lengthy and rather
torturous process that has dealt with a question touching upon deep
wounds of the past. No one can deny that the Orthodox have an acute
sense of being the victims of Catholic aggression, and many still see
the Eastern Catholic churches as a part of their own flock that has
unjustly been removed from their communion. And many Byzantine
Catholics in Eastern Europe are convinced that their suffering under
communism was aided and abetted by the local Orthodox churches
into which they were officially absorbed. Considering this history, the
fact that the international commission was able to produce a com-

mon document on this topic is nothing short of miraculous and is testimony to the wisdom, openness and sheer Christian charity of those who produced it. It stands as a sign of hope that Catholics and Orthodox will eventually put the past behind them and achieve the reconciliation for which Christ prayed.

September 25, 1994
Chicago, Illinois

Since September 1994 there have been no further meetings of the international commission for dialogue. In July 1995 the Inter-Orthodox Commission for the Theological Dialogue with the Roman Catholic Church met at the Ecumenical Patriarchate and proposed unanimously that the next plenary session continue the study of uniatism. In April 1997 a joint committee met in Rome and drafted a document entitled, "The Ecclesiological and Canonical Implications of Uniatism." Another meeting of the Orthodox members of the dialogue took place at the Ecumenical Patriarchate in December 1997. It reviewed the Rome document and stressed the importance of continuing the dialogue with the Catholic Church. The Joint Coordinating Committee then met at Ariccia, near Rome, from June 15 to 20, 1998. It continued work on the draft document and decided that the eighth plenary session of the dialogue should take place from June 7 to 15, 1999, at Mount St. Mary's College in Emmitsburg, Maryland, as a guest of the Catholic Archdiocese of Baltimore. In the meantime, regular contacts have been maintained between the Catholic Church and the various Orthodox churches, especially the Ecumenical Patriarchate and the Russian Orthodox Church.

October 1998

Appendix II

The Contemporary Relationship between The Catholic and Oriental Orthodox Churches

Today the term "Oriental Orthodox Churches" generally refers to a communion of six independent ancient eastern churches.[1] The common element among them is their non-reception of the christological teachings of the Council of Chalcedon, which was celebrated in 451.[2] These churches are the Armenian Apostolic Church,[3] the Coptic Orthodox Church, the Ethiopian Orthodox Church, the Syrian Orthodox Church, and the Malankara Orthodox Syrian Church in India.[4] In addition, an independent Orthodox Church of Eritrea was established following that country's independence from Ethiopia in 1993. All are members of the World Council of Churches and have committed themselves to the contemporary ecumenical movement. In total,

---

[1] The Assyrian Church of the East, descended from the ancient East Syrian or "Nestorian" church which rejected the christological teachings of the Council of Ephesus in 431, is not included in this study, although it is at times incorrectly referred to as one of the Oriental Orthodox churches. Because of its christological tradition, the Assyrian church is not in communion with any other church.

[2] See W. de Vries, "The Reasons for the Rejection of the Council of Chalcedon by the Oriental Orthodox Churches," *Wort und Wahrheit*, Supplementary Issue No. 1 (Vienna: Herder, 1972) 54-60.

[3] The Armenian Apostolic Church is made up of two independent Catholicosates which are separate members of the World Council of Churches. The Catholicosate of Etchmiadzin, in the former Soviet republic of Armenia, is recognized as the first see. The Catholicosate of Cilicia is based at Antelias, Lebanon. In addition, two Armenian Patriarchates in Istanbul and Jerusalem are autonomous churches dependent on Etchmiadzin.

[4] The Malankara Orthodox Syrian Church is autocephalous and includes about half of the total 2,000,000 Oriental Orthodox faithful in India. The other half makes up the autonomous Malankara Syrian Orthodox Church, which is dependent upon the Syrian Orthodox Patriarchate in Damascus.

there are probably about thirty million Oriental Orthodox faithful in the world today.[5]

In the 1960s, these churches began a process of rapprochement with both the Catholic and Orthodox[6] churches. This paper examines the renewed relationship of the Oriental Orthodox churches with the Catholic Church, which took place through unofficial theological consultations, visits between Popes and hierarchs of these churches, and official theological dialogues with the Coptic Orthodox and Malankara Orthodox Syrian churches. The paper begins with a chronological presentation of the way in which the ancient christological dispute has been addressed and shows how major progress has been made as a result of the symbiotic relationship that developed between theologians meeting unofficially on the one hand, and church leaders meeting officially on the other. The second section focuses on ecclesiology, in which significant divergences remain to be resolved, despite the mutual recognition of each other as churches.

1. Christology

The Oriental Orthodox said little about christology in their earliest encounters with Pope Paul VI. But the Pope seems to have been convinced that the ancient disputes over christological terminology should no longer prevent the two churches from professing their faith

---

[5] See membership statistics provided in Ans J. vander Bent, ed., *Handbook: Member Churches, World Council of Churches*, Fully Revised Edition (Geneva: World Council of Churches, 1985).

[6] I use the term "Orthodox" without the adjective "Oriental" to refer to the Orthodox churches of the Byzantine tradition that are in communion with the Patriarch of Constantinople, whom they recognize as a point of unity. On relations between the Oriental Orthodox and Orthodox churches, see André de Halleux, "Actualité du néochalcédonisme: Un accord christologique récent entre Orthodoxes," *Revue théologique de Louvain* 21 (1990) 32-54, and Paulos Gregorios, William Lazareth, Nikos Nissiotis, eds., *Does Chalcedon Divide or Unite? Towards Convergence in Orthodox Christology* (Geneva: World Council of Churches, 1981).

in Christ together.[7] In his welcoming speech to Armenian Catholicos Khoren I of Cilicia in May 1967, Pope Paul said:

> With you We give glory to the one God, Father, Son, and Holy Spirit; with you We acclaim Jesus Christ, Son of God, Incarnate Word, our Redeemer, the founder and head of the holy Church, his mystical body.[8]

During his visit to Armenian Patriarch of Constantinople Shnork Kalustian in July 1967, Pope Paul pointed out the importance of the Council of Ephesus' teaching as the basis of the unity of the two churches:

> It is a great consolation to meditate upon the vision of Christ presented to the Church and to the world by that holy assembly. That vision, too, we share in common. God, made man for our salvation, is the God we confess in our Creed and preach to the world.[9]

And in his speech to Armenian Catholicos Vasken I (Etchmiadzin) in May 1970, Pope Paul stated that the different expressions of the one faith are due in large part to non-theological factors:

> If we have come to divergent expressions of the central mystery of our faith because of unfortunate circumstances, cultural differences and the difficulty of translating terms worked out with much effort and given precise statement only gradually, then research into these doctrinal difficulties must be undertaken again in order to understand what has brought them about and to be able to overcome them in a brotherly way.[10]

---

[7] From the Catholic point of view, the idea that the dispute was essentially a question of terminology had been officially expressed as early as 1951, when Pope Pius XII stated in his encyclical *Sempiternus Rex* that these Christians "verbis praecipue a recto tramite deflectere videantur" ("seem to depart from the right path chiefly in words"). *Acta Apostolicae Sedis* 43 (1951) 636.

[8] *Acta Apostolicae Sedis* 59 (1967) 510.

[9] *Information Service* [Secretariat for Promoting Christian Unity] 3 (1967/3) 13.

[10] *Information Service* 11 (1970/III) 5-6.

The Pope went on to quote Nerses IV, a twelfth-century Armenian Catholicos, who wrote that the term "two natures" would be acceptable insofar as it indicates the absence of any confusion of humanity and divinity in Christ, against Eutyches and Apollinaris. Pope Paul then asked: "Has the time not come to clear up once and for all such misunderstandings inherited from the past?"[11]

In the *Common Declaration* signed at the end of Vasken's visit, both churches made a clear commitment to encourage theological research into the remaining difficulties:

> They exhort theologians to devote themselves to a common study leading to a deepening of their understanding of the mystery of our Lord Jesus Christ and of the revelation brought about in him. ... For their part, the Pope and the Catholicos will try to do all that is possible to support these efforts and will give them their pastoral blessing.[12]

The *Pro Oriente* foundation in Vienna took up this challenge and sponsored a historic series of discussions between theologians of the two communions. The first "Non-Official Ecumenical Consultation between Theologians of the Oriental Orthodox and the Roman Catholic Churches" took place in Vienna in September 1971. In the communiqué issued at the end of the meeting, the theologians affirmed that a common basis had been found in the apostolic traditions and the first three ecumenical councils. After rejecting both Eutychian and Nestorian christologies, they expressed their common faith in Christ in these words:

> We believe that our Lord and Saviour, Jesus Christ, is God the Son Incarnate; perfect in his divinity and perfect in his humanity. His divinity was not separated from his humanity for a single moment, not for the twinkling of an eye. His humanity is one with his divinity without commixtion, without confusion, without division, without separation. We in our common faith in the one Lord Jesus Christ, regard his mys-

---

[11] Ibid., 6.

[12] *Acta Apostolicae Sedis* 62 (1970) 416.

tery inexhaustible and ineffable and for the human mind never fully comprehensible or expressible.

We see that there are still differences in the theological interpretation of the mystery of Christ because of our different ecclesiastical and theological traditions; we are convinced, however, that these differing formulations on both sides can be understood along the lines of the faith of Nicea and Ephesus.[13]

This text reveals an effort to avoid terminology which had been the focus of ancient disputes. Indeed, the words "person" and "nature" never appear. It is an effort to create a new vocabulary, using new concepts to express the one faith which underlies both traditional formulations.

The importance of this theological breakthrough was quickly realized. When the Syrian Patriarch Ignatius Yacoub III visited Rome one month later, Pope Paul was already echoing the findings of the *Pro Oriente* meeting when he said that theologians discussing the issue "are convinced ... that these various formulations can be understood along the lines of the early councils, which is the faith we also profess."[14]

This thought was also reflected in the *Common Declaration*, which was signed at the end of the Patriarch's visit:

> Progress has already been made and Pope Paul VI and the Patriarch Mar Ignatius III are in agreement that there is no difference in the faith they profess concerning the mystery of the Word of God made flesh and become really man, even if over the centuries difficulties have arisen out of the different theological expressions by which this faith was expressed.[15]

---

[13] "Communiqué," *Wort und Wahrheit*, Supplementary Issue No. 1 (Vienna: Herder, 1972) 182.

[14] *Information Service* 16 (1972/I) 3.

[15] *Acta Apostolicae Sedis* 63 (1971) 814.

In May 1973 Coptic Pope[16] Shenouda III visited Pope Paul VI in Rome. The profession of faith contained in the *Common Declaration* they signed at the end of the meeting had clearly benefited from the *Pro Oriente* formulation:

> We confess that our Lord and God and Saviour and King of us all, Jesus Christ, is perfect God with respect to His divinity, perfect man with respect to His humanity. In Him His divinity is united with His humanity in a real, perfect union without mingling, without commixtion, without confusion, without alteration, without division, without separation. His divinity did not separate from His humanity for an instant, not for the twinkling of an eye. He who is God eternal and invisible became visible in the flesh, and took upon Himself the form of a servant. In Him are preserved all the properties of the divinity and all the properties of the humanity, together in a real, perfect, indivisible and inseparable union.[17]

Despite the historic nature of this joint christological declaration, the theologians involved in the *Pro Oriente* consultations realized that more progress could be made. Christology, then, still figured strongly in their discussions at the second meeting which took place in September 1973. In the final communiqué, the theologians of both communions built on what had been said in the 1971 statement. They added that the mystery of Christ is incomprehensible, and that all concepts about him are limited. Thus correct christological formulations can be wrongly understood, and behind an apparently wrong formulation there can be a right understanding. This fact enabled them to affirm that "the definition of the Council of Chalcedon, rightly understood today, affirms the unity of person and the indis-

---

[16] The Coptic Patriarchs of Alexandria have had the title "Pope" since ancient times. His full title is "Pope and Patriarch of the Great City of Alexandria and of all Egypt, the Middle East, Ethiopia, Nubia, and the Pentapolis."

[17] *Acta Apostolicae Sedis* 65 (1973) 300.

soluble union of Godhead and Manhood in Christ despite the phrase 'in two natures.' "[18]

The statement also deals with problems of terminology:

> For those of us in the Western tradition, to hear of the one nature of Christ can be misleading, because it may be misunderstood as a denial of his humanity. For those of us in the Oriental Orthodox Churches to hear of two natures can be misleading because it can be misunderstood as affirming two persons in Christ. But both sides agree in rejecting Eutychianism and Nestorianism. ...
>
> Our common effort to clarify the meaning of the Greek terms *hypostasis* and *physis* in the trinitarian and christological contexts made us realize how difficult it was to find a satisfactory definition of these terms that could do justice to both contexts in a consistent manner.[19]

The communiqué also calls for new terminology that would express more effectively the mystery of Christ for people today.

Since 1973, Popes and heads of Oriental Orthodox churches have affirmed repeatedly that they share the same faith in Christ, an assumption taken for granted in most of their statements. For instance, during his visit to Rome in June 1983, Moran Mar Baselius Marthoma Mathews I, the Catholicos of the Malankara Orthodox Syrian Church of India, quoted Cyril of Alexandria's "one divine-human nature" formula as being part of the common faith of the two churches.[20]

Another significant christological text was issued in June 1984, at the conclusion of the visit of Syrian Orthodox Patriarch Ignatius Zakka I Iwas to Rome. The Pope and Patriarch maintained in their *Common Declaration* that past schisms "in no way affect or touch the substance of their faith," since the divisions arose from terminologi-

---

[18] "Communiqué," *Wort und Wahrheit*, Supplementary Issue No. 2 (Vienna: Herder, 1974) 175-176.

[19] Ibid., 176.

[20] *Information Service* 52 (1983/III) 74.

cal misunderstandings. They then made the following joint confession of faith in the mystery of the Word made flesh:

> In our turn we confess that He became incarnate for us, taking to himself a real body with a rational soul. He shared our humanity in all things but sin. We confess that our Lord and our God, our Saviour and the King of all, Jesus Christ, is perfect God as to His divinity and perfect man as to His humanity. This Union is real, perfect, without blending or mingling, without confusion, without alteration, without division, without the least separation. He who is God eternal and invisible, became visible in the flesh and took the form of servant. In Him are united, in a real, perfect indivisible and inseparable way, divinity and humanity, and in Him all their properties are present and active.[21]

Catholic and Coptic representatives meeting at Amba Bishoy monastery in February 1988 reaffirmed the christological agreement found in the 1973 *Common Declaration*. They also adopted this more concise formulation which was intended to make the christological accord more accessible to the faithful:

> We believe that our Lord, God and Saviour Jesus Christ, the Incarnate-Logos, is perfect in His Divinity and perfect in His Humanity. He made His Humanity One with His Divinity without Mixture, nor Mingling, nor Confusion. His Divinity was not separated from His Humanity even for a moment or twinkling of an eye. At the same time, we Anathematize the Doctrines of both Nestorius and Eutyches.[22]

This progress on christology was noted with satisfaction by the participants at the fifth *Pro Oriente* consultation in September 1988. They went on to emphasize the following:

> ... that the great mystery of the Incarnation of the Son of God could not be exhaustively formulated in words, and that within the limits of condemned errors like Arianism, Nestorianism and Eutychianism, a certain plurality of expressions was permissible in relation to the inseparable and unconfused hypostatic unity of the human and the di-

---

[21] *Information Service* 55 (1984/II-III) 62.

[22] *Information Service* 69 (1989/1) 8.

vine in one Lord Jesus Christ, the Word of God incarnate by the Holy Spirit of the Blessed Virgin Mary, consubstantial with God the Father in His divinity and consubstantial with us in his humanity.[23]

Another christological agreement was reached at the first meeting of the new Joint International Commission for Dialogue between the Catholic Church and the Malankara Syrian Orthodox Church of India, held at Kottayam in October 1989.[24] The statement was officially approved by the authorities of both churches and published on June 3, 1990. It includes this text on the relationship between Christ's humanity and divinity in paragraph 5:

> Our Lord Jesus Christ is one, perfect in his humanity and perfect in his divinity, at once consubstantial with the Father in his divinity, and consubstantial with us in his humanity. His humanity is one with his divinity — without change, without commingling, without division and without separation. In the Person of the Eternal Logos Incarnate are united and active in a real and perfect way the divine and human natures, with all their properties, faculties and operations.[25]

This put an end to any christological disagreement between the Catholic and Malankara Orthodox Syrian churches.

The *Common Declaration* signed by Pope John Paul II and Armenian Catholicos Karekin I at the end of the Catholicos' visit to Rome in December 1996 contained the following affirmation of agreement in the area of christology:

> [The Pope and Catholicos] particularly welcome the great advance that their Churches have registered in their common search for their unity in Christ, the word of God made flesh. Perfect God as to His divinity, perfect man as to His humanity, His divinity is united in Him to His humanity in the Person of the Only-begotten Son of God, in a

---

[23] "Communiqué," *Wort und Wahrheit*, Supplementary Issue No. 5 (Vienna: Herder, 1989) 149.

[24] See G. Daucourt, "First meeting for dialogue with Syrian Orthodox Church of India," *L'Osservatore Romano*, English weekly edition, November 27, 1989, 2.

[25] *L'Osservatore Romano*, June 3, 1990, 5.

union which is real, perfect, without confusion, without alteration, without division, without any form of separation.

The reality of this common faith in Jesus Christ and in the same succession of apostolic ministry has at times been obscured or ignored. Linguistic, cultural and political factors have immensely contributed towards the theological divergences that have found expression in their terminology of formulating their doctrines. His Holiness John Paul II and His Holiness Karekin I have expressed their determined conviction that because of the fundamental common faith in God and in Jesus Christ, the controversies and unhappy divisions which sometimes have followed upon the divergent ways in expressing it, as a result of the present declaration, should not continue to influence the life and witness of the Church today.[26]

A careful reading of the statements issued over the past 30 years indicates that the ancient christological dispute between the Oriental Orthodox churches and the Catholic Church has been substantially resolved. Even though different interpretations of the meaning of the Chalcedonian definition remain, the churches have been able to set aside the old disputes and affirm that their faith in the mystery of Christ which transcends all formulations is, in fact, the same.

2. Ecclesiology

Progress has also been made in the area of ecclesiology, although certain differences remain to be resolved. The nature of an ecumenical council has figured prominently in the theological discussion, since the Oriental Orthodox have received only the first three of the seven ancient councils accepted by the Catholic and Orthodox churches. The concept and exercise of primacy is another area of disagreement, especially since the Oriental Orthodox have no experience of primacy among their six independent churches. Not even a limited form of primacy exists similar to the role that the Patriarchate of

---

[26] *Information Service* 94 (1997/I) 30.

Constantinople plays among the Orthodox churches. A third sensitive area is the existence of the Eastern Catholic churches and the related question of proselytism between members of the two communions.

Before examining these areas of disparity, it is necessary to review the way both churches have consistently stated their recognition of the ecclesial reality of the other. Statements of this type are found at the very beginning of the series of visits between Popes and Oriental Orthodox hierarchs. In May 1970, when Catholicos Vasken I visited Pope Paul VI, he said, "We have remembered, as in a reawakening, that we have been brothers for the past two thousand years."[27] Paul VI responded:

> Let us give thanks to the Lord together that day by day the profound sacramental reality existing between our Churches is made known to us, beyond the daily differences and the hostilities of the past.[28]

And in their *Common Declaration* at the conclusion of the visit, the two church leaders affirmed that collaboration and research "must be founded on reciprocal recognition of the Christian faith and of common sacramental life, on mutual respect of persons and of their Churches."[29]

The *Common Declaration* of Paul VI and Coptic Pope Shenouda III in May 1973 stated that Catholics and Copts are rediscovering each other as churches despite the divisions of the past:

> These differences cannot be ignored. In spite of them, however, we are rediscovering ourselves as Churches with a common inheritance and are reaching out with determination and confidence in the Lord to achieve the fullness and perfection of that unity which is His gift.[30]

During his visit to Istanbul in 1979, John Paul II spoke to Armenian Patriarch Shnork of "the unity which already exists between us."

[27] *Information Service* 94 (1970/III) 9.
[28] Ibid.
[29] *Acta Apostolicae Sedis* 62 (1970) 416.
[30] *Acta Apostolicae Sedis* 65 (1973) 300-301.

And in response, Patriarch Shnork indicated that both are parts of the one Church:

> Such visits serve the praiseworthy purpose of deepening the love, respect, and mutual understanding between various parts of the Christian Church. We shall always pray that God may bless this renewal of relations, which is manifested through such visits.[31]

This recognition of the full ecclesial reality of both churches has been stated repeatedly during subsequent visits and in common declarations. For instance, in 1981 John Paul II made the following statement to Ethiopian Orthodox Patriarch Tekle Haimanot:

> The contacts which we have reestablished are now enabling us to rediscover the profound and true reality of this existing unity. Even the real divergences between us are being seen more clearly as we gradually free them from so many secondary elements that derive from ambiguities of language.[32]

Armenian Catholicos Karekin I and Pope John Paul II spoke of the deep spiritual communion that already exists between their churches in their 1996 *Common Declaration*:

> Pope John Paul II and Catholicos Karekin I recognize the deep spiritual communion which already unites them and the bishops, clergy and lay faithful of their Churches. It is a communion which finds its roots in the common faith in the holy and life-giving Trinity proclaimed by the apostles and transmitted down the centuries by the many Church Fathers, Church doctors, bishops, priests, and martyrs who have followed them. They rejoice in the fact that recent developments of ecumenical relationships and theological discussions carried out in the spirit of Christian love and fellowship have dispelled many misunderstandings inherited from the controversies and dissensions of the past. Such dialogues and encounters have prepared a healthy situation of mutual understanding and recovery of the deeper spiritual communion based on the common faith in the Holy Trinity that they

---

[31] *Information Service* 41 (1979/IV) 28.

[32] *Information Service* 47 (1981/III-IV) 100.

have been given through the Gospel of Christ and in the Holy Tradition of the Church.[33]

In later pronouncements, John Paul II and heads of Oriental Orthodox churches have listed areas of cooperation which this rediscovered relationship makes possible. The *Joint Communiqué* issued at the end of the visit to Rome of Armenian Catholicos Karekin II of Cilicia in April 1983 encouraged cooperation in the theological formation of clerics and laity, catechetical instruction, practical solutions of situations of common pastoral concern, social action, cultural promotion, and humanitarian services.[34]

In their *Common Declaration* (June 1984), Pope John Paul II and Patriarch Ignatius Zakka I Iwas considered the two churches so close that they even envisaged cooperation in pastoral care, including some sacramental sharing:

> It is not rare, in fact, for our faithful to find access to a priest of their own Church materially or morally impossible. Anxious to meet their needs and with their spiritual benefit in mind, we authorize them in such cases to ask for the sacraments of penance, Eucharist, and anointing of the sick from lawful priests of either of our two sister Churches, when they need them.[35]

The historic nature of this declaration goes without saying. It is the first time in modern history that the Catholic Church and a church separated from it have agreed mutually to allow some forms of sacramental sharing. The same declaration also envisages cooperation in the formation and education of clergy:

> It would be a logical corollary of collaboration in pastoral care to cooperate in priestly formation and theological education. Bishops are

---

[33] *Information Service* 94 (1970/III) 30.

[34] *Information Service* 51 (1983/I-II) 40.

[35] *Information Service* 55 (1984/II-III) 63.

encouraged to promote sharing of facilities for theological education where they judge it to be advisable.[36]

All this was made possible because of the Pope and Patriarch's common wish:

> ... to widen the horizon of their brotherhood and affirm herewith the terms of the deep spiritual communion which already unites them and the prelates, clergy, and faithful of both their Churches, to consolidate these ties of Faith, Hope, and Love, and to advance in finding a wholly common ecclesial life.[37]

Many modes of cooperation were envisaged in the 1996 *Common Declaration* of the Pope and Armenian Catholicos:

> The communion already existing between the two Churches and the hope for and commitment to the recovery of full communion between them should become factors of motivation for further contact, more regular and substantial dialogue, leading to a greater degree of mutual understanding and recovery of the communality of their faith and service.
>
> Pope John Paul II and Catholicos Karekin I give their blessing and pastoral support to the further development of existing contacts and to new manifestations of that dialogue of charity between their respective pastors and faithful which will bear fruit in the fields of common action on the pastoral, catechetical, social and intellectual levels.
>
> Such a dialogue is particularly imperative in these present times when the Churches are faced with new challenges to their witness to the Gospel of Jesus Christ arising out of the rapidly changing situations in the modern world so deeply affected by an extreme secularistic and secularizing pace of life and culture. It requires closer collaboration, mutual confidence and a greater degree of concern for common action. It presumes and requires an attitude of service which is not self-seeking and which is characterized by a mutual respect for the fidelity of the faithful to their own churches and Christian traditions.
>
> They appeal to their clergy and laity to carry out more actively and effectively their full cooperation in all fields of diaconia, and to be-

---

[36] Ibid.

[37] Ibid., 62.

come agents of reconciliation, peace and justice, struggling for the true recognition of human rights and dedicating themselves to the support of all those who are suffering and are in spiritual and material need throughout the world.[38]

Recent speeches and common declarations now frequently state that what unites the churches is far greater than what divides them; these communications also list common elements such as belief in the Trinity, the mystery of Christ, the apostolic traditions, the sacraments, the Theotokos, and especially the first three ecumenical councils.

In spite of all this, important areas of disagreement remain. Participants at the second *Pro Oriente* theological consultation in 1973 considered ecclesiological questions for the first time, and the third and fourth meetings were devoted entirely to this area. Ecclesiological issues also figured prominently at the fifth meeting.

The communiqué of the second consultation treated the question of ecumenical councils and the relationship between the papacy and councils in a tentative way. The members agreed that the first three councils have a "greater degree of fullness" because of their wider acceptance by Christians. Moreover, they "look forward to future regional and ecumenical councils with larger representation as the reunion of churches is hastened by the working of the Holy Spirit." On the relationship between Pope and Council, they praised the notion of collegiality expressed in the documents of Vatican II as "a move in the right direction according to which the role of the bishop of Rome is seen within the Council and not above it."[39]

The theologians were able to reach greater consensus on these issues in 1976 at the third *Pro Oriente* meeting. The communiqué described areas of agreement on the nature of the Church and the notion of conciliarity. The text begins by affirming that unity is Christ's

---

[38] *Information Service* 94 (1997/I) 31.

[39] "Communiqué," *Wort und Wahrheit,* Supplementary Issue No. 2 (Vienna: Herder, 1974) 176.

gift to the Church. This is a unity which allows for a "multiplicity of traditions," in which "diversity has to be held together by basic unity in fundamental matters."

The communiqué goes on to speak of the identity of the local and universal churches:

> One and the same Church, for there cannot be more than one, is manifested both locally and universally as a koinonia of truth and love, characterized by eucharistic communion and the corporate unity of the episcopate. The unity of the Church has its source and proto-type in the unity of the Father, the Son and the Holy Spirit, into which we have been baptized.[40]

Conciliarity is described as:

> ... the understanding of the Church as koinonia, so essential to the na-ture of the Church as the Body of Christ, and so clearly visible in the structure of its life and leadership from the very inception.[41]

The communiqué considers the council or synod both as a single event and as a continuing structure of the Church's life. Insofar as it is an event, the theologians stated:

> [We] could not agree on how and by whom such a worldwide council of our Churches should be convoked and conducted, nor could we agree completely on the procedure for the reception of past or future councils.[42]

Nevertheless, they agreed that churches have the right to convoke a council:

> ... whenever found necessary and possible though there is no neces-sity to hold ecumenical councils at given intervals as a permanent structure of the Church. We recognize the need of structures of coor-dination between the autocephalous Churches for the settlement of

---

[40] "Communiqué," *Wort und Wahrheit*, Supplementary Issue No. 3 (Vienna: Herder, 1976) 223.

[41] Ibid.

[42] Ibid.

disputes and for facing together the problems and tasks confronting our Churches in the modern world.[43]

The question of councils was taken up again in the communiqué issued by the fifth consultation in 1988. It reaffirms that the first three ecumenical councils provided the basis for the common faith of Catholics and Oriental Orthodox and acknowledged that the Oriental Orthodox are "not in a position formally to accept" the Council of Chalcedon and the ones following it. However, further study of the later councils was recommended. The communiqué also examined the nature of the reception of conciliar teaching and recognized it as a complex process that sometimes does not include formal reception of conciliar decisions as such.[44]

The fourth consultation (September 1978) discussed two more problems which divide the Catholic and Oriental Orthodox churches: the notion of primacy and the status of Eastern Catholic churches. Primacy was taken up again at the fifth meeting.

The communiqué of the fourth consultation describes primacy in the context of what it calls three integrally related elements in the life of the Church: primacy, conciliarity, and the consensus of the believing community. It recognizes, however, that "their relative importance has been differently understood in different situations."

The Oriental Orthodox understand primacy as being "of historical and ecclesiological origin," while Catholics see it as part of "the divine plan for the Church." Yet both sides acknowledge that primacy is connected with the continuing guidance of the Holy Spirit within the Church. The Catholic teachings about the primacy of the bishop of Rome "are to be understood in the context of their historical, sociological and political conditions and also in the light of the historical

---

[43] Ibid., 223-224.

[44] "Communiqué," *Wort und Wahrheit*, Supplementary Issue Number 5 (Vienna: Herder, 1989) 149-150.

evolution of the whole teaching of the Roman Church, a process which is still continuing."[45]

The Oriental Orthodox, on the other hand, "have not felt it necessary to formulate verbally and declare their understanding of primacy though it is clearly implied in the continuing life and teaching of their Churches."[46]

The consultation called for more research and reflection on primacy "with a new vision for our future unity."

With regard to infallibility, both sides affirmed that it "pertains to the Church as a whole." But they could not agree on "the relative importance of different organs in the Church through which this inerrant teaching authority is to find expression."

The participants stated that Catholics and Oriental Orthodox should strive toward the following goal:

> ... full union of sister Churches — with communion in the faith, in the sacraments of the Church, in ministry and within a canonical structure. Each Church as well as all Churches together will have a primatial and conciliar structure, providing for their communion in a given place as well as on regional and worldwide scale.[47]

The statement goes on to address the focus of such communion and the role that Rome might play in it:

> The structure will be basically conciliar. No single Church in this communion will by itself be regarded as the source and origin of that communion; the source of the unity of the Church is the action of the triune God, Father, Son and Holy Spirit. It is the same Spirit who operates in all sister Churches the same faith, hope and love, as well as ministry and sacraments. About regarding one particular Church as the center of the unity, there was no agreement, though the need of a special ministry for unity was recognized by all.

---

[45] "Communiqué," *Wort und Wahrheit*, Supplementary Issue Number 4 (Vienna: Herder, 1978) 233.

[46] Ibid.

[47] Ibid.

This communion will find diverse means of expression — the exchange of letters of peace among the Churches, the public liturgical remembering of the Churches and their primates by each other, the placing of responsibility for convoking general synods in order to deal with common concerns of the Churches, and so on.[48]

At the fifth consultation in 1988 the members recognized that both the Catholic and Oriental Orthodox churches possess some form of primacy, always related to the conciliar nature of the Church. In the Catholic Church the Bishop of Rome's primacy serves the unity of all the churches; the Oriental Orthodox experience primacy *within* each of their six independent churches, not at a level above them. Members of the consultation recommended further study of this question and acknowledged that in practice some form of both central coordination and local autonomy was needed.[49]

This lack of full agreement on the function of conciliarity and primacy within the Church explains why these topics are almost never mentioned in the speeches and common declarations issued as a result of visits between Popes and heads of Oriental Orthodox churches. The 1973 *Common Declaration* of Pope Paul VI and Pope Shenouda III contains the broad sentence, "We have, to a large degree, the same understanding of the Church, founded upon the Apostles, and of the important role of ecumenical and local councils."[50] The fact that nothing more specific could be said indicates the continuing divergence in the two churches' understanding of this important area in ecclesial life. In fact, after the 1973 meeting between Paul VI and Shenouda III, there were no visits between a Pope and the head of an Oriental Orthodox church for six years. The next contact occurred when a Coptic Orthodox delegation visited John Paul II in 1979. The delegation carried a letter to John Paul in which Shenouda

---

[48] Ibid.

[49] "Communiqué," *Wort und Wahrheit*, Supplementary Issue Number 5, (Vienna: Herder, 1989) 150.

[50] *Acta Apostolicae Sedis* 65 (1973) 300.

expressed his concern about the lack of progress in the area of ecclesiology.

The 1973 *Common Declaration* had set up a special Joint Commission between the Catholic and Coptic Orthodox churches to "guide common study in the fields of Church tradition, patristics, liturgy, theology, history and practical problems, so that by cooperation in common we may seek to resolve, in a spirit of mutual respect, the differences existing between our Churches."[51] By 1979, this commission had met four times in Cairo[52] and continued to make progress in the area of christology but not ecclesiology, as Pope Shenouda wrote in his letter to John Paul:

> In ecclesiology only very little real progress has been reached. This is why we thought it appropriate to delegate an official delegation of six members of the official Commission, in order to enhance the negotiations between our two Churches, which seem to have stopped at a point without reaching further steps of real progress in the achievement of the unity of our two Churches.[53]

In his speech to the delegation, Pope John Paul responded to some concerns raised in Pope Shenouda's letter. Although he did not address the question of conciliarity, he did speak on the role of the papacy in the dialogue:

> I know that one of the fundamental questions of the ecumenical movement is the nature of that full communion we are seeking with each other and the role that the Bishop of Rome has to play, by God's design, in serving that communion of faith and spiritual life, which is nourished by the sacraments and expressed in fraternal charity. A

---

[51] Ibid., 301.

[52] See reports on these meetings in *Proche Orient Chrétien*: "La commission mixte de l'Église copte orthodoxe et de l'Église catholique," 24 (1974) 68-69; "Première réunion de la commission mixte des Églises catholique et copte orthodoxe," 24 (1974) 175-178; "Deuxième réunion de la commission mixte," 25 (1975) 314-316; "[Troisième] Réunion de la commission mixte," 26 (1976) 360-361; "[Quatrième] Réunion de la commission mixte," 29 (1979) 107-109.

[53] *Information Services* 41 (1979/IV) 8.

great deal of progress has been made in deepening our understanding of this question. Much remains to be done. I consider your visit to me and to the See of Rome a significant contribution towards resolving this question definitively.[54]

One could raise a question about how Pope John Paul understood the visit of the Coptic delegation to Rome as "a significant contribution towards resolving this question definitively." Perhaps this statement gives an example of the kind of communion he would envisage taking place after the reestablishment of unity: occasional official visits between heads of sister churches to inform the universal primate about the lives of their churches, or the type of communion outlined in the fourth *Pro Oriente* communiqué.

In the same speech, Pope John Paul emphasized that the re-establishment of communion between the churches would not imply a loss of the identity of either of them:

> Fundamental to this dialogue is the recognition that the richness of this unity in faith and spiritual life has to be expressed in diversity of forms. Unity — whether on the universal level or the local level — does not mean uniformity or absorption of one group by another. It is rather at the service of all groups to help each live better the proper gifts it has received from God's Spirit. ... With no one trying to dominate each other but to serve each other, all together will grow into that perfection of unity for which Our Lord prayed on the night before he died.[55]

Unfortunately, the political situation in Egypt worsened soon after this visit, and Pope Shenouda was placed under house arrest by President Sadat in September 1981. This brought the dialogue between the Catholic and Coptic Orthodox churches to a virtual stand-

---

[54] Ibid., 7.
[55] Ibid.

still. It was only after Pope Shenouda's release in January 1985 that the commission could resume its work.[56]

In their *Common Declaration* of June 1984, Pope John Paul II and Syrian Patriarch Ignatius Zakka I Iwas added significant new elements to the developing ecclesiological consensus between the two communions. This declaration draws from the work of other interconfessional dialogues, and it places the Eucharist at the center of its understanding of the Church. Here the Eucharist is shown to be much more than one of the seven sacraments that Catholics and Syrian Orthodox have in common:

> Sacramental life finds in the holy Eucharist its fulfillment and its summit, in such a way that it is through the Eucharist that the Church most profoundly realizes and reveals its nature. ... The other Sacraments ... are ordered to that celebration of the holy Eucharist which is the centre of sacramental life and the chief visible expression of ecclesial communion. This communion of Christians with each other and of local Churches united around their lawful Bishops is realized in the gathered community which confesses the same faith.[57]

This is the first time that a common declaration makes such a connection between Church, Eucharist, and bishop. It represents an

---

[56] The first phase of the commission's work was concluded with the adoption of a brief christological statement in 1988. The second phase, which was to examine other issues, began with the commission's fifth meeting at Amba Bishoy monastery in October 1988. The discussion at this meeting centered on the mystery of the redemption and the final destiny of the human person. See report in *Irénikon* 61 (1988) 537-539, *Information Service* 68 (1988/III-IV) 164, and *Proche Orient Chrétien* 39 (1989) 330-333. The sixth session, which took place at the same monastery in April 1990, discussed the procession of the Holy Spirit and the *filioque*. See *Proche Orient Chrétien* 40 (1990) 301-303, and *Irénikon* 63 (1990) 213-215. The seventh session, held in April 1991, studied the situation of the faithful after death and the Catholic teaching on purgatory. It also set up a joint pastoral commission to deal with concrete local problems involving the faithful of the two communities. See *Irénikon* 64 (1991) 236-237, and *Proche Orient Chrétien* 41 (1991) 362-364. The discussion continued at the eighth meeting in February 1992: *Irénikon* 65 (1992) 63-65. The ninth meeting, scheduled for April 1993, had to be canceled because of technical difficulties.

[57] *Information Service* 55 (1984/II-III) 62.

ecclesiological advance which needs to be amplified in future statements.

Another question concerning relations between Catholics and Oriental Orthodox focuses on the Eastern Catholic churches. Until recently, Rome has presented its relationship with the Eastern Catholic churches as a model for the relationship that should exist between the Catholic Church and any eastern church that might come into communion with it.[58] The Oriental Orthodox, however, often take great offense at the very existence of these churches, which are frequently the direct result of Catholic missionary activity among the Oriental Orthodox faithful. They see in this a denial of the ecclesial reality of the Oriental Orthodox churches by the Catholic Church and claim that some Eastern Catholics continue to proselytize even now among the Oriental Orthodox faithful.

The first mention of the Eastern Catholic churches in encounters between Popes and Oriental Orthodox hierarchs is found in the speech Paul VI delivered in the presence of Armenian Catholicos of Cilicia Khoren I in May 1967. Perhaps not attuned to Oriental Orthodox sensitivities in this matter, the Pope expressed his affection for the Armenian tradition by recalling the *Decree for the Armenians* of the Council of Florence, the foundation of the Armenian College in Rome, the Armenian Catholic presence in Venice, and highly placed Armenian Catholics in the Roman Curia.[59] He made similar references in a speech during the visit of Catholicos Vasken I of Etchmiadzin in 1970.[60]

---

[58] See letter of Cardinal Willebrands to Russian Orthodox Metropolitan Juvenaly of September 22, 1979, where, in the context of a misunderstanding about a papal statement on the status of the Ukrainian Catholic Church, the Cardinal wrote, "There was no intention whatever of presenting the Union of Brest as the model for our relations with the Orthodox Churches today or as one for the contemplated future union." Text in T. Stransky and J. Sheerin, *Doing the Truth in Charity* (Ramsey: Paulist, 1982) 228.

[59] *Acta Apostolicae Sedis* 59 (1967) 511-512.

[60] *Information Service* 11 (1970/III) 5.

Oriental Orthodox concern about the activity of Eastern Catholics was mentioned indirectly in the *Common Declaration* of Paul VI and Shenouda III in 1973, which rejected all forms of proselytism as incompatible with the relationship that should exist between the two churches:

> ... We reject all forms of proselytism, in the sense of acts by which persons seek to disturb each other's communities by recruiting new members from each other through methods, or because of attitudes of mind, which are opposed to the exigencies of Christian love or to what should characterize the relationships between Churches. Let it cease, where it may exist.[61]

This statement was a response to Pope Shenouda's complaint that Coptic Catholics were proselytizing among Coptic Orthodox in Egypt. The Coptic Catholic Patriarch was reminded of this statement in a letter from Pope Paul soon thereafter.[62]

This issue has not been taken up in any of the speeches and common declarations since 1973. However, the fourth *Pro Oriente* meeting of 1978 made the following statement:

> The Oriental Catholic Churches will not even in the transitional period before full unity be regarded as a device for bringing Oriental Orthodox Churches inside the Roman communion. Their role will be more in terms of collaborating in the restoration of eucharistic communion among the sister Churches. The Oriental Orthodox Churches, according to the principles of Vatican II and subsequent statements of the See of Rome, cannot be fields of mission for other Churches. The sister Churches will work out local solutions, in accordance with differing local situations, implementing as far as possible the principle of a unified episcopate for each locality.[63]

---

[61] *Acta Apostolicae Sedis* 65 (1973) 301.

[62] "Lettre du Pape Paul VI au Patriarche copte catholique," *Proche Orient Chrétien* 24 (1974) 351-354.

[63] "Communiqué," *Wort und Wahrheit* Supplementary Issue No. 4 (Vienna: Herder, 1978) 233-234.

The position of the Catholic Church which emerges from these statements is twofold. While it affirms the right of the Eastern Catholic churches to exist, it also gives assurances that Catholics are not to proselytize among Oriental Orthodox Christians. Even so, many Oriental Orthodox remain suspicious of the true intentions of their Eastern Catholic counterparts and continue to feel with resentment that these churches are made up of their own faithful who have been unjustly taken away from them.

The contemporary relationship between the Catholic and Oriental Orthodox churches is unique, and the resolution of the christological divergences between the two communions is unprecedented. In no other ecumenical relationship has a dogmatic disagreement of this type been overcome so unequivocally, and with such official approbation. This was achieved without any official bilateral dialogue taking place.[64] The interplay of unofficial theological consultations and official pronouncements made by church leaders proved to be an effective means of resolving a centuries-old problem.

At the same time, the lack of any clearly defined ministry serving the unity of the various Oriental Orthodox churches has necessitated a rather piecemeal process by which levels of agreement with individual churches differ. The lack of a specific christological accord with the Ethiopian and Eritrean churches somewhat relativizes the importance of the understanding reached with the Copts, Syrians, Armenians, and Malankaras. Nevertheless, progress has been substantial and provides real hope for the future.

Ecclesiology remains the area of greatest disagreement. It is doubtful that any of the Oriental Orthodox churches will accept a

---

[64] It should be noted that the fifth *Pro Oriente* consultation in 1988 "urgently appeals to all the Churches represented here to set up a joint official body to engage in that formal dialogue between the Roman Catholic Church and the family of the Oriental Orthodox Churches which will have as its objective the achieving of full communion in faith and sacramental life." See text in *Wort und Wahrheit*, Supplementary Issue No. 5 (Vienna: Herder, 1989) 151.

form of unity with the Catholic Church that does not fully respect their administrative independence. And the Catholic Church must decide if full communion with another church necessarily means that the Bishop of Rome must have unlimited authority to intervene in the affairs of the other church. These issues will provide ample material for research and reflection in the years to come as the relationship between these churches reaches greater maturity.

Official Visits: Popes and Oriental Orthodox Hierarchs

1. Armenian Catholicos Khoren I to Paul VI
   Rome, May 9, 1967
   2 Speeches
   Acta Apostolicae Sedis 59 (1967) 510-12
   L'Osservatore Romano (May 10, 1967) 1

2. Paul VI to Patriarch Shnork Kalustian
   Istanbul, July 25-26, 1967
   2 Speeches
   Information Service (1967/3) 13-14

3. Armenian Catholicos Vasken I to Paul VI
   Rome, May 8-12, 1970
   a) 4 Speeches
   Information Service 11 (1970/III) 3-10
   b) Common Declaration
   Acta Apostolicae Sedis 62 (1970) 416-7

(First *Pro Oriente* Theological Consultation:
Vienna, Austria September 7-12, 1971)

4. Syrian Patriarch Ignatius Yacoub III to Paul VI
   Rome, October 25-27, 1971
   a) 4 Speeches
   Information Service 16 (1972/I) 3-5
   b) Common Declaration
   Acta Apostolicae Sedis 63 (1971) 814-815

5. Coptic Pope Shenouda III to Paul VI
   Rome, May 4-10, 1973
   a) 8 Speeches
      Information Service 22 (1973/IV) 3-10
   b) Common Declaration
      Acta Apostolicae Sedis 65 (1973) 299-301

(Second *Pro Oriente* Theological Consultation:
Vienna, Austria, September 3-9, 1973)

(Third *Pro Oriente* Theological Consultation:
Vienna, Austria, August 30 to September 5, 1976)

(Fourth *Pro Oriente* Theological Consultation:
Vienna, Austria, September 11-17, 1978)

6. Reception of Coptic Delegation by John Paul II
   Rome, June 23, 1979
   a) Letter from Pope Shenouda
   b) Speech by John Paul II
      Information Service 41 (1979/IV) 6-8

7. John Paul II to Armenian Patriarch Shnork
   Istanbul, November 29, 1979
   2 Speeches
   Information Service 41 (1979/IV) 28-29

8. Syrian Patriarch Ignatius Yacoub III to John Paul II
   Rome, May 13-16, 1980
   4 Speeches
   Information Service 44 (1980/III-IV) 92-95

9. Reception of Ethiopian Orthodox Delegation by John Paul II
   Rome, July 16-19, 1980
   Two Letters
   Information Service 44 (1980/III-IV) 97-98

10. Ethiopian Patriarch Tekle Haimanot to John Paul II
    Rome, October 17, 1981
    2 Speeches
    Information Service 47 (1981/III-IV) 100-101

11. Armenian Catholicos Karekin II to John Paul II
    Rome, April 15-19, 1983
    a) 2 Speeches
    b) Joint Communiqué
    Information Service 51 (1983/I-II) 37-41

12. Syrian Catholicos of India Moran Mar Baselius
    Marthoma Mathews I to John Paul II
    Rome, June 2-5, 1983
    2 Speeches
    Information Service 52 (1983/III) 72-75

13. Syrian Patriarch Ignatius Zakka I Iwas to John Paul II
    Rome, June 20-23, 1984
    a) 2 Speeches
    b) Common Declaration
    Information Service 55 (1984/II-III) 59-63

14. John Paul II to Mar Basileus Paulos II, Catholicos of the
    Malankara Jacobite Syrian Orthodox Church
    Kottayam, India, February 7, 1986
    Speech of Pope John Paul II
    Information Service 60 (1986/I-II) 12-13

15. John Paul II to Syrian Catholicos of India Moran
    Mar Baselius Marthoma Mathews I
    Kottayam, India, February 8, 1986
    a) Speech of John Paul II
       Information Service 60 (1986/I-II) 13-14
       Star of the East 8 (1986) 8-9
    b) Speech of Catholicos Marthoma Mathews I
       The Star of the East 8 (1986) 5-7

(Fifth *Pro Oriente* Theological Consultation:
Vienna, Austria, September 18-25, 1988)

16. Ethiopian Patriarch Abuna Paulos to John Paul II
    Rome, June 11, 1993.
    a) Speech of John Paul II
       L'Osservatore Romano, 11-12 June 1993, p. 4.

17. Armenian Catholicos Karekin I to John Paul II
    Rome, December 10-14, 1996.
    a) Common Declaration
    b) Speech of John Paul II
    c) Speech of Catholicos Karekin I
       Information Service 94 (1997/I) 27-31

BIBLIOGRAPHY

This bibliography contains only the major works that were consulted in compiling this book, plus a limited selection of books in English on various aspects of the eastern churches for further reading.

Anglican-Orthodox Dialogue: The Dublin Agreed Statement 1984. London: SPCK, 1985. Contains all Anglican-Orthodox agreed statements from 1976 onwards.

Annuario Pontificio 1998. Vatican City: Editrice Vaticana, 1998.

Atiya, A. *A History of Eastern Christianity.* London: Methuen & Co., 1968. A history of the Assyrian and Oriental Orthodox Churches.

Attwater, Donald. *The Christian Churches of the East* (2 Volumes). Milwaukee: Bruce, 1961.

Autocephaly: The Orthodox Church in America. Crestwood, New York: St. Vladimir's, 1971. Documentation and essays on the status of the OCA from an OCA perspective.

Barrett, D., ed. *World Christian Encyclopedia.* Oxford: Oxford University Press, 1982. Exhaustive statistical presentation of Christianity in every country.

Betts, R.B. *Christians in the Arab East.* Athens: Lycabettus, 1978.

Bolshakoff, S. *Russian Mystics.* Kalamazoo: Cistercian Publications, 1980.

Borelli, J. and J. Erickson, eds. *The Quest for Unity: Orthodox and Catholics in Dialogue.* Crestwood, NY and Washington, DC: St. Vladimir's Seminary Press and the United States Catholic Conference, 1996. Contains all the documents produced by the international and North American dialogues.

Bria, I., ed. *Martyria/Mission: The Witness of the Orthodox Churches Today.* Geneva: WCC, 1980.

Bulgakov, S. *The Orthodox Church.* Revised translation by L. Kesich. Crestwood, NY: St. Vladimir's, 1988.

Cabasilas, Nicholas. *The Life in Christ*. Crestwood, NY: St. Vladimir's, 1974. Classic 14th century work on liturgical/sacramental spirituality.

Chrysostomos, Bishop, with Bishop Auxentios and Archimandrite Ambrosios, *The Old Calendar Orthodox Church of Greece*. Etna, California: Center for Tradtionalist Orthodox Studies, 1991.

Clément, Olivier. *Conversations with Ecumenical Patriarch Bartholomew I*. Crestwood, NY: St. Vladimir's Seminary Press, 1997.

Code of Canons of the Eastern Churches: Latin-English Edition. Washington, DC: Canon Law Society of America, 1992.

Constantelos, D. *Understanding the Greek Orthodox Church: Its Faith, History and Practice*. New York: Seabury, 1982.

Cragg, Kenneth, *The Arab Christian: A History in the Middle East*. London: Mowbray, 1991.

Daniel, David. *The Orthodox Church of India*. New Delhi: Miss Rachel David, 1972.

Davis, Nathaniel. *A Long Walk to Church: A Contemporary History of Russian Orthodoxy*. Boulder, Colorado: Westview Press, 1995.

Descy, Serge. *The Melkite Church: An Historical and Ecclesiological Approach*. Newton, Massachusetts: Sophia Press, 1993.

Δίπτυχα τῆς Ἐκκλησίας τῆς Ἑλλάδος 1998. Athens: Apostoliki Diakonia, 1997.

Directory of Orthodox Parishes and Clergy in the British Isles 1988/89. Welshpool: Stylite Publishing, 1988.

Dvornik, F. *Byzantium and the Roman Primacy*. New York: Fordham University Press, 1966.

Efthimiou, M., and G. Christopoulos. *A History of the Greek Orthodox Church in America*. New York: Greek Orthodox Archdiocese, 1984.

Ellis, J. *The Russian Orthodox Church: A Contemporary History*. London and Sydney: Croom Helm, 1986.

Every, G. *Understanding Eastern Christianity*. Bangalore: Dharmaram Publications, 1978.

Fortescue, A. *The Lesser Eastern Churches*. London: Catholic Truth Society, 1913.

Fries, Paul and Tiran Nersoyan, eds. *Christ in East and West*. Macon, Georgia: Mercer University Press, 1987.

Geanakoplos, Deno, *A Short History of the Ecumenical Patriarchate of Constantinople (330-1990): "First Among Equals" in the Eastern Orthodox Church*. Brookline, Massachusetts: Holy Cross Orthodox Press, 1990.

Gill, J. *The Council of Florence*. Cambridge: Cambridge University Press, 1959.

Gregorios, P., W. Lazareth, N. Nissiotis, eds. *Does Chalcedon Divide or Unite? Towards Convergence in Orthodox Christology*. Geneva: World Council of Churches, 1981. Essays on the christological and ecclesiological issues that divide the Orthodox Church from the Oriental Orthodox Churches.

Hill, H., ed. *Light from the East: A Symposium on the Oriental Orthodox and Assyrian Churches*. Toronto: Anglican Book Centre, 1988.

Horner, N. *A Guide to Christian Churches in the Middle East*. Elkhart, IN: Mission Focus, 1989.

Hussey, J.M. *The Orthodox Church in the Byzantine Empire*. Oxford: Claredon Press, 1986.

Janin, R. *Églises orientales et rites orientaux*. Paris: Letouzey & Ané, 1955.

Kilmartin, E. *Toward Reunion: The Orthodox and Roman Catholic Churches*. New York: Paulist Press, 1979.

Limouris, G., and N. Vaporis, eds. *Orthodox Perspectives on Baptism, Eucharist and Ministry*. Brookline, MA: Holy Cross, 1986.

Litsas, F., ed. *A Companion to the Greek Orthodox Church*. New York: Greek Orthodox Archdiocese, 1984.

Lossky, V. *The Mystical Theology of the Eastern Church*. Cambridge: James Clarke & Co., 1957.

Maloney, G. *A History of Orthodox Theology Since 1453*. Belmont, MA: Nordland, 1976.

Maximos, Metropolitan of Sardis. *The Oecumenical Patriarchate in the Orthodox Church: A Study in the History and Canons of the Church.* Analekta Vlatadon 24. Thessalonika: Patriarchal Institute, 1976.

Meyendorff, J. *Byzantine Theology: Historical Trends and Doctrinal Themes.* New York: Fordham University Press, 1974.

Meyendorff, J. *The Orthodox Church.* Crestwood, NY: St. Vladimir's, 1981.

Meyendorff, J., et al. *The Primacy of Peter in the Orthodox Church.* Leighton Buzzard: The Faith Press, 1963.

Meyendorff, J. *A Study of Gregory Palamas.* Crestwood, NY: St. Vladimir's, 1974. Best study available in English on this crucial 14th century Byzantine theologian.

Oriental Orthodox-Roman Catholic Interchurch Marriages and Other Pastoral Relationships. Washington, DC: National Conference of Catholic Bishops and the Standing Conference of Oriental Orthodox Churches, 1995. Includes texts of Common Declarations and other important documentation.

Oriente cattolico: cenni storici e statistiche. Vatican City: Congregation for Oriental Churches, 1974. Statistical and historical survey of all Eastern Catholic Churches.

Orthodoxia 1997-1998. Regensburg, Germany: Ostkirchliches Institut, 1997. A list of all the bishops of non-Catholic eastern church along with biographical information.

Ouspensky, L., and V. Lossky. *The Meaning of Icons.* Revised edition, Crestwood, NY: St. Vladimir's, 1982.

Patelos, C., ed. *The Orthodox Church in the Ecumenical Movement: Documents and Statements 1902-1975.* Geneva: WCC, 1978.

Pelikan, J. *The Christian Tradition: A History of the Development of Doctrine.* Volume 2: *The Spirit of Eastern Christendom (600-1700).* Chicago: University of Chicago Press, 1974.

Pennington, B. *One Yet Two: Monastic Tradition East and West.* Kalamazoo, MI: Cistercian Publications, 1976. Papers from an Orthodox-Cistercian Symposium, 1973.

Podipara, P.J. *The Thomas Christians*. Bombay: St. Paul Publications, 1970.

Pospielovsky, D. *The Russian Church Under the Soviet Regime 1917-1982* (2 volumes). Crestwood, NY: St. Vladimir's, 1984.

Ramet, Pedro, ed. *Eastern Christianity and Politics in the Twentieth Century*. Durham and London: Duke University Press, 1988.

Ramet, S. *Nihil Obstat: Religion, Politics, and Social Change in East-Central Europe and Russia*. Durham and London: Duke University Press, 1998.

Runciman, S. *The Eastern Schism: A Study of the Papacy and the Eastern Churches During the XIth and XIIth Centuries*. Oxford: Clarendon Press, 1955.

Runciman, S. *The Great Church in Captivity: A Study of the Patriarchate of Constantinople from the Eve of the Turkish Conquest to the Greek War of Independence*. Cambridge: Cambridge University Press, 1968.

Schmemann, A. *For the Life of the World: Sacraments and Orthodoxy*. Crestwood, NY: St. Vladimir's, 1973.

Schmemann, A. *The Historical Road of Eastern Orthodoxy*. Crestwood, NY: St. Vladimir's, 1977.

Schulz, H. *The Byzantine Liturgy: Symbolic Structure and Faith Expression*. New York: Pueblo Publishing Company, 1986.

Špidlík, T. *The Spirituality of the Christian East: A Systematic Handbook*. Cistercian Studies 79. Kalamazoo, MI: Cistercian Publications, 1986.

Stormon, E., ed. *Towards the Healing of Schism: The Sees of Rome and Constantinople. Public Statements and Correspondence between the Holy See and the Ecumenical Patriarchate 1958-1984*. New York: Paulist, 1987.

Surrency, Archimandrite Serafim. *The Quest for Orthodox Unity in America. A History of the Orthodox Church in North America in the Twentieth Century*. New York: Sts. Boris and Gleb, 1973.

Index of Churches and Their Head

Albania, Orthodox Church of, 92

Albanian Byzantine Catholics, 187

Albanian Orthodox Diocese of America, 118

Aleksy II, Patriarch, 67

Alexandria, Patriarchate of, 51

America, Orthodox Church in, 98

American Carpatho-Russian Orthodox Greek Catholic Diocese of the USA, 112

Anarghyros Printesis, Bishop, 178

Anastasios, Metropolitan, 95

Ancient Oriental Churches (see Oriental Orthodox Churches, 23)

Aram I, Catholicos, 26

Antioch, Patriarchate of, 54

Armenian Apostolic Church, 24

Armenian Catholic Church, 151

Assyrian Church of the East, 15

Autocephalous Orthodox Churches, 44

Autonomous Orthodox Churches, 102

Bartholomew I, Patriarch, 51

Baselius Mar Thoma Matthews II, Catholicos, 39

Belarus, Orthodox Church in, 65

Belarusan Autocephalous Orthodox Church, 129

Belarusan Byzantine Catholics, 186

Belarusan Council of Orthodox Churches in North America, 118

Berhane-Yesus Demerew Souraphiel, Bishop, 157

Bidawid, Patriarch Raphael I, 148

Bulgaria, Orthodox Church of, 76

Bulgarian Catholic Church, 179

Byelorussia (see Belarus, 65)

Carpatho-Russian Orthodox Greek Catholic Diocese of the USA, 112

Catholic Eastern Churches, 139

Chaldean Catholic Church, 146

China, Orthodox Church of, 108

Christodoulos, Archbishop, 89

Chrysostomos, Archbishop, 86

Constantine, Metropolitan, 116

Constantinople, Patriarchate of, 45

Coptic Catholic Church, 154

Coptic Orthodox Church, 27

Cyprus, Orthodox Church of, 83

Cyril Mar Baselios Malancharuvil, 161

Czech and Slovak Republics, Orthodox Church in, 96

Damianos, Archbishop, 104

Daoud, Ignatius Moussa I, Patriarch 159

Dimitry I, 121

Dinkha IV, Mar, Catholicos-Patriarch, 20

Diodoros I, Patriarch, 60

Dorotheos, Metropolitan, 98

East, Ancient Church of the (see
    Assyrian Church of the East, 15)
Ecumenical Patriarchate (see Patriar-
    chate of Constantinople, 45)
Eritrean Orthodox Church, 40
Estonia, Orthodox Church in, 109
Ethiopian Catholic Church, 156
Ethiopian Orthodox Church, 30

Finland, Orthodox Church of, 105
Filaret, Patriarch, 128

Georgia, Catholics in, 187
Georgia, Orthodox Church of, 80
Ghattas, Patriarch Stephanos II, 155
Greece, Orthodox Church of, 86
Greek Catholic Church, 177

Hakkim, Patriarch Maximos V, 164
Hirka, Bishop Ján, 183
Hungarian Catholic Church, 184

Ignatius IV, Patriarch, 57
Ignatius Moussa I Daoud, Patriarch, 159
Ignatius Zakka I Iwas, Patriarch, 37
Ilia II, Catholicos-Patriarch, 86
India, Orthodox Church of (see Malank-
    ara Orthodox Syrian Church, 37)
Italo-Albanian Catholic Church, 145

Jacobite Church (see Syrian Orthodox
    Church, 34)

Japan, Orthodox Church of, 107
Jean Pierre XVIII Kasparian, Patriarch,
    154
Jerusalem, Patriarchate of, 57
John, Archbishop (Finland), 107

Karekin I Sarkissian, Catholicos, 27
Kasparian, Patriarch Jean-Pierre XVIII,
    154
Katre, Rev. Ilia, 118
Keresztes, Bishop Szilárd, 185
Knanaya Christians,
Konovalov, Archbishop Sergei,
Kous, Sviatoslaw, 119

Lubachivsky, Cardinal Myroslav Ivan,
    169

Macedonian Orthodox Church, 130
Malabar Catholic Church, 149
Malabar Independent Syrian Church of
    Thozhiyoor,
Malankara Catholic Church, 159
Malankara Orthodox Syrian Church, 37
Malankara Syrian Orthodox Church, 36
Manoogian, Torkom II, Patriarch, 26
Mar Dinkha IV, 20
Maronite Catholic Church, 142
Mar Thoma Syrian Church of Malabar,
    38
Maxim, Patriarch, 79
Maximos V Hakkim, Patriarch, 164
Melkite Catholic Church, 161

Metropolia, The (see Orthodox Church in America, 98)

Mihail, Archbishop, 132

Miklovš, Bishop Slavomir, 179

Moldova, Orthodox Church in, 66

"Monophysite" Churches (see The Oriental Orthodox Churches, 23)

Moscow Patriarchate (see the Orthodox Church of Russia, 60)

Mount Sinai, Orthodox Church of, 103

Mureşan, Metropolitan Lucian, 176

Nasrallah Sfeir, Patriarch, 144

"Nestorian" Church (see Assyrian Church of the East, 15)

Nicholas, Metropolitan, 97

OCA (see Orthodox Church in America, 98)

Old Believers, 121

Old Calendar Orthodox Churches in Greece, Romania, and Bulgaria, 133

Oriental Orthodox Churches, 23

Orthodox Church, 43

Paulos, Patriarch, 34

Pavle I, Patriarch, 72

Petros VII, Pope and Patriarch, 53

Phanar (see Patriarchate of Constantinople, 45)

Philipos I, Patriarch, 41

Poland, Orthodox Church of, 89

Pre-Chalcedonian Churches (see Oriental Orthodox Churches, 23)

Printesis, Bishop Anarghyros, 178

Procyk, Judson, Metropolitan, 172

Proykov Christo, Bishop, 181

Raphael I Bidawid, Patriarch, 148

Romania, Orthodox Church of, 72

Romanian Catholic Church, 173

Romanian Church United with Rome (see Romanian Catholic Church, 173)

Russia, Orthodox Church of, 60

Russian Byzantine Catholics, 185

Russian Orthodox Archdiocese in Western Europe, 116

Russian Orthodox Church Outside Russia, 123

Ruthenian Catholic Church, 169

Saint Catherine's Monastery (see Church of Mt. Sinai, 103)

Sawa, Metropolitan, 92

Semedi, Bishop Ivan, 173

Serbia, Orthodox Church of, 68

Sergius Konovalov, Archbishop, 117

Sfeir, Patriarch Nasrallah, 144

Shenouda III, Pope, 30

Silvestrini, Cardinal Achille, 142

Sinai, Orthodox Church of Mount, 103

Slovak Catholic Church, 182

Stephanos II Ghattas, Patriarch, 155

Synod, The (see Russian Orthodox Church Outside Russia, 123)

Syrian Catholic Church, 157

Syrian Orthodox Church, 34

Syro-Malabar Catholic Church, 149

Teoctist I, Patriarch, 75

Theodosius, Metropolitan (America), 102

Theodosius, Metropolitan (Japan), 108

Thomas Christians, 20

Torkom II Manoogian, Patriarch, 26

True Orthodox Christians of Greece, Church of, 134

Ukraine, Orthodox Church in, 65-66

Ukrainian Autocephalous Orthodox Church, 126

Ukrainian Catholic Church, 165

Ukrainian Orthodox Church in the USA, 113

Ukrainian Orthodox Church-Kiev Patriarchate, 126

Ukrainian Orthodox Church of Canada, 119

Vitaly, Metropolitan, 125

Varkey Vithayathil, Archbishop 151

Volodymyr Sabodan, Metropolitan, 128

Wasyly, Metropolitan, 120

Western Europe, Russian Orthodox Archdiocese in, 116

Yugoslavia, Byzantine Catholics in Former, 178

Yugoslavia, Orthodox Church in (see Serbia, Orthodox Church of, 68)